HUBERT

HUBERT

An Unauthorized Biography of the Vice President

BY

ALLAN H. RYSKIND

ARLINGTON HOUSE

New Rochelle *New York*

Library of Congress Catalog Card Number 68-22456

MANUFACTURED IN THE UNITED STATES OF AMERICA

Acknowledgments

In writing this book the author relied heavily on the following basic research materials: the Minneapolis *Star*, the Minneapolis *Tribune*, the New York *Times*, the *Congressional Record* and the *Congressional Quarterly*. Extremely useful to me in the chapter regarding the left-wing, right-wing split in the Democratic-Farmer-Labor Party was an article by Professor G. Theodore Mitau in the Spring 1955 issue of *Minnesota History*.

Two biographies on Humphrey also proved very valuable: Winthrop Griffith's *Humphrey: A Candid Biography* and Michael Amrine's *This Is Humphrey*. Other books that were helpful: TheodoreWhite's *The Making of a President, 1964;* Victor Lasky's *JFK: The Man and the Myth;* Clifton Brock's *Americans for Democratic Action;* Max Kampelman's *The Communist Party vs. The CIO;* and David J. Saposs' *Communism in American Politics.*

I would also like to thank the following people for permitting themselves to be interviewed for this book either orally or by letter: Max Kampelman, Orville Freeman, William Connell, Bradshaw Mintener, Svend Petersen, Cyril King, Rollo Mudge, Walter Judd, Harold Stassen, G. Theodore Mitau, Joseph Ball, William Kirkpatrick, Karl Mundt, Strom Thurmond, Sheriff Ed Ryan and Donald Lambro.

I wish, too, to give lavish thanks—though she would prefer cash—to my wife J'aime, who diligently scoured numerous reference works to secure important facts and who typed the completed manuscript.

While the above and many others were helpful to me, a number of persons who provided me with information will take sharp issue with what I have written; so I wish to stress that the author alone bears full responsibility for the views contained herein.

Contents

1

The Splendid Tease

In late August, 1964, President Johnson—who has been called the ringmaster of the American political world—was busily setting the stage for the Democratic National Convention in Atlantic City. The convention promised no real fireworks. The Presidential nomination obviously was all sewed up, and for sheer public exhilaration it would be hard to top July's "Cow Palace Revolution" in San Francisco, a revolution which had seen the Southern and Western majority of the GOP finally sweep out the Eastern Establishment that had ruled Republican nominating conventions for almost 30 years. Whether one had been for or against Barry Goldwater, his nomination produced a surge of excitement, not only within the confines of the GOP, but throughout the country and abroad.

American conservatives, who had long waited for this moment, saw in the Arizonan a rugged, handsome political gladiator. Here was a man to lead the country away from collectivism at home and appeasement abroad. Here was a man who bluntly espoused less government rather than more, a man who, astonishingly enough, talked of victory over the Communist enemy, rather than "building bridges" to (and for) the enemy.

To the conservative, Goldwater was far from the maniacal demon portrayed by such liberal luminaries as cartoonist Herblock and columnist Walter Lippmann. His philosophy was not new, and it certainly would have been understood by a Jefferson, or even a William Howard Taft. But it seemed—and was—revolutionary to a majority of the people living in America in 1964, people whose political consciousness arrived with the era of the New Deal and Franklin Delano Roosevelt. While the conservative thrilled, others had different reactions. The public at large, it appeared, was bewildered by the Goldwater nomination. Abroad, free world capitals were curious and alarmed, steeped in American press folklore that Goldwater would thrust the nation into fascism and racism and let loose the fury of the atom in a nuclear war. America's foes, too, took notice, with sharp, negative reactions emanating from Moscow and Peking.

Could Johnson, then, possibly hope to upstage the GOP performance at the Cow Palace? Obviously not, but he would come close. With his keen sense of political drama, the President knew there would be only one point of vital interest at the Democratic convention: the Vice Presidency. And he was to milk that interest for all it was worth. Not until the last possible moment would the public—or even the candidate—learn of LBJ's choice. The President's purposeful delay in naming his running mate was to become what columnist Joseph Alsop would call "The Splendid Tease."

The tease, no doubt, was less exciting than the drama played out in San Francisco, but still it captured the public's attention. And with good reason. For the persisting thought in people's minds was that LBJ's running-mate—assuming the Democrats won—would very likely become a future President of the United States. In recent years, many Vice Presidents—Truman, Nixon and Johnson himself—had been elevated to the Presidency or had become Presidential nominees. The awareness that a Vice President could be catapulted out of obscurity to head the nation had been forcefully driven home by the assassination of John F. Kennedy. Moreover, there was the unpleasant but politically significant fact that Kennedy's successor had been the victim of a massive coronary in July of 1955. Thus, the nomination for Vice President was of intense interest and LBJ, showman that he always is, would carefully create a climate of suspense before making his final choice known.

To sustain the suspense, the White House, or White House intimates, dropped dozens of names as potential VP nominees. The newspapers bandied about such leading political figures as Mayor Robert Wagner of New York, California's Governor "Pat" Brown, who headed the most populous state in the nation, and Senate Majority Leader Mike Mansfield. Sargent Shriver, who had married a Kennedy, was in the running. So were Eugene McCarthy, a liberal Senator from Minnesota, and Thomas Dodd, a liberal Connecticut Senator, who had the reputation of being a vigorous anti-Communist. These men had in common another political asset: they were all Roman Catholic, a factor of prime importance to the Democrats with their reliance on the big-city vote. As to non-Catholics, there was Senate Democratic Whip Hubert Humphrey, long an intimate of the President and a favorite of liberals and big labor.

Defense Secretary Robert S. McNamara was also under serious consideration. McNamara, it turned out, would come within an eyelash of getting the President's nod. Formerly president of Ford Motor Company, he was a special favorite of LBJ.

Touted as a Republican by the newspapers, McNamara in actuality had been helping Democrats for many years. He was Ford's top executive when that company raised over $250,000 for the JFK-LBJ campaign in 1960. He actively supported Michigan's liberal Senator Philip A. Hart in 1958[1] and had much admiration for union leader Walter Reuther, a powerful influence in liberal Democratic circles. (McNamara's first pick for a top Pentagon manpower job was, in fact, Reuther's right-hand man, Jack Conway.)[2] But McNamara also had high standing in the business community, a factor which, it was felt, would hurt the GOP. In addition, much of the public was attracted to the Defense Secretary's image as a defender of the dollar.

The defense budget, it was true, had climbed steadily under McNamara's reign and both Congress and the military were fuming over his choice of weapons to fight present and future wars. But the more McNamara was criticized, the more the public appeared to like him. The press had portrayed him as a budget-cutter—and the country bought it.

Unquestionably, however, the leading contender for the Vice Presidential spot was none of the above, but the then Attorney General, Robert F. Kennedy.

The late President's brother did not have everything going for him. Indeed, he faced several obstacles. As Vice President, LBJ had never particularly liked Bobby's brusque and abrasive manner. And there was good reason to suspect Bobby of having pushed the case of Bobby Baker—Lyndon's protegé—to the attention of the public for the purpose of pushing Lyndon off the Kennedy ticket in 1964. That many Kennedy intimates were talking openly of "scrubbing" Lyndon in 1964 was mentioned on several occasions by staff members of the Democratic National Committee. Yet, initially, Bobby was the frontrunner.

For all of LBJ's distaste for Bobby, he found it difficult not to put him on the ticket. As part of the Kennedy Administration, Bobby had built up powerful friends and allies in the Democratic Party. And he was, most important of all, brother to the late JFK, whose good, unlike Caesar's, had not been interred with his bones. In life, JFK had been able to capture the imagination of many. He had verve and style. A glittering phrasemaker, he could buoy the hopes of millions with brilliant rhetoric. In perspective, however, he had been something less than a successful President, as most people are accustomed to thinking of the term successful. He had won the Presidency by less than one-tenth of one per cent of the popular vote, bringing no Congressmen in on his coattails. His big domestic programs—medicare, federal aid to education, the farm program, immigration—were either defeated, or passed by his successor. In foreign affairs, he had botched things badly. Asia: He publicly talked of the necessity of defending Laos against the Communists—and didn't, thus permitting that country to become a vital Communist corridor which would feed the Viet Cong guerrillas in South Vietnam. Africa: He helped the United Nations launch a war against one of the few Congolese moderates, Moise Tshombe, whom the Congolese would later have to recall from exile to save their country from chaos. Latin America: The Bay of Pigs had become an international symbol of defeat. True, JFK would partially redeem that failure by forcing Khrushchev to remove his missiles from Cuba, yet he was never to get rid of Castro—and if the Bay of Pigs had been successful, there never would have been a Cuban missile crisis.

Still, when an assassin's bullet felled the young President on November 22, 1963, when he was on a political mission to Texas, the world was horrified and genuinely mournful. Grief poured from many and strange places. A woman member of the Soviet's UN delegation was said to have wept. Soon towns and public buildings in America were bearing the name of Kennedy. Idlewild in New York and Cape Canaveral in Florida were to become Kennedy Airport and Cape Kennedy, respectively.

Alive on November 21, 1963, JFK was an unknown quantity, but in death not only JFK, but the name Kennedy itself had attained a mystical hold over people. Certainly it enthralled the delegates to the Democratic convention. And Bobby Kennedy was well aware of the magic name he held. Indeed, as a result, Bobby and his friends would artfully set the stage seeking to compel LBJ to accept Bobby as the VP candidate.

What *Time* magazine would call a "burning boomlet" for Bobby had already been set in motion before the convention. Chicago's Mayor Daley, a long time associate of the Kennedy clan, made it known he favored Bobby. Indiana's Birch Bayh, who headed the Youth for Johnson group at the convention, was busily stacking his misnamed organization with pro-Bobby people. Northern and Midwestern governors and state and county party chairmen were working for the Attorney General, in some cases secretly. It had been arranged, too, that a film tribute to JFK would be shown to the delegates *before* the nomination for Vice President. And then came a spectacular report: that Jacqueline Kennedy, JFK's widow, would come to the convention to plead the case for her late husband's brother. With Jackie's presence and the eulogies for the late President Kennedy tugging at the delegates' heartstrings, it became the profound hope of the Kennedy people that the convention would sweep Bobby into the VP spot on a wave of emotionalism.

As the boomlet started to boom, however, LBJ finally came

to a difficult decision. He felt he had to block the Bobby bandwagon. On Monday, July 27, three weeks before the convention, he told Bobby of his intentions. When he requested Bobby to repudiate publicly any Vice Presidential ambitions, Bobby balked. On Thursday, LBJ took the matter into his own hands. He told the public, in regard to his VP choice, "I have reached the conclusion that it would be inadvisable for me to recommend to the convention any member of my Cabinet or any of those who meet regularly with the Cabinet."

LBJ's words had fooled no one. The statement had eliminated from consideration McNamara, Shriver, Rusk and a galaxy of other potential VP candidates, but the entire political world realized LBJ was actually aiming his blow at Bobby. The moment was a nervous one for the President, for he realized that no matter how he couched the terms of Bobby's elimination, he was testing his strength with the powerful Kennedy forces in the party. Having been in office less than a year, LBJ felt he did not yet have a firm grip on the party machinery. Kennedy allies were still in government—LBJ had been afraid to remove many of them—and they still had control over many of the Democratic machines in the big cities. He knew, too, that the Kennedy wing looked upon him as a usurper of the throne.

As it turned out, LBJ had exaggerated his worries. His "dump Bobby" move caused some bitterness and unpleasant muttering, but there was no revolt. Johnson breathed easier. Suddenly the Bobby threat had vanished.

At first blush, Hubert Horatio Humphrey did not seem a likely choice as LBJ's running mate. The 53-year-old Humphrey had come a long way from soda jerk at his father's drugstore to Senate Democratic Whip, but one could think of a number of reasons why he shouldn't adorn the national Democratic ticket. Though popular in his state of Minnesota, where he had been elected mayor of Minneapolis and then Senator, he had not stirred the blood of those outside it. He had half hankered for the VP spot under Stevenson in 1952, but Adlai didn't feel Humphrey could aid his election chances. He desperately sought the Vice Presidency in 1956, but once again Adlai didn't like the idea. When Stevenson threw the nomination for the VP spot open to the convention, the delegates chose Tennessee's Estes Kefauver. In 1960, Humphrey decided to test his popularity directly with the voters—and lost disastrously. He entered the Wisconsin Presidential primary—and was whipped. Though favored by the newspapers and the polls in Protestant West Virginia, his Presidential hopes were to be snuffed out by Kennedy, who at the time was a relatively inexperienced politician.

In 1964, Humphrey suffered another handicap; he was anathema to the South. Having Humphrey on the ticket, the pros feared, would play directly into Goldwater's "Southern strategy" and might turn the South into permanently Republican territory. The South, it was known, had compiled a long list of grievances against the man from Minnesota.

In 1948, Humphrey—risking party harmony, which had already been hurt by the Henry Wallace third-party movement—shattered a delicately arranged civil rights compromise worked out by the party convention with a dramatic 10-minute talk calling for a strong civil rights plank in the platform. Humphrey reaped tremendous political benefits from the speech. It was to catapult the then mayor of Minneapolis onto the national scene and play an important role in his victory that year over incumbent GOP Senator Joseph H. Ball. But the speech would cause a divisive split in the Democratic Party. The Humphrey talk triggered the immediate walkout of the Alabama and Mississippi delegations and became the catalyst for the States Rights Party, a conservative Southern Democratic group which, along with the Wallace movement, plagued the Democratic Party in 1948.

In later years, Humphrey seemed to temper his assaults on Southerners and his drive for militant civil rights planks. Yet on September 17, 1963, he blamed the infamous church bombing in Birmingham of four young Negro girls not on the warped minds which committed that vicious crime, but on the entire South. He would blame it squarely on the Southern Establishment, "those men who own and control the banks and the factories, newspapers, the radios, the televisions, who own the land, who are the big contributors to the politicians. . . ."[3] Moreover, just prior to the convention, Humphrey floor-managed the precedent-making 1964 civil rights bill, which would put the South's racial and social system in the hands of zealous federal bureaucrats.

Humphrey appeared to have other grave defects from a political point of view. A founder and former national chairman of the liberal Americans for Democratic Action, he was still listed as its vice chairman. The ADA's virulent brand of radicalism had never seemed particularly popular with rank-and-file Democrats. The ADA called for scrapping internal security mechanisms and institutions designed to deal with the Communists, including the House Committee on Un-American Activities and the Senate Internal Security Subcommittee; it baited free enterprise and proposed a host of socialist programs. Humphrey did not pursue the ADA line to the last dotted "i," but he followed it slavishly enough to have earned a national reputation as a radical.

As if this weren't enough, many businessmen, even those who contributed to the Democratic Party, felt he was "anti-business." Newsmen and Establishment sources, of course, pumped out pages of print claiming the "New Humphrey" was really a friend of the business community, and Humphrey himself went out of his way to cultivate that image. Yet only four years before Humphrey had courted his voting public in the Wisconsin Presidential primary in semi-Marxist tones. In the midst of a campaign drive in Racine, for example, Humphrey joined with picketers to sing the militant labor song "Solidarity Forever" at the main gates of the J. I. Case Company.[4] The New York *Times* reported that Humphrey predicted the "union would bring the company to its knees in a week." As late as September, 1963, he was accusing "the economic power of the Northern and Eastern banks, insurance companies and other corporations" of fostering racial bombings in the South.[5]

Nevertheless, with McNamara and Bobby Kennedy eliminated as Vice Presidential candidates, the political world turned its eyes toward Humphrey.

In spite of his radical outlook, Humphrey had built up some strong support for himself, if not throughout the country, at least within the framework of the Democratic Party. Big labor, which controlled nearly 250 delegates at the convention, had invested much in Humphrey over the years. It had put him over as mayor of Minneapolis some 19 years before. It paved his way to the Senate in 1948 and it was now in his corner for the Vice Presidency. When President Johnson asked AFL-CIO president George Meany for his first three VP choices, Meany only had one: Humphrey.[6] Humphrey, too, had begun publicly to soften his anti-business image. And newsmen who toadied to Humphrey were doing their energetic best to radiate this softened image in the press. He became, in the parlance of the day, a "moderate."

There was another important factor working for Humphrey: he was in the good graces of President Johnson. Indeed, Humphrey had managed to entwine himself in the affections of every Democratic President since his election to the Senate. He has always been sensitive to power. On the public record it is hard to find a single issue of importance where he has chosen to cross swords with the White House—when it has been occupied by a Democrat. Nor did Humphrey seriously buck the Democratic leadership when he served in the Senate, an ingredient in Humphrey's make-up that was not to be overlooked by Johnson.*

Johnson and Humphrey had always had a certain rapport. Both had come to the Senate in 1949 and were to become social as well as political friends. They came from similar backgrounds. Both had been school teachers, both loved politics, and both had their political thinking shaped largely by the depression.

*Michael Amrine, a prominent member of the nationally known disarmament committee, SANE, has put out a highly favorable biography of Humphrey. Called *This Is Humphrey*, with a foreword by President Johnson, Amrine says (page 159): "Humphrey followed the party line most devotedly in his first year in the Senate, 1949, when he voted with the majority 94 per cent of the time. Since then his score has never been above 92 per cent and in 1950 was 88 per cent. In 1953 it was 89 and in 1954 it was 88 per cent again. As the *Congressional Quarterly*, a highly authoritative, non-partisan report on politics computes such things, he was well ahead of the party in all these years. The average Democratic Senator was with the party about 75 to 80 per cent of the time."

When LBJ ascended to leadership of the Senate Democrats by 1953, Humphrey entered the leadership shortly afterwards because of Johnson's intercession. As Theodore White notes, Humphrey became "the first Northern Democratic liberal of the Bourbon inner circle."

When JFK became President in 1961, it was Johnson who saw to it that Humphrey would end up in the post of Senate Whip.

Because of his close ties with Johnson, Humphrey was actively seeking the Vice Presidential nomination. His campaign had several parts. Again, Theodore White reports, there was the feverish public campaign put on by Humphrey's Minnesota partisans and energetically directed by Max Kampelman, a long-time Humphrey intimate, and William Connell, Humphrey's chief executive assistant. Masked from public view was the secret operation led by Humphrey, himself, and James Rowe, Humphrey's campaign manager in West Virginia four years previously. An intimate of LBJ as well, Rowe would prove invaluable as a message carrier between Humphrey and the President.

After Bobby had been scrapped, it was Rowe who came to Humphrey bearing Johnson's thinking about the Vice Presidency. If Humphrey truly desired to secure the Vice Presidential nomination, he had to make it "crystal-clear, come hell or high water, directly to the President that he would be a *Johnson* man as Vice President of the United States."[7]

Responding to the message carried by Rowe, Humphrey talked to the President by telephone. In words that were "crystal-clear," Humphrey told Johnson that he fully understood the President and that, if he were to be selected, he would give President Johnson his complete loyalty.

It was Tuesday afternoon, August 25, in Atlantic City. Sometime Wednesday a Vice President was scheduled to be nominated. Sitting in one of his rooms at the convention, Rowe received a signal from his pocket-radio beeper to call on LBJ aide Walter Jenkins, sequestered in the Deauville Hotel. When he arrived at the hotel, Rowe received a message from LBJ in

Washington. The President wanted Humphrey to read the interview given correspondents on Monday for the Vice Presidency. Repeating what he had said almost a month earlier, he told Rowe that the Vice President must have no public disputes with the President, that he must clear his every speech, his every public thought, with the President. Late in the afternoon, Rowe found Humphrey with Walter Reuther in the Hotel Traymore and delivered the message regarding LBJ's VP choice.

Later in the day, a second message was delivered to Humphrey by Rowe. This one seemed to cinch the nomination. LBJ wanted both Humphrey and his wife Muriel to stand by for a plane trip to Washington. In Humphrey's view, this must mean he had the President's blessing. Certainly he would not have asked his wife to come down too just to tell him "No."

Humphrey slept late Wednesday morning, breakfasted with his son, Douglas, then waited for the President, who was scoring the script, to call. Around 3 p.m., he received a call from Jenkins. Jenkins changed the plans somewhat: Muriel was not to come. Humphrey was also told that he was to fly down to Washington with another Senator. At Bader Airport, just outside Atlantic City, Humphrey saw Senator Thomas Dodd of Connecticut getting into the six-seat Piper Aztec which was to fly them to the capital.

The news that Dodd was accompanying Humphrey had produced the electric effect Johnson had desired. Here it was, the night of the VP nomination, and still neither the public nor the Atlantic City delegates nor the nominee himself knew who LBJ's choice would be. And now Johnson, by skillful maneuvering, had managed magnificently to heighten the suspense.

Was Dodd a serious candidate? It was true that he was a dark horse, but he had been mentioned frequently. Moreover, he had a number of plusses Humphrey obviously lacked. The more one considered Dodd's assets, the more he appeared as a likely candidate.

The Connecticut lawmaker was as liberal on domestic matters as Humphrey and would be acceptable to the liberally-inclined delegates assembled in Atlantic City. He was a Catholic and would help to keep in the party those Catholics who did not ordinarily vote Democratic but had been attracted to the Democrats with the advent of Kennedy. Dodd, also, had long been a friend of the President. He was one of the few Northern liberals who had supported Johnson over Kennedy in 1960.

But these were the least important qualifications as far as some Democratic "pols" were concerned. What was important to them was that Dodd could wreak havoc with the GOP strategy of accusing the Democrats of being "soft on communism."

Johnson, of course, had not yet really been tested in foreign policy, but he had inherited the Kennedy legacy of retreating before the Communists from Laos to the Bay of Pigs. And he had followed some rather dubious policies himself after the assassination. He had, for example, bestowed an award on the controversial Dr. J. Robert Oppenheimer, pushed through Congress legislation underwriting wheat sales to the Soviet Union, and conferred seriously with such radical disarmament advocates as Seymour Melman, who had once endorsed a campaign against civil defense in New York.

Dodd clearly could squash the Communist issue completely. As a member of the Senate Foreign Relations Committee, he had developed a well-deserved reputation of being an uncompromising anti-Communist, particularly in the field of foreign policy. His lengthy but highly learned speeches in the Senate were sometimes the only available information in this country on the Communist threat from abroad. With Dodd on the ticket, who would dare accuse the Democrats of being lenient with the Reds?

Humphrey, himself, must have realized some of Dodd's political attractiveness as he boarded the plane. On the flight toward Washington, he soberly pondered his situation. He had desired to be the Vice Presidential candidate on at least two other occasions, but never had he worked so desperately for the nomination as he had in the summer of 1964. Surely Johnson had not led him on this way only to cast him aside. Yet there was no denying that Dodd had assets Humphrey didn't have.

When both Senators finally arrived at the White House, it

was Dodd who had a private conference with the President first. Shortly after six, LBJ released Dodd to a mob of reporters, then sought Humphrey in the Cabinet Room and asked him to step into the Oval Office. When Humphrey entered the room, he found himself in the presence of Defense Secretary Robert McNamara, Secretary of State Dean Rusk and Presidential Assistant McGeorge Bundy.

Putting his arm around Humphrey, the President said, "Hubert, how would you like to be my Vice President?" Humphrey said he would. Again, Johnson wanted to discuss with him an important detail: Humphrey had to remember that he couldn't disagree with the President in public and had to stand by him at all times.[8] Again, Humphrey painfully told the President he would never do anything disloyal.

"The Splendid Tease" was almost over. When LBJ, a few hours later, requested the delegates in Atlantic City to nominate Humphrey, Alabama's delegates immediately rose to place in nomination the name of Gov. Carl Sanders of Georgia. Sanders declined the nomination. At 12:27 a.m. on August 27, Humphrey was nominated by the convention. On November 3, 1964, he was elected Vice President, riding to victory, like a lot of other Democrats, on the President's "coattails."

2

"As the Twig is Bent . . ."

Hubert Horatio Humphrey, evangelist for the Welfare State, would probably scorn the story of Horatio Alger—the tale of a poor boy who, with industry and skill and without federal handouts, struggles his way from rags to riches. Yet Humphrey's own life story is full of Horatio Alger touches. Born in a small town of less than well-to-do parents, he has carved himself a path that has led to awesome success and awesome political power. Luck and shrewdness, the characteristics of that other Horatio, played a part. But boundless energy, skill, quickness and a combative spirit were more decisive in carrying him to high achievement in the political arena.

Perhaps it was in the blood. The family tree blossomed with rugged individualists whose traits one immediately associates with the sturdy American pioneer. His father's ancestors left Wales in 1648 to come to America. Humphrey's great-great-great grandfather, Elijah Humphrey of Dudley, Massachusetts, served in the Revolutionary War. Both his great grandfather and grandfather earned their livelihoods from the soil, with grandfather John Humphrey becoming a Master Farmer and an organizer in the Minnesota Grange. Humphrey's father, Hubert Horatio Humphrey, Sr., broke with the farm tradition to become a pharmacist and small businessman. He married Christine

Sannes, who came from a small seaport at the southern tip of Norway.

Grandfather Sannes was a bold adventurer with a swashbuckling spirit. Winthrop Griffith, a former aide to Humphrey, writes that Sannes spent his youth at sea working on Norwegian ships "which sailed the trade routes from Scandinavia and Europe to China and Africa." He captained one of the first ships that went through the new Suez Canal. In the 1880's, Sannes abandoned both his native Norway and the sea and took his family to South Dakota, where he bought "360 acres of rich lowland between Lily and Wallace."[1]

Sannes was a diligent pioneer. "When Humphrey was a boy," notes Griffith, "he helped his grandfather mow the grasses at the edge of the roadway, swept the yard between the red barns and livestock sheds, and weeded a garden of flowers in front of the white frame house. During evening visits he lolled at the old man's feet listening to tales of the sea and proclamations about the evil of debt, the honor of labor and the pursuit of excellence."[2]

The Humphrey who was to become Vice President was born in Wallace, South Dakota on May 27, 1911. In 1915, Humphrey's father moved the family to the sleepy farming community of Doland, S.D., where Humphrey spent most of his formative years. It was here he grew up with his two younger sisters, Fern and Frances, and his older brother, Ralph.

The young Hubert Humphrey (like the mature man) had similarities to a perpetual motion machine. In grade school he sold newspapers, starred in the plays, organized baseball teams in summer and cold weather sports in winter. His favorite winter game was one of his own making called "Napoleon at Waterloo." Humphrey relished it and remade history in the process. As Griffith describes the game: "On a snowy slope outside town he directed the boys to form two armies, one French and one British. A Doland lad who had been born in England was always assigned the role of the Duke of Wellington. Humphrey always appointed himself Napoleon. He had a burning ambition to beat the British; each Saturday afternoon he did. With bigger snowballs and more aggressive tactics than the nine-year-old 'Duke of Wellington,' Humphrey rewrote the history of Napoleon's final summer defeat at the hands of the British."[3]

Humphrey's childhood, generally, was happy, but he once had a serious bout with influenza complicated by pneumonia. The entire town learned he was on the verge of death. Humphrey, only nine at the time, recalls that he himself felt he would die. He would wake in the night with grisly dreams of death still lingering in his memory. But the senior Humphrey refused to accept this fate for his youngest son. Being a pharmacist, he knew of a radically experimental drug, which luckily could be acquired without doing battle with today's rigorous Food and Drug regulations. Humphrey, of course, recovered.

His energies did not diminish upon reaching high school. He played football, basketball, and baseball, ran track, acted in high school drama productions and evolved into a star debater. He even found time to sing in the Glee Club. Entering boldly into politics in his junior year, he was elected president of his class. It was, it might be added, not very difficult to participate in many activities. The school was small. Humphrey's senior class, for example, had only 20 students. But Doland High School fielded excellent debating and athletic teams in spite of its size. Humphrey was part of his high school relay team which took first place in the state track meet, and his famous talkative streak was instrumental in capturing the state debating tournament.

Fiercely competitive in everything he tried, Humphrey also excelled in scholarship, receiving A's in all save two subjects. In 1929 he was a senior. When the class valedictorian was selected, he turned out to be Hubert Humphrey.

From his mother, Humphrey inherited a reverence for family life and a sense of duty. Good humored and with a gift for poetry, she brightened the family home life. His father left a deeper mark, for it was from him he imbibed his politics. "Dad" Humphrey died in 1949, but Humphrey has said that "his mind, his spirit, his soul are ever present in my daily life . . ."

Dad Humphrey was ebullient and gregarious, like his son. "When he laughed," according to one observer of the Humphrey family, "he would shake all over. People remember that he shook the furniture when he was really amused."[4]

Possessing a roving curiosity, he was an omnivorous reader and a lively conversationalist. Some South Dakotans, notes Humphrey biographer Michael Amrine, described Dad Humphrey as "the greatest talker they ever knew," a trait that must run in the Humphrey genes. When Dad and son got together, according to old timers, verbal winds could blow to hurricane velocity.

Dad Humphrey not only read and talked voluminously, he taught his sons to do both. He had them read the papers, Ben Franklin, Tom Paine and Tom Jefferson. An avid student of politics, he was spellbound by William Jennings Bryan—he would read Bryan's "Cross of Gold" speech to his family once or twice a year—and he worshipped at the shrine of Woodrow Wilson. Indeed, politics was his major topic of conversation and the young Humphrey absorbed his enthusiasm for it.

But Dad Humphrey did more than just talk. Though a Democratic internationalist in the heart of Republican isolationism, the senior Humphrey was elected city councilman, mayor of Doland (a post more honorary than political), a member of the South Dakota state legislature and a delegate to three Democratic National Conventions. His successes were more of a tribute to the man than to his politics. When he died in 1949, thousands of people—politics aside for the moment—came out of the farms and villages to pay their last respects to their druggist friend.

Dad Humphrey's politics, passed on to his son, were infused with a potent mixture of Wilson internationalism and the radical spirit of Populism. He idolized Wilson and thought him one of America's greatest Presidents. When the League of Nations was scuttled, he was stunned and later insisted that participation in it by the United States could have prevented Hitler's rise to power.

His economic ideas paralleled those of the Populist movement which swept the South and the West during the 1890's. Blaming both business and the Eastern bankers for the economic troubles of the farmer and the small businessman, the Populists demanded government intervention to break the power of "monopoly capital."

The long agricultural depression in the latter half of the 19th century attracted to Populism the American farmer, who became acutely aware of the power of the Eastern banker; mortgage foreclosures were a common occurrence. Laborers and small businessmen sympathized with the Populists. But these elements weren't the movement's only source of strength. The first national convention of the movement in 1892 was also filled with representatives of the Knights of Labor, the single-tax people, the anti-monopolists and other radical elements.

While many of the principles of the party were hazy and simplistic, many were also far in advance of their time. Among the ideas espoused were women's suffrage, direct election of the President, a graduated income tax and farm subsidies. The Populists called for nationalization of the telegraph, telephone and the railroads—the latter a special symbol of despotism to farmers who were often compelled to pay arbitrarily high rates because the railroads sometimes exercised monopoly control.

When the Democratic National Convention met in 1896, the Populists and their followers had infiltrated it to such an extent that the delegates nominated Dad Humphrey's hero: William Jennings Bryan.

Populist theories pervaded Dad Humphrey's thinking. When a large private firm proposed to buy the Doland power and light company from the town and turn it into a profitable, tax-paying venture, Dad Humphrey bitterly fought in favor of keeping the utility municipally owned. Doland, he insisted, shouldn't be turned over to some "soulless corporation."[5]

Like his son, Dad Humphrey could be sent into orbit when he argued, and he barked out Biblical phrases from the Old Testament prophets while passionately pouring out his views.

With many a farmer and businessman, he shared a particular fear of and distaste for the banks. Part of this deep antagonism sprung from personal experience. When young Hubert Humphrey was 16, both banks in Doland failed. Hubert Jr. came home from school one day and saw his mother standing in front of the house crying. Through her tears, she explained that his Dad would have to sell the house in which the Humphrey family had lived for many years. For Mrs. Humphrey, the home had been her whole world.

The bank failures not only affected the Humphrey home, but the Humphrey drugstore. During the years in Doland, the entire family worked in the store. Young Humphrey was born above it and reared there, and actively helped with the business. The store was quite modern for the times. While most stores stocked only medicine, the Humphrey store carried such non-medicinal items as radios and ice cream. Meals were also served. Animal vaccine, which the farmers desperately needed, was also available and the young Humphrey helped the farmers vaccinate their hogs. When Doland's two banks collapsed in 1927, the senior Humphrey saw economic ruin staring him in the face. His own savings were wiped out along with those of other Doland citizens. Customers were unable to pay old bills. In September, 1929, young Humphrey entered the University of Minnesota. In October, the bottom fell out of the stock market. The symptoms of a sick economy which had revealed themselves in Doland two years previously had now spread across the nation. Prosperity vanished. Prices plummeted. The 1929 depression hit Doland with another jolt and more farmers found themselves penniless. In 1931, during his sophomore year, young Humphrey received a long distance call from his dad. His father said he was calling it quits in Doland. To keep the family business going, he was moving to the bigger city of Huron and he needed his son to help him out.

In the spring of a good year, South Dakota is lush with fields of corn and alfalfa and wheat waiting to be harvested in the autumn. But drought is the farmer's ever threatening enemy. There had been precious little rain in the early 30's and the summers parched the prairie land. In November 1933, the citizens of Huron, as well as inhabitants of other parts of the state, saw an ominous yellow-gray cloud on the horizon; it turned black, then rolled over the Prairie State carpeting communities and farms with thick, gritty dust. It was the first of more than 90 dust storms that choked and suffocated the state within the next year.

The depression had left much of the nation in gloom. But times were even darker in the Dakotas. Crops withered and blew away in the dry and dusty land. Cattle starved. At times the dust was so thick that street lights had to be turned on in the day-time. Hordes of locusts and insects came to plague the people. Many farmers packed up their bags to go, but the Humphreys remained.

Dad Humphrey hawked more pig serum and veterinary medicine and expanded his stock of non-drug items, but times stayed difficult. The farmers who refused to go found that seed wouldn't respond to the stubborn soil. With the farmers possessing little cash, the Humphrey store turned to barter: the farmers could get drugs for whatever they could grow. The Humphrey drugstore, though constantly on the verge of going under, managed to survive. Young Hubert had been important to its survival, and had himself become a registered pharmacist after attending pharmacy college in Denver from January through May in 1933. ("Denver was real cram learning," but Humphrey philosophically remarked that this was "about the only way I have ever learned anything—I have never had the opportunity to take my time to learn things in a leisurely and reflective way.")[6]

Things were not entirely bleak, even in the depths of the dust and the depression. Families found themselves closer together; townsmen pitched in to help each other out in a fashion that built community spirit. Young Humphrey, in spite of his full schedule at the drugstore, managed to have his diversions. He participated in Young Democratic activities, gave speeches to small groups, and became scoutmaster for a Methodist church troop. In 1935, he began to squire around a pretty blond girl named Muriel Buck. Born in Huron, she went through high school, then studied piano at Huron College for several years. Her parents came from English, Pennsylvania Dutch and Holland Dutch ancestry. Muriel found young Humphrey an intense young man, bursting with ambition and drive. He obviously felt cooped up in Huron and Muriel was a sympathetic listener. In 1935 she caught a glimpse of his ambition. The young Humphrey had been able to go to Washington, D.C., as a guide for Huron's Boy Scout troop. Fascinated by the Capitol and Congress, he wrote to "Bucky":

> . . . I can see how someday, if you and I just apply ourselves and make up our minds to work for bigger things, we can live here in Washington. . . . I set my aim at Congress.

Humphrey and Muriel were married on September 3, 1936. When they came home from their honeymoon, young Hubert appeared determined to leave Huron. He was tired and weary of drought and dust storms. In September 1937, he had made up his mind to finish the education he had left behind six years before. The couple left for the University of Minnesota. They could hardly have realized at the time that it was Humphrey's first big step toward national politics.

3

". . . So Inclines the Tree"

The University of Minnesota became a breeding ground for liberals and radicals during the days of the New Deal. It also became a launching pad for Hubert Humphrey's political career. Between the time he entered the university and his first stab at running for mayor of Minneapolis was a scant five and one-half years.

With characteristic energy and exuberance, he plunged himself into his studies; but he also attained a nucleus of friends—both students and teachers—who would later prove important in advancing his political fortunes. In his graduate days, and even beyond, the university provided Humphrey with invaluable friends and allies. The university professors were taken with Humphrey, for he was not only intelligent but his distinctly liberal views paralleled their own. It was only natural that when the time was ripe they would want to cast him upon political waters.

Sharing a common philosophy with his professors, Humphrey's thoughts were shaped and polished by the university's political science department, whose influence spread far beyond its immediate boundaries. Dr. William Anderson, now retired, was head of the department and was known as an ardent New Dealer. Another favorite teacher of Humphrey's was Benjamin Lippincott. A champion of socialism, Lippincott had edited in

1938 *On the Economic Theory of Socialism,* in which he expounded his anti-capitalist views. Not only did he assert that "socialism is practicable" and would "seem to be the only solution" in our present day society, but he also insisted that "a socialist economy is far more in harmony with democracy than is a capitalist."[1]

Humphrey, to be sure, was not the only protege of Anderson and Lippincott. Notes Humphrey biographer Michael Amrine:

> These teachers, now elder statesmen, were the spiritual or intellectual godfathers of many men who have made recent history. Few teachers can count so many of their 'boys' in the United States Senate. Besides Minnesota's Humphrey and Eugene McCarthy, a lad named Gale McGee became a Senator from Wyoming and another young fellow, Wayne L. Morse, who was an assistant professor at the university from 1924 to 1928, is now a Senator from Oregon. Morse and Humphrey shared honors in 1959 when the University of Minnesota presented them with its highest honorary award, the Outstanding Achievement Award.[2]

Dozens of people connected with the university have been instrumental in promoting Humphrey's career. A young, pro-New Deal professor, Evron M. Kirkpatrick, had a pronounced influence on Humphrey's life. For many years he was his campaign adviser and is now executive director of the American Political Science Association, which has its headquarters in Washington. Orville Freeman, a young student at the university, teamed up with Humphrey politically and later rose to be a three-term governor of Minnesota and then Secretary of Agriculture. When Humphrey was mayor of Minneapolis, he put Freeman, a World War II veteran, in charge of veterans affairs. Max Kampelman, a lawyer, became a student and a teacher at the university and wound up as Humphrey's legislative counsel in Washington from 1949 to 1955. Like many of Humphrey's university associates, Kampelman had radical views. A former Public Affairs Committee Chairman of Americans for Democratic Action in Minnesota, Kampelman supported socialist Norman Thomas for President in 1948.[3] He remains a close associate of Humphrey today, operating out of a Washington law office.

With Muriel earning enough money to put him through college, Humphrey sped through the university like a tornado. He completed requirements for his degree in a short two years and wound up with a straight A average, membership in Phi Beta Kappa and a *magna cum laude* in political science.

Graduating in 1939, Humphrey received a fellowship at Louisiana State University at Baton Rouge where he went to acquire a master's degree.

Louisiana was in a seething state of political turmoil following the assassination of Huey Long. Extortion, bribery and thievery, though hardly unknown in politics, existed in almost unparalleled proportions in the land of the bayous, with millions of tax dollars finding their way illegally into the pockets of Huey's political heirs. With the crumbling of his machine, however, Huey's henchmen were being rounded up and herded off to jail. The day Humphrey arrived in Louisiana, the state police were swarming over Baton Rouge attempting to quell a riot. The president of LSU, a Long appointee, had recently been nabbed for some crime after trying to beat a hasty escape to Canada.

The "Kingfish's" Louisiana was actually a pioneer welfare state, and the young Humphrey might have learned a thing or two about excessive welfarism or the dangers of concentrating vast power in one man or one ruling body. But if he ever reflected on the evils of Louisiana's politics, his thoughts on the matter are not prominently recorded.

Humphrey might even have found a twinge of sympathy for Huey's reign, as there were many striking similarities between it and the New Deal Humphrey so greatly admired. Huey, like Humphrey, thought of himself as an agrarian Populist. He prated against the vested interests, the corporations and the banks, allying himself with the "common man" and the farmer. Like many a New Dealer, he spread the folklore that two per cent of the people owned 70 per cent of the nation's wealth. At the height of his powers a virtual dictator, he ran roughshod over the state constitution, aggressively pushing the government into the business of building schools, constructing toll-free bridges, erecting hospitals and initiating public works projects. The cement of patronage, corruption and the effective use of the state's vast powers enabled him to stay in office until he was felled by an assassin's bullet. Humphrey arrived in Louisiana with the Long gang on its last legs and the political machinery in shambles. But Humphrey may have been more impressed with Long's legacy of state welfare services than his legacy of corruption.

Whatever his feelings, he found it easy enough to make friends at LSU with Huey's son, Russell. An economic Populist himself, Russell Long entered the Senate with Humphrey in 1949 and has risen to the position of Majority Whip, the post Humphrey held before he became Vice President.

Steeped in Populism and a product of the University of Minnesota, Humphrey naturally tended to favor welfarism and an active federal government. His master's thesis at LSU is an important window to his thoughts at this time. Called *The Political Philosophy of the New Deal,* it hails political liberalism and the advent of Franklin Roosevelt's welfare state. There is nothing to indicate that his opinions of welfarism on the national level were jaundiced in any way by his view of the corruption of state power in Louisiana resulting from Long's "miniature New Deal." So exuberant is his praise for the New Deal that the late Henry Wallace once read Humphrey's thesis and autographed it, "Dear Hubert, you get an A."

Most biographers tend to skip over the contents lightly, but they provide a valuable insight into Humphrey's political beliefs. Though he was only 28 when he wrote it, his ideas have not changed markedly over the years.

The roots of the New Deal, in Humphrey's view, stem from Jeffersonian democracy and Woodrow Wilson's "New Freedom." But it also "owes much to the Populist program. In many respects, it is but the latest edition of its predecessor. The financial policy of the New Deal, like many other of its leading policies such as labor organization, public works and business regulation, goes back to the Populist agitation of the nineties."[4]

The thesis is replete with unconscious ironies and revelations.

Even at this early date, Humphrey indicates he is opposed to "the totalitarian doctrines proposed by the Communists." Yet his own explanation of why the New Deal came into existence is clearly Marxist in orientation.

"The New Dealer," he explains, "noticed that control had shifted from industrial capitalism to finance capitalism. The objective of business was no longer the seeking of legitimate economic expansion; instead, emphasis was laid on the exploitation of investors and the consuming public by stock market manipulation and monopoly price maintenance. It was evident that the spread between capacity to produce and ability to consume had constantly widened; imperialism revealed its inability to provide all the needed outlets for surplus capital."[5]

Humphrey continued: "Class lines were being clearly drawn; the danger of class hostilities was no longer remote but already in evidence. Then, too, under the operation of the so-called capitalistic free market the owners or the controllers of the means of production, because of their greater strength, size and organization, could continue to maintain themselves perhaps for a long time; but their security would depend upon the steady debasement of the standards of living of the other classes of society."[6]

Humphrey footnotes historian Louis Hacker for this intriguing interpretation of American history, but it is clearly socialist in tone and temperament. His notions that the depression was triggered by "finance capitalism" and that alleged American imperialism was non-productive in nature could have been culled from Lenin's *Imperialism, The Highest Stage of Capitalism.* By no means was Humphrey consciously parroting Marx or Lenin, but many of their views on economics had obviously permeated his thinking through his liberal university teachers.

The early Humphrey, moreover, is well aware that the New Deal catered to radical Left groups in the United States, but he thinks there is nothing alarming in the matter. Indeed, as mayor of Minneapolis and Senator from Minnesota, he tried wooing these very same elements.

"There is a fourth and new type of liberal emerging—the democratic collectivist," says Humphrey. "The rise of organized labor's power has given impetus to this new progressive politician. His leanings are to the 'left,' toward a program of democratic socialization. He is, like the Administrative liberal, a gradualist, but is not so prone to compromise and temporize. He regards unionism not only as a method for better circulation of purchasing power but as a new cultural base for democracy. This liberal force has found its chief political power in the C.I.O. [Congress of Industrial Organizations]. The most casual observer has sensed the political pressure of this group, and the New Deal Administration has met its demands on numerous occasions."[7]

Humphrey sees the New Deal as leaning toward the Left end of the political spectrum, but, interestingly enough, he also sees a parallel between it and fascism. Astonishing also—in view of his political record since—is his apparent recognition of the fact that a massive increase in federal power could undermine the nation.

Humphrey appears fascinated that the "same world-wide economic collapse which brought Hitler to power in Germany in 1933, brought Roosevelt and the New Deal to America. . . .

". . . in the month of March, 1933, the positions of Roosevelt and Hitler were strangely similar. Both had risen to power on the crest of a wave of protest against things as they were. Both men and both nations faced problems of unemployment, financial collapse and the task of inspiring a bewildered and despairing people."[8]

The "international implications of a total world bound together into an economic unit were not realized by democratic statesmen until the enemy was long on the march. The forces of fascism recognized the economic and political interrelationships of the 20th century world. Nazism, to be successful by its own definition of success, must encompass the world. Statesmen of Democracy [e.g., FDR] are just beginning to see that security can be attained for one only if the conditions of security are available to all."[9]

There are other parallels which people associate with fascism. The New Deal, says Humphrey, "has given much more assistance to organized labor than it has to unorganized labor; it has materially aided the commercial farmer while doing comparatively little for the tenant and submarginal producer. It has lent the financial support of the government to big business, while doing little or nothing in the form of loans and credits for small business." And again: "No doubt, the New Deal has offered its major assistance to the owners of property and to corporate business."[10]

Humphrey states that "the tendency toward centralization of governmental power in Washington has received unprecedented encouragement"[11] and he points to the possibility that the New Deal "may have set in motion a cold, pragmatic philosophy that can ultimately lead to a fascist system."[12]

In a statement that could have been uttered by Barry Goldwater, Humphrey remarks that the "great danger of executive leadership and New Deal practices lies in the deadening influence it may have on individual initiative and responsiveness. If the citizen feels that government can do all for him, that he need not worry for the 'morrow, then the aim of releasing individual creativeness has been defeated. . . ."[13]

Having tossed out these caveats, Humphrey then dismisses them from his mind, praising the New Deal as the savior of the Republic. He sees the similarities between New Dealism and fascism only up to a point. "The quest for security," says Humphrey, "has become a dynamic movement of such intensity that, in the hope of attaining economic security, one nation after another has sacrificed the principles of political liberty." But Humphrey does not believe this has occurred in America under Roosevelt and the New Deal. "This, we may say, is true of the Fascist nation. With the promise of employment, bread and national prestige, millions of people have surrendered their very soul."[14]

For Humphrey, the New Deal seems different. It has "utilized the power of government to establish a balance between American class relations and a balance in the economic system.

"The readjustments cannot be termed revolutionary in the historical meaning of the term, but implicit in all of the program has been a call for a changed conception of economy and life.

Exploitation and speculation are to be curbed in the interest of security and stabilization. Personal liberty is to be adjusted in terms of the common welfare and the social good. The task of government has been enlarged to the development of an economic declaration of rights, an economic constitutional order. Human values have been emphasized and property values judged in light of their relationship to the common welfare. . . .

"It appears that for the New Deal the essence of a liberal society is that it makes the common good available not to a privileged class but to all, in so far as the capacity of each permits him to share it.

"The democratic tradition in America is a long struggle to secure for every man the privilege of property and the liberty that attends it. The New Deal has adhered to this tradition. . . ."[15]

It would be only a few years before Humphrey would try putting his political views into practice. At first, however, he and his wife returned to the University of Minnesota, where Humphrey seriously thought about a teaching career. Within a year, he completed all courses for a doctorate, again with a straight A average, but he never began his Ph.D. dissertation. Politics and work occupied his time. With the aid of Dr. Kirkpatrick, he became a political science instructor at the university and taught there until the summer of 1941. He then went to the Works Progress Administration, where he held jobs as supervisor of teaching and as director of war production training and reemployment. In 1943, he worked with the War Manpower Commission, of which he eventually became assistant director.

But 1943 was a far more eventful year for Humphrey. He decided to run for mayor of Minneapolis. He has been running for office ever since.

4

Humphrey's Ladder

Dr. Walter H. Judd, a former Republican Congressman from Minnesota, has an intriguing story to tell about Humphrey. According to Judd, who keynoted the 1960 Republican National Convention, Humphrey came to him shortly after Judd had won his first election to Congress in 1942. Judd had been urged to run because of the prominence he had gained as a medical missionary in China, and for his early and persistent warnings that the United States might find itself at war with Japan. At the time of Judd's election, Humphrey had developed a keen interest in running for office himself. A novice politically, he wanted to know something of the mechanics of a campaign, and he felt that Judd, newly successful, could offer him much in the way of smart advice.

Judd recalls that Humphrey met him in his doctor's office, and that Humphrey said he wanted to enter politics not so much for the sake of a career but because it would enable him to become a better teacher. Humphrey said his political science friends at the University of Minnesota had advised him, "We don't know beans about practical politics, so why don't you contact Judd to see how it's done?" Judd also remembers that Humphrey suggested he was a Republican, and had voted for such Republicans as Harold Stassen for Governor of Minnesota,

Wendell Willkie for President and Joe Ball, Humphrey's eventual opponent for Senator.

Judd told Humphrey that he himself knew next to nothing about practical politics, that the only race open in the near future was the non-partisan office of mayor of Minneapolis in 1943, but he would put Humphrey in touch with some of his own active campaign workers for advice and assistance. Judd called one of them to arrange a meeting and four or five of Judd's supporters had lunch with Humphrey, at which time they decided to help him run and kicked in money to start the fund for Humphrey's first campaign for mayor. Today Dr. Judd feels rather non-plussed at having helped initiate Humphrey's career, since Humphrey later evolved into the kingpin Democratic leader in Minnesota.

That Humphrey actually favored Willkie or Ball or Stassen over any good Democrat is highly questionable in view of Humphrey's background and his subsequent politics, but it is quite possible he conveyed that impression in order to acquire some help from Judd. Humphrey is not above taking on the political coloration of his immediate audience. Liberal Democrat Humphrey did at one time seriously entertain the idea of becoming a Republican, however, when Minnesota's powerful Cowles publications offered to support him for political office if he would do so. Humphrey wrestled with the thought for several days, but finally turned it down. These stories suggest, as does his career, that in spite of his deeply ingrained liberal views he is also something of a pragmatist when it comes to reaching for power.

Whether as a result of Judd's advice or not, Humphrey plunged into the mayoralty campaign with his usual boundless energy. Support came from the AFL's Central Labor Union, a few businessmen, and the "university contingent," including 16 of his former professors. Dr. Kirkpatrick, Arthur Naftalin, a University of Minnesota law student (later mayor of Minneapolis), and William Simms, a University of Minnesota graduate, became his right-hand men. Working into the wee hours of the morning, Humphrey made about 15 speeches a day, shook innumerable hands and stuffed literature into envelopes. He had himself photographed reading Wendell Willkie's *One World*, thus fostering the impression he was a serious student of foreign affairs as well as domestic problems. (Willkie, of course, was a Republican, but a liberal one—just the person to appeal to Minnesota's Republicans, Democrats and Independents.)

There were few lively issues in the campaign, though Humphrey talked about cleaning up juvenile delinquency, possibly changing Minneapolis' antiquated charter and making Minneapolis ready for the post-war period. He attacked incumbent Marvin Kline as a "do nothing" mayor, but most of his assaults directed at Kline fell rather flat.

He accused the Kline Administration, for example, of being lax in enforcing the liquor laws. Kline retorted that one of Humphrey's main supporters, George Murk, head of the musician's union, had had his place closed down twice for the illegal sale of liquor. Humphrey also flayed Kline for supposedly doing little to help Sister Kenny, who had come to Minneapolis to carry on her work in helping polio patients. When asked if this were true, Sister Kenny gave a ringing defense of Kline, insisting that at times he was the only person who had helped her. "I do not like politics," she said, "but it is only fair to say that Mayor Kline has given me wholehearted support."[1]

Humphrey also experienced some other embarrassing moments. Vincent R. Dunne, the Socialist Workers Party (Trotskyite) candidate for mayor in the primary, urged the election of Humphrey—an endorsement promptly rejected. "I emphatically repudiate any endorsement or support by Dunne or the Socialist Workers Party . . ." snapped Humphrey. "Mr. Dunne is a revolutionist whose principles and objectives have been repudiated time and again by the Minneapolis labor movement."[2]

Kline momentarily enlivened the mayor's contest when he charged that "racketeers are back in this campaign, upon the side of my opponent, armed with vicious and diabolical schemes to discredit what I have done." Shortly after newspapers containing Kline's charge reached the street, Humphrey, crimson with rage, burst into the Mayor's office demanding an apology. Humphrey never got it, but neither was Kline able to substantiate his charges.

Humphrey lost his campaign in the June election by 4,900 votes, yet actually he had done remarkably well to have scored such an impressive tally his first time out in politics. Though nearly broke from his campaign, Humphrey refused to brood about defeat, and in a short time he returned to the political wars. He soon decided the time was ripe for a new task: fusing the Democratic and Farmer-Labor parties together. And thereby hangs the tale of one of Humphrey's truly startling accomplishments.

To understand the merger, however, one should also have some knowledge of the Farmer-Labor Party. The Farmer-Labor Party in Minnesota was really an outgrowth of the famous Nonpartisan League, a Populist group which swiftly attracted followers in both North Dakota and Minnesota after its formation in 1915. After the Minnesota League's failure to merge with the Democrats in the early 1920s, League adherents campaigned as the Farmer-Labor Party. The new party met with small successes at first, and then began to fade away until the Great Depression. Equally with businessmen, farmers and laboring people were thrown into despair. Minnesotans, like the rest of the country, looked for a messiah and found one in Floyd B. Olson, a radical who streaked across the political horizon like some brilliant meteor.

A champion of the downtrodden, Olson blew new life into the Farmer-Laborites. After a year at the University of Minnesota, he knocked about the world as salesman, miner and common laborer. He returned to Minneapolis to put himself through law school at night. He won the post of Hennepin County Attorney, where he learned to think of petty criminals as victims of an unjust social order. Though defeated in the 1924 gubernatorial race, Olson, running as a Farmer-Laborite, swept to victory in 1930. In 1932, Olson brought in a Democratic legislature on his coattails. He received 50.6 per cent of the vote on a Farmer-Labor ticket, whereas 32.3 per cent went for the Republican candidate and 16.4 per cent for the Democrat. Important parts of his program, writes historian G. Theodore Mitau in his *Politics in Minnesota,* were subsequently signed into law: protection for farmers against foreclosures, a state income tax, abolition of labor injunctions and of "yellow dog" contracts. The more extreme planks, however, such as public ownership of utilities and factories and the like, were rejected.

Olson won again in 1934, though this time by only a plurality of the vote. During his three terms as governor, he managed to weather one storm after another, including Communist intrigue, marches on the state capital and bitter factional struggles in his own party. But as Mitau writes, Olson thrived on controversy. Indeed, his liberalism combined with his impressive political victories and his ability to ride out storms made Olson possible Presidential timber in the eyes of Washington. At the young age of 45, however, Olson's life was snuffed out by stomach cancer.

Olson's fellow Farmer-Laborite, Elmer Benson, succeeded Olson to the governorship. Yet while Olson had the ability to harness the radical and conservative elements in the Farmer-Labor coalition, Benson had no such skill. His difficulties were compounded by a renewed drive by the Communists to attain power. Olson had played ball with the Communists, but Benson capitulated to them completely.

According to David J. Saposs' *Communism in American Politics,* the Communists by 1936 "became the dominant factor in the Farmer-Labor Party. Steve Godler, a prominent Communist Party member who defected because of the Moscow purge trials, testified: 'In a period of two years we see a radical change in the tactics of the Communist Party of Minnesota. . . . They have taken over the Farmer-Labor Party and Farmer-Labor Association. . . . It does not constitute a majority of the rank and file . . . (but they) seized certain strategic positions. . . .' "[3]

Clarence Hathaway, a Minnesotan and in 1936 a key official in the national Communist hierarchy, corroborated all this in the December, 1936, issue of *The Communist.* In his article, "The Minnesota Farmer-Labor Victory," he wrote:

The most important turning point in the life of the Farmer-Labor Party was its last state convention, its nominating convention held last spring. Some forty or fifty active, leading members of the Communist Party participated as delegates in the Farmer-Labor Convention. . . .[4]

Communist methods of infiltrating the Farmer-Labor Party were simple enough. The Farmer-Labor Association, composed of Farmer-Labor clubs from local neighborhoods, was the controlling organization. In addition to these local clubs, the association had affiliates among local unions. In 1937, when the CIO was just beginning to organize in Minnesota, Communist agents applied their talents and energies to both the CIO and the Farmer-Labor Party. From out of state, Communist "carpetbaggers" were called in to man the operation. They captured the Farm-Holiday Association; then they took over the Farmer-Labor clubs organized by the Young Communist League, thereby capturing the Junior Farmer-Labor Association. "Through these maneuvers," says Saposs, "the Communist Party attained a dominant position in the Farmer-Labor Association and was able to control the Farmer-Labor Party and to become the key factor in its conventions, primaries and elections."[5]

With the advent of Benson, who had been boosted up the political ladder by Olson, the Communists moved in swiftly to capture top positions in the party. After Olson's sudden death in 1936, Benson decided to run for governor. He won by an unprecedented majority of 680,342 to 431,841. According to Saposs, "Benson surrounded himself with advisers who were either Communists or pro-Communists. His private secretary . . . was described as at least having the confidence of the Communists. One witness before the [House] Un-American Activities Committee, a former active Communist, declared: 'I want to vary a statement on the Governor's secretary, Roger Rutchek. I do not know whether he is a member of the Communist Party or not. However, I do know this—that he attended the meeting, which was a closed meeting of the Communist Party at Daniel Hall; I, myself, was present and saw him there on October 17, 1936, during the campaign.' Another former Communist Party member confirmed this occurrence, stating that the purpose of the meeting was to discuss 'the Democratic and Farmer-Labor fusion for Benson.' The personnel director of the State Relief Administration and subscription solicitor for the *Northwest Communist* was also a close adviser of Governor Benson. Another was the editor of this Communist paper. On the whole, 'leading Communists had ready access to Benson.'

"Benson was active in various Communist front meetings. At the House Un-American Activities Committee hearings a picture from a Communist leaflet and a clipping from the New York *Herald Tribune* (August 7, 1937) were displayed, showing Benson at the head of a parade of the League for Peace and Democracy in New York City. This photograph shows paraders carrying hammer and sickle insignia and wearing Communist Party bands, and also shows Benson surrounded by prominent Communists. It was brought out that during the gubernatorial campaign of 1938, Browder, then secretary of the Communist Party, journeyed to Minnesota to endorse Benson's candidacy."[6]

The Farmer-Laborites foundered upon the Communist issue. Concerned members began leaving the party in droves. By 1938 the party was bitterly divided and Benson narrowly eked out a primary victory. In the general election Republican Harold Stassen, with the aid of blistering anti-Farmer-Labor articles filed by Joseph Ball in the St. Paul *Dispatch-Pioneer Press*, routed Benson 678,839 to 387,263. Whether generally realized at the time or not, the voters had administered the *coup de grâce* to the Farmer-Labor Party.

With its defeat, the Republican Party began a powerful resurgence, threatening to hold sway over the state for years to come. The Democratic Party, which had polled less than both the Republicans and Farmer-Laborites for the previous 20 years, was in no position to challenge the GOP. To Humphrey and others, the task was clear: to promote the idea of welding the Democratic and Farmer-Labor parties together.

For twenty years there had been fitful attempts to join the Democrats and the Farmer-Laborites. Though both parties had supported FDR since 1932, there were strong reservations about a merger. The Democrats, essentially an urban party, had strong support among the Irish and Catholic communities. And their upper-middle class leadership bridled at the virulent strains of radicalism that coursed through the Farmer-Labor Party.

Farmer-Laborites, who catered more to Scandinavians than to Irish, had their own reservations, including the belief that the Democrats were opportunists who had compromised with southern bourbons and the moneyed interests.

Despite the wariness with which the two parties looked at each other, the merger fever soared in 1944, with "unity needed for FDR" the war whoop of the merger proponents. Roosevelt had carried the state three times, with solid support from the Farmer-Labor Party. But there was much doubt that FDR could carry the state in 1944. There had been a big swing away from the Administration due to the inequities in the draft and mismanagement of food, fuel and other critical commodities. The farmers were also thought to be in revolt. Surging Republican strength, moreover, was an additional factor speeding merger plans, as the GOP now controlled the governorship and both U.S. Senate seats.

Humphrey had clearly seen the meaning of the fusion strategy. A liberal Democrat by nature who had tasted defeat by only a narrow margin in the 1943 mayoralty race, Humphrey realized he could create for himself a secure power base by arranging such a merger. And he was zealously determined to achieve that end. The man who had forthrightly repudiated a Trotskyite in the spring of 1943 was now willing to work with the fellow-travelling Benson, who, with Humphrey and others, played a major role in the fusion campaign. Humphrey was also willing to accept the support of Stalinists and other assorted radicals who dominated the CIO in Minneapolis at this time. With the vision of a united Democratic Party dancing in his head, Humphrey blinked at left-wing and Communist support. True, he was not the only one who accepted such backing, but it is still worth noting that Humphrey, who is given great credit for having booted the Communists out of the Democratic Party in Minnesota in 1948, appeared more than willing to let the Communists in via the merger route in 1944. And like almost all coalitions with the Communists, this one was also subverted.

Desperately anxious for the role of midwife to the merger, Humphrey went to Washington in 1943 for the purpose of getting approval from Postmaster General Frank C. Walker, who doubled in brass as the chairman of the Democratic National Committee. Despite letters of introduction, he was initially given the brush-off. Humphrey fumed as people whom he considered of little consequence saw important officials, while he was given the runaround. At one point, say his biographers, he exploded at a minor functionary, ". . . you ought to get wise to what's happening out in Minneapolis, we came within five thousand votes of the mayorship of the fourteenth largest city."

Finally, after nearly despairing of the task, the 32-year-old Humphrey got in touch with an old family friend, Cecil Howes, who introduced him to Walker at the Willard Hotel. A now slightly nervous Humphrey outlined his plan for a merger and Walker bought it. This key meeting put over the fusion of the two parties.

The task of yoking them was far from simple. There were over 250 meetings between them before the eventual birth of the Democratic-Farmer-Labor Party in April of 1944. Humphrey worked diligently, stumping the state for the merger with such pro-Soviet apologists as Benson and Secretary of Agriculture Henry Wallace, who had come out to Minnesota to help the fusion movement. Organized labor, both the AFL and the CIO, pushed the unity plans, with the left-wing CIO a most enthusiastic supporter. The Minneapolis *Morning Tribune* describes conferences going on all day at the Dyckman Hotel in Minneapolis, with Oscar Ewing, national Democratic committee vice chairman "advising every step."[7] The merger sessions at the Dyckman were presided over by Elmer F. Kelm, Democrtaic state chairman, Elmer Benson, chairman of the Farmer-Labor Association and Paul Tinge, chairman of the Farmer-Labor Party. Tinge had been connected with both the AFL and CIO and in 1944 became director of political activity in the Minnesota area for the CIO's far-Left United Electrical Workers.

While the marriage plans were being hammered out, rumbles of discontent were heard from members of anti-Communist elements who apparently feared the Bensonites and their sympathizers were being awarded too many influential positions.[8] These feelings of concern appear to have been well-founded, judging from the subsequent subversion of the DFL. Time and again, the Democrats were forced to give up leverage to their more radical brethren in the Farmer-Labor Party. The April 18 Minneapolis *Morning Tribune* reports that "Oscar Ewing . . . put pressure on the Democrats to yield point after point to their new playmates."[9] The state central committee, upon agreement, was divided as equally as possible between the two parties. With Ewing, Humphrey and others, the overriding issue was unity, and who cared if the left-wingers were placed in strategic posts?

It is revealing to see just who some of the radicals were who wound up in influential spots in the new Democratic-Farmer-Labor Party. Charles Egley, a member of the National Farmers Union, emerged as vice chairman of the state central committee. In January of 1944—only a few months before the merger—Egley's name headed a list of sponsors of the twentieth anniversary party for the *Daily Worker*, the official Communist Party publication. Mrs. Arthur LeSueur was named as vice chairwoman of the state central committee. Her husband had also sponsored the anniversary celebration for the *Worker*. Mrs. LeSueur was a fervent radical in her own right who later supported Henry Wallace and his Communist-manipulated Progressive Party.

DFL delegates to the Democratic National Convention in Chicago included Elmer Benson and the secretary-treasurer of his left-wing Farmer-Labor Association, Viena P. Johnson. Senator Joseph Ball related that "she played the Communists' game in the Farmer-Labor Association when I observed her activities as a newsman"[10] in the late 1930's. Sander Genis was also a delegate. A 1944 Special House Committee on Un-American Activities report says that Genis was "notorious" for his "Communist front affiliations."[11] Another delegate, Carl Flodquist, had been a long-time Soviet apologist. He is known to have continued his radical activities up through November, 1961, when he was expelled from Local 386 of the Brotherhood of Painters, Decorators, and Paperhangers of America for "subversive activities."[12] Paul Tinge and Mrs. Susie Stageburg both were named delegates. Tinge's appointment as political action director of the UEW had been initiated by Ernest de Maio, identified as "a secret member of the Communist party."[13] Tinge was actually picked by the convention delegates to be the party's state secretary and candidate for Lieutenant Governor on the 1944 DFL ticket. Theodore S. Slen was the national committeeman. Slen was not a flaming radical, but he was willing to make deals with the Benson crowd and in 1946 he claimed he personally would rather have "avowed Communist" support than the backing of John L. Lewis.[14]

The newly formed DFL was not Communist dominated in 1944, but the essential point is that there seemed to be no determined effort to prevent pro-Soviet radicals from attaining power within its organizational structure. Elmer Benson and his followers had turned the Farmer-Labor Party into a pro-Communist operation in the late 1930's; now, in the mid-1940's, they were being permitted another chance to turn the DFL into a similar vehicle. Concerning the merger, Winthrop Griffith, Humphrey's friendly biographer and former assistant, writes: "Far-Left elements of the old Farmer-Labor Party retained major influence in the new party. Communists first infiltrated and then controlled the leadership of the Young DFL organization. They then moved into official positions in county and district divisions of the parent party. From there hard-core Communists stepped up to hold strategic positions in the state DFL organization. By 1946 DFL leadership was dominated by Communists."[15] Certainly Griffith's hero deserves part of the blame.

Humphrey played it cool politically when the DFL was formed. Because he had led the merger move and had come within a few thousand votes of becoming mayor, the DFL delegates began a drive to draft him as a gubernatorial candidate. It was clearly not to Humphrey's advantage to accept the nomination, as most seasoned political observers agreed that any DFL gubernatorial candidate would find the road rocky in 1944.

It was also evident that Humphrey didn't desire it. A proposal to draft Humphrey, however, was made from the convention floor. At midnight Saturday, April 15, after listening to the draft clamor from the delegates, Humphrey returned to the platform to announce his decision not to run. His voice rising with passion, Humphrey declared:

> I want to go into the armed forces if I am acceptable. I want to be with those other young men and women in the armed forces, and you can't deny me that privilege. I cannot be your candidate for governor.

Humphrey emphasized that after the war there would be many problems of readjustment, and he wanted to be in a position to understand them. "The movement is bigger than any individual," he said, "but the individual is important in the armed forces, for it is of individuals that divisions and armies are made."[16] Faced with this dramatic appeal, the convention balked at the draft. As it turned out, Humphrey never did go into the armed services for reasons which are still submerged in a sea of confusion. Politically, to be sure, Humphrey did the right thing in rejecting the nomination, for the DFL gubernatorial nominee, as experts had predicted, was swamped by his Republican opponent.

Humphrey also managed to evade the losing side at the July Democratic National Convention held in Chicago. The DFL delegation was pledged to support FDR and his Vice President Henry Wallace, but the party bosses had engineered a move to dump Wallace because of his extreme liberalism and replace him with a Missouri Senator, Harry S. Truman. Wallace was not willing to be dumped. At one of his own rallies, Wallace spoke glowingly of the youthful Humphrey, told of his candidacy for mayor, and then said he wanted him to make one of the seconding speeches for him. At one point in the convention proceedings, Humphrey had grabbed the Minnesota standard to lead a parade for Roosevelt and Wallace around the stadium. But when the time came for Humphrey to deliver his talk, he was sitting on the floor with his typewritten speech in hand.[17] Some reports had it that the DFL delegation didn't want Humphrey to deliver the speech because he had been taking too much of the limelight. For whatever reasons Humphrey failed his friend Wallace, it proved politically convenient as the delegates replaced Wallace with Truman. In the formation of the DFL, Humphrey of course had received much help from senior Democratic officials who did not want Wallace, and it is always possible that Humphrey was returning a favor when he didn't give that seconding speech.

When the convention was over, Humphrey began campaigning for the DFL ticket. Though he had refused to take the DFL gubernatorial nomination because he had wanted to join the military, this did not stop Humphrey from accepting the position of DFL campaign manager for Roosevelt and Truman. This time Humphrey had chosen the right job, as FDR, unlike the DFL gubernatorial candidate, carried Minnesota for the fourth straight time. The DFL, due largely to Humphrey, was now well on its way to becoming a truly challenging force to the GOP in Minnesota. Fusion and FDR's win notably advanced Humphrey's own political career. As a result, Humphrey, within less than a year, was to do battle—not in the armed forces—but with his old adversary, Minneapolis Mayor Marvin Kline.

5

The First Rung

Speaking before the men's club at Minneapolis' First Congregational Church on January 8, 1945, Hubert Humphrey propounded a thesis of American foreign policy which even during those Soviet-accommodating days must have seemed rather startling. Though at this time the Allied armies were battering the Nazi forces into submission, Humphrey warned that a re-emergence of new "rightist" governments was the clear and present danger now haunting Europe. Communism, he felt, was not much of a threat at all. The way to deal with the Soviet Union? Humphrey suggested that the United States put its stamp of approval on the U.S.S.R.'s aggressive appetites in Eastern Europe. He explained:

The closer the United Nations come to victory the more obvious and apparent become some of their differences. We have always had these differences and there is no reason to believe that the war would minimize them. I do not believe that Americans should be unduly alarmed over minor differences with Russia. If it will be but remembered that it was not until 1933 that we even recognized the Soviet Union as a state, and that bitterness through misunderstanding and deliberate perpetration of falsehood has been the pattern between Russia and America, then it becomes more obvious why differences may occur. I would say that we have to keep in mind what Russia wants and needs. I would list them in this manner:

A practical program of collective security as outlined in the Dumbarton Oaks proposal, establishing the Security Council.

Border states which are friendly to the Soviet Union and governments in those states which will not serve as agents of anti-Soviet forces.

An outlet into the Mediterranean.

A rectification of her boundaries with Poland and Rumania.

The inclusion of the Baltic states into the Soviet Union.

I would say that these are the major demands of the Soviet Union, none of which are in any way impossible of solution, and all of which fit very nicely into a more secure and stable Russia.

It is to be remembered that Russia has been living in a society opposed to its institutions of government and economics. Russian leadership has been fearful. This psychology of fear has motivated her to be highly nationalistic, sensitive and at times, militant. The answer to a fear psychosis is the establishment of conditions which promote and guarantee security.

Russia, more than any other major power because of her past history and because of evidence of intrigue against her, is going to demand conditions of security and obtain them, even if she has to do it through a system of alliances and outright absorption of neighboring states. The best assurance of a cooperative and peaceful Russia is the establishment of an international organization strong enough to guarantee the peace.

The major political danger arising in Europe is not that of communism but is rather the greater danger of the old Rightist ruling forces of the past seeking to dam up the change that is certain to sweep over the continent. . . .

It appears that Europe is going to the Left. This does not necessarily mean communism or socialism, but it does represent a revolutionary change in the thinking of a great part of the people. It means that in the old world purely private and monopolistic, capitalistic enterprise is losing ground.

I think the best example of this whole movement can be found in France's DeGaulle, who symbolized to a great extent the movement toward the Left. Before that, DeGaulle was a member of the French military hierarchy. He was even reported to have been a Royalist, yet today DeGaulle's statements reveal that he is capable of accepting the nationalization of French key industries. Even the conservative mind in France feels that DeGaulle's program of nationalization is acceptable. . . .[1]

Humphrey had been a political science instructor at both the University of Minnesota and Macalester College during the

1940's, but this speech hardly reflected glory on his teaching abilities. History has demolished his outspoken belief that communism was not the major threat to Europe during those times. There was, furthermore, something callous in Humphrey's suggestion that the West should approve the Soviet Union's incorporation of the Baltic states and large slices of Poland. As a self-proclaimed liberal, shouldn't Humphrey have been as strongly opposed to Stalin's aggressive designs as to Hitler's? Neither the Baltic states nor Poland had revealed any enthusiasm for Soviet domination. In 1939, the Soviets had received assurances from Hitler, both orally and in the Nazi-Soviet pact, that there would be no opposition to Soviet seizure of the eastern half of Poland and the Baltic states. When the Soviets gobbled up the half of Poland bequeathed to them by Hitler, they cruelly suppressed the population and deported tens of thousands of Poles into the interior of Russia. They were scarcely less harsh in their treatment of the Baltic states. After trumping up charges of anti-Soviet activities, the Soviets sent the Red Army marching into these tiny nations in 1940. Waves of arrests, mass deportations and the cruel suppression of all opposition became the order of the day. Humphrey, however, didn't mind telling Minnesotans that it was best for the United States to endorse these Soviet actions.

Intended or not, Humphrey's speech, geared as it was to the pro-Moscow line, undoubtedly helped him gain left-wing labor support in Minneapolis, support which he was certain to need in his second shot at Mayor Marvin Kline. In the 1943 race, Humphrey had the backing of much of organized labor, but not nearly as much as he would have liked. When he finally entered the campaign against Kline in 1945, organized labor was solidly behind him. Humphrey picked up, for example, the unanimous endorsement of the powerful United Labor Committee for Political Action, which was composed of delegates from the railroad unions and the AFL and CIO central bodies.

Indeed, Humphrey had ensured himself of labor support by refusing to run unless labor agreed to back him. Before receiving endorsement from the United Labor Committee, Humphrey insisted through his representatives that he would not even bother to file unless he was assured of the Committee's backing.

Organized labor put on a whirlwind campaign for Humphrey by registering pro-Humphrey voters, distributing pro-Humphrey literature and making sure the Humphrey voters got to the polls. But it was the left-wing labor unions which appeared to give Humphrey the most loyal support.

The state CIO, which was beating the drums for Humphrey, had been manipulated by the Communists for a number of years. This fact is recorded by Max Kampelman, later a Humphrey aide, in his *Communist Party vs. the CIO.*

Many of the top members of the CIO during the early and middle forties were open members of the Communist Party. These included Clarence Hathaway, former editor of the *Daily Worker,* and William Mauseth, who became press agents for the United Electrical Workers, the largest pro-Communist union in Minnesota. The president of UE District 11, of which Minnesota was a part, was Ernest DeMaio, a "secret member of the Communist party."[2] Robert I. Wishart, president of the Hennepin County (Minneapolis) CIO Council during the Humphrey campaign and one of Humphrey's biggest supporters, had during the forties "sponsored, been present at, and cooperated with CIO-UE meetings called to honor national Communist leaders visiting the Twin Cities; he had been one of 144 CIO leaders who hailed the *Daily Worker* on its twentieth anniversary in January, 1944; and he had joined a number of their Communist-front organizations, including the National Federation of Constitutional Liberties, and the Citizens Committee to Free Earl Browder, officially listed as 'subversive' by Attorney General Biddle."[3] In 1947, Wishart timidly began severing some of his left-wing ties, but until that period he had been an ardent follower and promoter of Communist causes.

The state CIO's weekly newspaper *Minnesota Labor* saturated its available space with pro-Humphrey material and Humphrey warmly welcomed its aid. Yet *Minnesota Labor* was completely pro-Communist oriented. At the time Humphrey was running in 1945, Sam K. Davis, a long-time Communist activist, was *Minnesota Labor's* manager. William Mauseth, a Stalinist, was a member of its executive board. One issue reporting on Humphrey's receiving support from organized labor also carried William Mauseth's review lauding a pamphlet written by Communist George Morris on the Trotskyite fifth column in the labor movement. In a subsequent issue, Soviet author Ilya Ehrenburg glorified Soviet Russia's war effort. Dr. Harry F. Ward, the fellow-travelling Methodist minister, wrote ecstatically about "Uncle Joe" Stalin:

> For the past few weeks nothing has stirred the admiration of Mr. and Mrs. America so deeply as the march of Uncle Joe's boys toward Berlin. That is understandable for every American knows, as the U.S. Army newspaper *Stars and Stripes* puts it, that 'Joe Stalin is the champion Nazi-killer.' They know that the march of the Red Army to Berlin means the speedy end of the war. . . .[4]

Kampelman again proves a useful source of information on the subject. "Communist party meetings," he noted, "were publicized in *Minnesota Labor* as were Russian films; articles were written by Communists; Communist-sponsored May Day meetings were supported; and editorial opinions always supported the Communist position."[5] Not until 1947 were the Communists eased out.

The CIO even more than the AFL had been concentrating its political efforts in Minnesota in 1945, and Humphrey, as well as other labor-oriented candidates, stood to gain as a result. The state CIO formed a legislative service appearing weekly in *Minnesota Labor* which went to some 40,000 members in the Gopher State. This service, in addition to interpreting measures before the Minnesota legislature from the viewpoint of the CIO, also listed voting records of U.S. Representatives and Senators on every bill in which organized labor was interested. Every legislator coming from a district with CIO constituents was listed in a weekly vote chart as voting "right," "wrong," "absent and not voting," or "present and not voting." Labor leaders reported that, as a result, a number of representatives and senators were becoming particularly sensitive to issues in which labor was interested.[6]

The CIO was extending its influence in other ways as well. The CIO national organization was beginning to reach the general public through radio, a weekly newspaper, colorful and well-illustrated pamphlets, comic strips, public forums and trained speakers. And the CIO unions in Minnesota proved to be a funnel for the propaganda dispensed at the national level. In addition to all of this, the Political Action Committee of the CIO had been busily working since the fall of 1944 in registering thousands of new voters in Minneapolis. Nor was the CIO content with just this feverish activity. In May of 1945, the National Citizens Political Action Committee, an entity distinct from CIO-PAC, selected Minnesota's fellow-travelling Elmer Benson as its chairman.[7] This organization, which had the blessings of Sidney Hillman, chairman of CIO-PAC, had been created to reach voters who were not laborers but who had the same radical slant as the CIO. Benson's organization worked hard for Humphrey.

It would be entirely unfair to suggest that labor, and left-wing labor in particular, was the sole source of Humphrey support. The Cowles publications, both the Minneapolis *Star Journal* and the Minneapolis *Morning Tribune,* endorsed Humphrey's candidacy. So did veterans committees, independent Republicans and some businessmen. But organized labor, much of it pro-Communist or far-Left oriented, unquestionably supplied the high-powered fuel for the campaign. The power of labor was dramatically revealed in the May 14 primary. Humphrey upset all tradition when he swept up 49 per cent of the total vote cast for 14 candidates. Furthermore, he ran almost 2-to-1 ahead of his nearest opponent, Mayor Marvin Kline. The Minneapolis *Morning Tribune* reported that 20 of 22 "labor-indorsed candidates were nominated" for other local posts.[8] Earl Almquist in the *Tribune* remarked that Humphrey's "endorsement by the united labor political committee, although Humphrey does not come from the ranks of union labor, contributed more than any other one factor in making him the leader in the primary mayoralty race. . . ."[9]

Humphrey's primary victory received enthusiastic reactions

from the *Minneapolis Labor Review*, official organ of the AFL's Minneapolis Central Labor Union, and the state CIO's *Minnesota Labor*. While both papers played up Humphrey's win in lead page-one stories, it was the leftist *Minnesota Labor* which gave Humphrey the more laudatory reviews. In addition to a news story, *Minnesota Labor* carried a lengthy page-one editorial titled "100,000 Votes for Humphrey," setting this as a goal for the general election on June 11. Commented the paper:

> Humphrey campaigned on a program of carrying forward the Roosevelt policies as applied to Minneapolis. And who was better qualified to do just that than Humphrey, who managed the campaign that put Minnesota in the Roosevelt column?
>
> In Humphrey, the people saw a public servant who sought to place city politics on a plane that Roosevelt had placed national and international politics. In Humphrey they saw a man who understood that the overwhelming majority of the people wanted a city they could be proud of, and the fact that he had united labor support did not blind him to the fact that the less well organized sections of the population had interests identical with those of labor.
>
> The very unity of the labor movement behind Humphrey was in itself a guaranty of a prosperous and progressive community. They saw in Humphrey the man most capable of unifying the people of Minneapolis for the program of advancing the city to the place it will occupy among the great cities of America. Humphrey earned that tremendous vote in his own right.

Any complacency about the final result, warned the paper, was extremely dangerous and could bring about the "reckless dissipation of the fruits of the partial victory gained last Monday. It can be expected that the forces of Mayor Marvin L. Kline will stoop to every form of political trickery and slander to confuse the issues. Mayor Kline is a past master at this game as was amply proved by his campaign against President Roosevelt last fall.

"This is the time to mobilize for action. . . . The goal is 100,000 votes for Humphrey. Hard, alert work will sweep the vote beyond that goal."[10]

While Humphrey had been more energetically seeking labor support in 1945 than in 1943, he did not noticeably change his campaign style against Kline. As in the first campaign, he assailed Kline for being a "do-nothing" mayor, for having been lax in law enforcement, and for the fact that the mayor was frequently absent from various board and commission meetings. There were some new twists, also. He tried to portray Kline as a high-tax, big-spending mayor who was squandering the city taxpayer's money. Humphrey bemoaned the fact that "our city is in debt over $50,000,000. Last year our city operated on a deficit of approximately $800,000. It is important that the people of Minneapolis be informed of these facts."[11] Playing up to the property owners, Humphrey claimed that it was imperative to overhaul the tax structure to bring "needed relief to property owners who today are shouldering too heavy a tax burden."[12]

While Humphrey was calling for lower taxes and less debt, he was also calling for more city services and public works. Where would Humphrey get the money? He would not try to hike the taxes of the folks in Minneapolis who would benefit from the services; he would try to get the state and federal governments to pay for what services he felt were needed in Minneapolis. The Minneapolis *Morning Tribune* asked Humphrey: "Do you think post-war development projects in Minneapolis should be largely financed by grants from the federal government or local funds?" Humphrey replied: "As much federal assistance as can be obtained. . . ."[13]

No doubt it was a good political ploy to suggest to his future constituents that someone other than themselves would finance their welfare schemes. Humphrey also indicated he was for setting up a commission to help in streamlining the government's structure. For some time, municipal experts in Minneapolis had been campaigning for a new charter that would strengthen the hand of the mayor and reduce the inefficiency of government.

Humphrey was not above employing some highly emotional issues to win votes. When teenage hoodlums had engaged in anti-Semitic incidents in northern Minneapolis, Humphrey immediately blamed Mayor Kline for having fostered the malevolence because of his failure to institute a "community program" to combat anti-Semitism. Humphrey also played on the heartstrings of those voters who had idolized FDR. The President had died in Warm Springs, Georgia in April, 1945. About a week after his death, a crowd braved a cold, pelting rain to attend a rally in Minneapolis' CIO hall for Hubert Humphrey. The rally, called by the United Labor Committee for Political Action, had representation from 78 organizations, including groups not affiliated with trade unions.

On one side of the hall, a huge banner proclaimed: A VOTE FOR HUMPHREY IS A VOTE FOR ROOSEVELT'S POLICIES. A large portrait of the late President hung on the backdrop of the stage, with a spotlight playing on the face. *Minnesota Labor* reported: "It [FDR's fighting countenance] caught and dominated the feelings of those in the audience. They had all taken part in the last electoral fight for the Roosevelt policies, and determination that those policies would be kept alive was written on their faces as they sat there a week after his burial.

"Humphrey, the standard-bearer of the liberal ticket, who managed the successful Democratic-Farmer-Labor campaign for Roosevelt last fall, pledged in a fighting speech to carry into municipal government the ideals of the late commander-in-chief. . . ."[14]

Kline fought back hard, latching on to the issue of Humphrey's radical support. Speaking at a seventh ward rally, the mayor charged that the "announced return to Minnesota of Benson, chairman of the National Citizens Political Action Committee, and of John Jacobsen, state regional director of CIO-PAC, shows the 'big guns' are coming into battle. They no longer trust the ability of Humphrey to carry the fight with his facile oratory," he continued. "The voters, including many in the ranks of labor, are beginning to realize he speaks only empty platitudes.

"The left-wing Farmer-Laborites are crying for help," Kline continued. "But the right-wingers of this party, and the Democrats and Republicans, will not permit our state to revert to what it was under the Benson administration. They realize now that Humphrey is only the mouthpiece for Benson, Roger Rutchik and others of that crowd."[15]

A Kline campaign newspaper, circulated through the city, splashed a story on the front page assaulting Benson and Rutchik for using the Humphrey campaign as a stepping stone to ride back to power in the state. This prophecy turned out to be all too true.

But when the campaign ground to a halt, it was Humphrey, not Kline, who had won this second title bout. He did not receive the 100,000 votes the CIO was aiming for, but he received close to 84,000, trouncing Kline by some 30,000 votes. Humphrey's majority was reported to be the most decisive received by any mayoralty candidate in 14 years.

Many trumpeted Humphrey's good fortune, but once again the leftist elements in Minneapolis and elsewhere saw Humphrey's victory as a signal triumph which they had helped to create. The *Daily Worker* commented: "Labor and liberal forces in Minneapolis won a sweeping victory in the city elections yesterday, electing Hubert H. Humphrey, Jr., mayor, and breaking a 13-to-13 deadlock in the City Council. Liberal forces now have 14 seats in the council. . . . The campaign of the defeated Mayor Marvin L. Kline was one of Red-baiting, Jew-baiting, attacks on the CIO, on the Soviet Union, personal attacks on former Governor Benson and his secretary, Roger Rutchik. . . . Humphrey's main slogan was to make Roosevelt's national policies applicable to Minneapolis for jobs, security, a greater Minneapolis, and for support of Roosevelt's national and international policies."[16]

But the leftist-leaning CIO in Minnesota heralded the Humphrey win with even greater gusto. John M. Jacobsen, regional director of the CIO Political Action Committee, declared the victory for Humphrey and a majority of liberal aldermen "a victory for progress and a defeat for reaction." Jacobsen claimed that it "furnishes a strong foundation for waging a successful campaign in the 1946 elections."[17] CIO-PAC state chairman Robert Wishart remarked: "We in the CIO are proud of the role our PAC played in the state and the nation last fall in the re-election of President Roosevelt. The job has been done again on the municipal level in the election of Hubert H. Humphrey as mayor of Minneapolis."[18]

Sander Genis, state CIO president, said: "It is extremely gratifying to all of organized labor in Minnesota that a liberal and progressive man has been elected mayor of our largest city. . . . I offer my congratulations to Hubert H. Humphrey. He conducted a brilliant and able campaign and we are confident that he will carry out his duties as mayor in the same fashion."[19]

There were even more CIO laurels to be placed upon Humphrey. The CIO's *Minnesota Labor* reported: "A standing ovation was given Hubert H. Humphrey when he dropped in at the meeting of the Hennepin County CIO council Wednesday night to express his appreciation for the part that the CIO played in the election of a liberal mayor and a liberal council. Humphrey declared that the same spirit of cooperation that existed during the election campaign must be transferred to the incoming mayor and council to bring into being the program presented to the city. . . . If we can keep the unity that existed in the election campaign, there's nothing that we cannot do. . . .

"Humphrey," *Minnesota Labor* continued, "singled out the election of Mrs. Nellie Stone to the library board as showing that the 'people of Minnesota had the best interest of democracy at heart.' He praised the work of Robert I. Wishart, president of the Hennepin County CIO council, as a vital force in the United Labor for Political Action. 'Bob brought a new force into the political movement of Minneapolis,' said Humphrey."[20]

Did Humphrey realize then that Nellie Stone was at that time a Communist, and had just six months before sponsored the twentieth anniversary celebration for the *Daily Worker*?* And did he know that Wishart had been part of the arrangements committee for that august occasion?

*In 1951 Mrs. Nellie Stone in a letter addressed to "fellow workers and friends" announced that she had "severed my relationships with the Communist and Progressive Party last October." She explained that she had not intended to make her withdrawal public, considering it a private matter, but had issued the letter because "so many people continued to identify me with Communist Party activities." An account of her repudiation of the Communist Party can be found in the Minneapolis *Morning Tribune* of March 3, 1951, p. 11.

6

Labor's Candidate I

Minneapolis is in bad shape financially. The city does not have enough money to finance its schools. It does not have money for a badly needed program of public works—such things as a safety building for the police and fire departments and a new library building. It is coming dangerously close to having an inadequate airport.

Taxes are high and going higher. They are rivaled in size only by the debt, which has been accumulated over many years and has not been reduced substantially even during the most prosperous period the citizens of this community have ever known.

The city is losing population to its suburbs, and the value of the property which remains in the city is falling, reducing the yield to the city despite the increasing tax rates. . . .

The city does not get sufficient return on the funds it contributes to the state. The city lacks a good, efficient government in which responsibility can be pegged and from which action can be obtained. The city lacks coordination of revenues and expenditures. There is no correlation of the city and its suburbs, which together form an independent metropolitan area.

John Q. Minneapolis looks to his city council for help in these matters. And what does he get? A kick in the pants. John Q. asks for more taxicabs to make Minneapolis transportation more adequate, and his request is refused by the council at demand of the Central Labor Union.

He asks who controls the liquor interests in the city and why the licensing system is not improved, and he gets no answer.

He asks a place to park his car in the loop, and he is told parking rates should be increased. He asks for a better city government, and he gets no support.[1]

Such was the Minneapolis *Morning Tribune*'s stinging indictment against "Humphrey's town" when Humphrey was running for re-election in 1947. The cause of all these troubles? The labor bosses. The *Tribune* and the rest of the Cowles-owned publications bore down hard on the issue as the campaign shifted into high gear.

"Minneapolis would roar in protest," a Minneapolis *Star* editorial barked out in May, "if a political dictator or a business dictatorship tried to take over the city government. Why then should it tolerate the same kind of dictatorship by a group of labor bosses?

"These bosses now control the city council and other municipal agencies. They are fighting hard to retain the council majority, and to extend their power if possible. By the stamp of labor indorsement upon compliant alderman candidates, these bosses have been able to defeat independent candidates who usually run without any organization backing."[2]

The Minneapolis *Morning Tribune* also ripped into the union-controlled council. "The present city council," noted the *Tribune*, "has a majority of self-styled 'liberals' who are in fact controlled by a group of bosses just as effective in their way as the better known bosses of other cities. These 'liberals' must sign pledges to the Central Labor Union and vote as the CLU dictates.

"When one of these 'liberal' aldermen leaves the council, these bosses hand-pick the man they want to fill the vacancy. It doesn't matter whether the man they pick is qualified or whether he will be interested in improving the city for the good of all the people. The only question so far as the bosses are concerned is 'Will he vote the way WE want him to vote.' "

In the twelfth ward, the *Tribune* noted, the alderman was George Matthews, commonly known as the chief of the political bosses of Minneapolis. When Matthews left the council to become a Hennepin County commissioner, the hand-picked candidate to fill out his term was George Todd. Remarked the *Tribune:*

> It develops now that Todd may not be qualified to run for public office because he has not had his civil rights restored since his conviction in 1930 on a charge of violating the federal prohibition act. With this disclosure, the political bosses of the CLU have been scrambling to set the record right by getting Todd's civil rights restored. There is no question about Todd's affairs since he served the sentence in Leavenworth. But there is a question about his qualification for the council seat he is trying to fill.
>
> For the voters there is some question about the group of political bosses which lines up candidates in this manner to protect and enhance the special interests they represent.[3]

Two days previously, on June 5, the *Tribune* had assailed the city's labor machine in an editorial called the "Carbon Copy Candidates." The title was particularly apt, for five pro-union candidates had given literally identical written responses to questions concerning city government put forth by the Minneapolis *Morning Tribune*. Asked if they favored a municipal wheelage tax, for example, all five had answered: "This likewise must be determined by the people, so I do not have any control over the matter." The five made identically evasive answers to all the other questions. While the councilmen skirted the issues, they also made it clear they were not endorsing measures opposed by the AFL's Central Labor Union. Commented the *Tribune* on the astonishing answers these councilmen had given:

> The self-proclaimed 'liberal' candidates for the city council now have provided the best evidence that there is a 'machine' which dominates them in running city affairs. The *Morning Tribune*, in an attempt to give the voters of this city the best possible information about their candidates, has been publishing daily a summary of the views of those candidates. Eleven questions were put to each council candidate.
>
> Careful readers of the Wednesday *Morning Tribune* noticed that the replies to these questions by Syl F. Blosky and Stanley Anderson were identical. This wasn't an error!
>
> The replies submitted by Blosky and Stanley *were* identical. In the *Morning Tribune* today readers will find the replies by William J.

Meagher. These replies are identical with those given by Blosky and Anderson.

In the Friday *Morning Tribune* readers will find the replies by Oscar Cleve. They will be identical with those given by Blosky, Anderson and Meagher.

And in the Saturday *Morning Tribune,* readers will find the replies by George Todd. Those, too, will be identical with those given by Blosky, Anderson, Meagher and Cleve.

Who are these men? . . . .

They are self-proclaimed 'liberal' aldermen. . . .

These are some of the men who deny they are dominated by the Central Labor Union or any other group!

Yet they bow so obediently to directions that they submit identical replies to a questionnaire which is intended to show their own thinking on vital subjects in Minneapolis. . . .

These are the carbon copy councilmen!

The editorial went on to note that two other candidates, one a "hand-picked candidate of the CLU" and another with CLU backing, gave strikingly similar, if not quite identical, replies. "If the carbon copy candidates are elected to the city council again," snapped the *Tribune,* "they will be glorified errand boys for the Central Labor Union. They will merely warm chairs in the council and draw their salaries and allowances for bringing in their carbon copies of the CLU decision on city affairs."[4]

It is hardly an overstatement to say that union influence pervaded the Minneapolis power structure under Humphrey's reign. Rudolph Lee, manager of the Minneapolis Research Bureau of the Chamber of Commerce, reported in March of 1947—a few months before the June mayoralty election—that the Minneapolis General Hospital was being "run by the labor unions." Lee said that unionized employes, approximately half the hospital staff, "to a considerable degree have taken over management of the institution" and declared there had been a breakdown in discipline, resulting largely from employees' squabbles and the increasing activities of business agents ("business agents" were actually union representatives).[5] The accusation was "denied" by Mayor Humphrey, but not convincingly. Nor were the charges hard to believe since militant union leader

Robert Wishart, a Humphrey appointee, was a member of the Minneapolis Welfare Board and chairman of the committee which directed the affairs of the Minneapolis General Hospital and other city health institutions.[6]

In May the *Tribune* editorially blistered the Central Labor Union and the unionized city council for the manner in which they dominated the city's transportation system by refusing to provide enough cabs for the town's citizens. "After more than six months of campaigning," remarked the *Tribune,* "Minneapolis still is limping along with second-rate taxicab service. The city council, dominated by organized labor, has refused to approve issuance of 25 new licenses. The Central Labor Union has not been moved by statistics proving Minneapolis has about the poorest taxicab service of any city in the nation, nor by the statement of hospital superintendents that they could not get cabs for discharged patients, by businessmen that they cannot get cabs to go about their work, or by veterans who want to operate cabs.

"In short, the CLU has decided that Minneapolis will not have better cab service no matter what the needs. The self-proclaimed 'liberals' of the city council have gone along 100 per cent with the CLU in this 'the public be damned' attitude. . . ."[7]

George Murk, a left-wing Farmer-Laborite, a strong supporter of Humphrey (and *vice versa*), and head of the Minneapolis Musicians' Association, "governed" the hiring policies of musicians with an iron hand. A crude operator, he milked producers who put on musical entertainment. Under Murk's policies, for example, a producer who wished to present a concert singer, musician, or entertainer in a building such as the taxpayer-owned Minneapolis Auditorium had to hire 15 of Mr. Murk's musicians, even though they might be entirely unessential to the program. Murk's outrageous demands, of course, discouraged such performances. Furthermore, unless the "stand-bys" actually played their instruments, the salaries were not paid to the musicians but went into the treasury of the Minneapolis Musicians' Association to be used for "charitable purposes."

There were a myriad of other areas where the unions were wielding decisive power by early 1947. Labor dispute after labor dispute found Humphrey on the side of the union leaders, with the city's legal apparatus actually used to aid strikers intent upon forcing companies to knuckle under to union demands. A few months before winning reelection in June, Humphrey publicly acknowledged he did not enforce the law against mass picketing in the Northwestern Bell telephone strike.

The schools, on the brink of one financial crisis after another, appeared at the mercy of the militant AFL Federations of Men and Women Teachers, though it was not until early 1948 that the federations would shut down all 92 of the city's public schools and surround them with marching pickets. The central question in the strike was ostensibly salary, but the real issue—and the one that had plagued the schools for some time—was whether the board of education and the superintendent or the teachers' federation was going to administer the schools. When Humphrey made a "compromise" offer to end the strike, the *Star* chastised the mayor for "advocating a surrender to the federations which would increase their power and prestige over the superintendent and the board."[8]

Humphrey also displayed favoritism toward the unions in the crucial area of charter reform. Since Humphrey first began campaigning for mayor, he talked incessantly about the need for a reorganization of the city government. Experts believed the government needed streamlining, as there appeared to have been a mushrooming of semi-independent boards and commissions over the years. Even more important to reform, however, was reducing the power of the unions. The charter commission was not particularly anti-union, but it strongly recommended that any new charter cut down the number of aldermen from 26 to 13. When organized labor feared that the reduction would threaten its control over the city council, it vigorously opposed the commission's recommendation. Humphrey, in turn, vigorously supported labor's opposition.

Taking Humphrey to task, the Minneapolis *Morning Tribune* commented:

> To achieve the reforms and the reorganization the city needs, the city must first of all have a new charter. . . .
>
> Now organized labor in Minneapolis is 'putting the heat' on the mayor to wipe out some of the gains the new charter would give the city. Particularly, labor objects to the proposal that the city have 13 instead of 26 aldermen.
>
> No sooner had organized labor made known its demands than the mayor gave strong support to those objections. It was complete capitulation on the part of the mayor.[9]

By 1947 the three-man civil service commission, which governed the hiring and firing of city employees, was also dominated by the unions, but it was not until almost mid-1948 that the Cowles papers decided to roast Humphrey for his packing of the commission.

What prompted the criticism was Humphrey's decision to replace the outgoing George Phillips, head of the Central Labor Union, with one Rubin Latz, business agent for the laundry workers' union. A devoted worker for the DFL, Latz had pleaded bankruptcy when he was hauled into court for failure to pay back debts to grocers, doctors and friends. He had failed to pay his property taxes in some years and had actually been indicted November 7, 1927, by the Hennepin County Grand Jury for conspiracy in a "dry cleaning racket." Latz was never convicted. In addition, for some curious reason, Latz continued to change the spelling of his first name, alternately using Reuben, Rubin and Ruben. Latz was hardly a criminal, but neither did his record inspire confidence. James Laughlin, chairman of the Veterans Good Government League, circulated material documenting the blemishes on Latz's record, wondering why Humphrey had selected him.

Yet Humphrey's reasons were obvious: Latz was a loyal DFL member and, more important, loyal to the unions. About a month prior to Humphrey's naming of Latz, in fact, Phillips claimed Humphrey had actually promised the CLU that he would appoint Latz to the commission. Humphrey asserted he had made no such deal with the CLU, but one month later Latz was Humphrey's man.[10]

Though professing to have a "high regard" for Latz, the Minneapolis *Star* was far from pleased with his appointment. In a heated editorial, the *Star* commented:

The civil service commission is composed of two union business agents and the state chairman of the Democratic-Farmer-Labor Party. The term of one of the business agents, George Phillips, expires soon. Phillips and the Central Labor Union endorsed Latz as Phillips' successor. Mayor Humphrey appointed Latz to the vacancy.

Suppose the situation were reversed. Suppose the civil service commission were composed of the state chairman of the Republican Party and two conservative employers. Could any mayor defend the appointment of another employer to the commission, however qualified and public-spirited that employer might be?

By tradition the civil service commission is composed of representatives of the workers, the employers and the public. Humphrey upset that balance early in his administration. Now he seeks to perpetuate the one-sided arrangement.[11]

In view of Humphrey's pro-unionism, it was hardly surprising that the city's debt continued to soar or that the city had the second highest property tax rate among major cities in the United States.[12]

Nor should it have been a shock that eight months after Humphrey's re-election in June, Minneapolis' financial condition was so precarious that Vice President Rollin G. Andrews of the J. M. Dain investment company warned of the detrimental influence labor was having on the city's credit rating. Andrews spoke with authority since his company, in conjunction with a New York firm, had purchased 90 per cent of the bonds issued by Minneapolis over a 20-year period. Given only an "A" rating by Moody's Investment Service, Minneapolis had the lowest rating at which a city of its size and type could expect to dispose fairly easily of its bonds, and Andrews suggested that its less-than-healthy financial condition was due to the power of "selfish" labor leaders.[13]

The Cowles press kept hammering away at the "union boss" theme during the 1947 election, but strangely enough it supported Humphrey over his opponent, Frank J. Collins. A conservative lawyer, a Republican and a veteran, Collins vigorously opposed DFL and union domination of Minneapolis. His victory would not only have seriously diminished the powers of organized labor, but would have cut short the budding political career of Humphrey, who already had his sights set on Republican Joe Ball's Senate seat in 1948.

For reasons best known to the publishers, however, the Cowles papers supported Humphrey by maintaining the fiction that he was somehow not a cog in the union machine. This was the purest of fancies, for Humphrey not only owed his political fortunes to union support, but the unions owed their tight grip on Minneapolis to Mayor Humphrey.

As the man who had been instrumental in putting the DFL together, Humphrey had forged a powerful vehicle through which the unions could gain political control of Minneapolis. If the unions controlled the city, it was thanks to Humphrey's work in creating the DFL. If the unions controlled the city council, it was thanks to Humphrey's support of labor candidates in 1945. It was Humphrey who had packed the commissions and boards in favor of the unions; it was Humphrey who had put union leader Robert Wishart on the welfare board; it was Humphrey who sought to perpetuate union domination of the city bureaucracy by putting union business agents in control of the civil service commission; it was Humphrey who supported the unions and their hand-picked candidates intent upon controlling the schools. And it was Humphrey, too, who proudly boasted of the way in which he had refused to uphold the laws against the unions.

Even as the Cowles papers were trying to differentiate between Humphrey and the "unionized" candidates during his '47 race, Humphrey was ingratiating himself with organized labor. Already eyed by union leaders as their choice to be the DFL Senate candidate in 1948, Humphrey stroked their fancies by campaigning hard to defeat the Taft-Hartley bill, a measure aimed at checking uncontrolled union power. Dubbed by both the AFL and the CIO as a "slave labor" act, the bill had passed the Republican-dominated 80th Congress in 1947 as a result of the post-war wave of union violence and crippling nationwide strikes. The bill declared a number of coercive union activities as illegal, including the closed shop and secondary boycotts. It also permitted the government to obtain a court order to delay strikes endangering the nation's safety for 80 days and allowed states to pass laws forbidding compulsory unionism. With union power the most potent threat to Minneapolis' welfare, Humphrey should have favored its passage.

Instead, he leaped into the fray against it. A little over a week before the mayoralty election, Humphrey appeared on a nationwide broadcast to denounce Taft-Hartley as a threat to free enterprise and free collective bargaining and to urge President Truman to veto it. The program was sponsored by the American Federation of Labor.[14]

Humphrey's role in opposition to Taft-Hartley not only aided him in the mayoralty race, but was political money in the bank for his cherished goal: the DFL's Senate nomination in 1948. Humphrey knew that the unions desperately wanted to knock off Ball, who had campaigned to make the provisions governing the unions in Taft-Hartley even stricter. By vigorously opposing the law (and assuming he would win re-election), Humphrey felt the unions would eagerly support him for the Senate—an assumption that proved wholly accurate.

Humphrey was also tipping his cap to labor by backing labor-endorsed candidates for various city positions. The papers, for example, reported that Humphrey "endorsed" at a meeting held a few days before the May primary W. Glen Wallace, Glenn Thompson and Abel O. Norbeck, labor-backed candidates for the second ward council seat, board of education and library board, respectively.

When this was publicly revealed, the mayor made a half-hearted attempt to deny he had endorsed any of the three, no doubt with the intention of perpetrating the myth that he was free from union control. His "denial," however, was weak.

Regarding reports that he had endorsed Wallace, Humphrey said: "Wallace is the aldermanic candidate in my ward and has been one of my major supporters in the city council. He is a high-grade fellow, and I told him that whatever I could do to help him I would, and he told me the same. Mrs. Humphrey is on a volunteer committee supporting him, and I have authorized 'Humphrey' and 'Wallace' cards to be distributed in the ward."[15]

Still, Humphrey denied this was an "endorsement." He also admitted he had some kind words for Norbeck at the meeting, but insisted that wasn't an endorsement either.

In reference to Glenn Thompson, Humphrey said:

> I told the club that Glenn Thompson was an old friend of mine and that I intended to vote for him. There is a great difference between outright sponsoring or endorsing and saying I am going to vote for someone.[16]

What that great difference was only a Philadelphia lawyer could fathom.

Just prior to the general election in June, moreover, Humphrey permitted his name to be used to swing the public behind two pro-labor office seekers for the school board. Thompson and Owen Cunningham, both union-endorsed school board candidates, ran ads in the Minneapolis *Morning Tribune* demonstrating that Humphrey was enthusiastically in their corner. The ads were actually reproductions of letters Humphrey had written both men. To Cunningham, Humphrey had said:

> Good luck to you in this campaign, Owen! Both Mrs. Humphrey and I are going to put our ballots in the box for you and we are going to speak to our friends and ask them to do the same. I have no doubt but that you will be reelected.[17]

Humphrey had written a similar letter to Thompson, saying in part:

> I think we are fortunate to have you as a candidate. . . . I think you will be interested to know that Mrs. Humphrey was much impressed with the statement of your qualifications. Both she and I are going to cast our vote for you on election day, and we will be glad to say a word to our friends too.

Here's wishing you all the luck in the world! Minneapolis needs people of courage and integrity in its government.[18]

(Humphrey's support of Thompson would come back to haunt him, as Thompson, who was elected, became a militant member of the school board and helped to foment the 1948 strike that shut down Minneapolis' schools—an event that hurt Humphrey politically.)

Aside from his aid to these candidates, Humphrey publicly admitted "endorsing" Robert I. Wishart, candidate for the city council.[19] Humphrey openly supported Wishart even after Humphrey's electrifying statement in March that the Democratic-Farmer-Labor Party had been taken over by Communists and leftists. Wishart was still in league with the leftists at this time, but Humphrey undoubtedly felt a particular loyalty to the man who had diligently worked to put Humphrey in office and who was still a big power in Minneapolis because of important posts he held in the city administration and because of his position as president of the Hennepin County CIO council.

But Humphrey's close ties to the unions were even more graphic. In late February, 1947, a city-wide conference of labor and liberal groups was held in Minneapolis for the purpose of adopting a municipal program and endorsing office seekers. The conference, sponsored by the Hennepin County Democratic-Farmer-Labor committee, was, in reality, dominated by organized labor. The conference chairman, in fact, was George P. Phillips, head of the Hennepin group and president of the AFL's Central Labor Union.

The gathering adopted a number of pro-union proposals, including a graduated income tax (with the first $4,000 of income exempt), a gross earnings tax on privately owned public utilities, higher taxes on commercial properties and other similar schemes. Vigorously upholding "the principles of taxation based on ability to pay," the taxation plank also opposed any municipal sales tax or payroll tax. In short, the labor conference was proposing that Minneapolis' wealthy and middle classes bear all the financial burdens of the city's services.

The more than 200 delegates also pledged to support the "program of progressive" education of the Minneapolis school board and urged an extensive public works program.

The majority of delegates, furthermore, voted to make endorsements contingent upon the endorsees signing a pledge to work on behalf of the platform. There was another feature as well. Frankly serving notice that partisanship had permanently entered into the city's supposedly non-partisan elections, the conference made it plain that the current campaign was preparing the battleground for national and statewide elections in 1948.

"Our campaign this year," Phillips himself told the delegates, "is also a preparation for 1948. Minneapolis by itself cannot carry through reform—we must look to the state and to the nation.

"Next year, 1948, is a Presidential year. It also is the year Joe Ball will come up for re-election—and, we hope, defeat."[20]

The partisan nature of the conclave was scarcely hidden from public view, yet the first person this highly pro-labor conference endorsed was Mayor Hubert Humphrey. Humphrey, furthermore, not only publicly approved the pro-labor platform hammered out by the conferees, but was to claim in May that "I wrote that program."[21] Whether he actually did so is open to some question, but he certainly championed most of its provisions. Humphrey's support for the conference and its program revealed perhaps as much as did any other single act that Humphrey was labor's pawn.

The significance of this program was explained by the Minneapolis *Morning Tribune:*

> This 'progressive' program is a set of demands by organized labor, particularly the Central Labor Union. Organized labor confronts candidates with this list of demands and requires that they agree to it to get the support of its members.
>
> That, however, is not the end of the matter. If the labor-endorsed candidate wins election, the CLU demands iron-clad adherence to the dictates of the organized labor group. If the CLU decides it is opposed to any proposal before the city's council or boards, those officials who were elected with CLU support must vote in opposition to the proposal. If they venture to express an independent opinion,

they face loss of the CLU support in the next election. The labor support then is given some other candidate who is more willing to bend to the dictates of the CLU.

The result is government of Minneapolis by machine. . . . The question which comes before the voters . . . is not one of 'liberal' vs. 'conservative.' It is a question of whether Minneapolis is going to perpetuate government by a machine.

It is a question of whether Minneapolis is going to have city officials who, when they are elected, will be able to vote and act in the interest of all the people instead of the few. It is a question of whether the city will be governed from the city hall or the offices of the CLU.[22]

From the evidence, Humphrey opted to have the city run by the CLU.

7

Labor's Candidate II

Union labor definitely was king in Minneapolis. But it was not only the city council, the commissions, the hospitals and the transportation system that were union-dominated. Even the administration of law enforcement—in which Humphrey took particular pride since he selected the police chief—was subservient to union power.

While Humphrey had bowed to labor's dictates in many areas, he had originally defied some powerful union bigwigs in 1945 when he appointed Ed Ryan—a 1943 supporter of his—to the post of police chief of Minneapolis. For reasons which are still difficult to unravel fully, several union leaders opposed Ryan, even though he had always been rather friendly toward union labor and considered himself a DFL supporter. Some trace union resentment to the fact that, as Ryan says, he kept a file on Communists when he was working in the internal security division of the Minneapolis police force from 1940 until Humphrey's appointment in 1945. Robert Wishart, the left-wing labor leader who had supported Humphrey, was one influential union leader who opposed Ryan.

Humphrey went along with Ryan, however, because of the insistence of one of his key 1943 and 1945 backers: Bradshaw Mintener, then general counsel and vice president of Pillsbury Mills, Inc. Mintener, a liberal Republican, had backed Humphrey because he believed Humphrey was sincere in his claim that he wanted to clean up crime in Minneapolis. Even today, Mintener speaks highly of Humphrey's efforts in this area. Now living in Washington, Mintener says he made it clear he would be quite unhappy if Ryan—the first member of the Minneapolis police force accepted by the FBI Academy—wasn't selected for the position. Humphrey agreed, but Wishart balked. Finally, after an all-night powwow in the mayor-elect's office on July 4, 1945, Wishart walked over to Mintener and reluctantly agreed to accept Ryan. Not everything went Mintener's way, however, and labor made sure that several high-ranking police officers more favorable to labor were also placed close to the new police chief. In 1946, furthermore, Humphrey persuaded Ryan to run for sheriff* of Hennepin County, and a new police chief, Glenn MacLean, replaced him. Unlike Ryan, MacLean did not have bitter enemies in labor's camp. He was easily "cleared" beforehand by union leaders.

Before making his selection, Humphrey saw to it that MacLean was approved by the United Labor Committee for Political Action—a strong supporter of Humphrey during his 1945 campaign.[1] Both George Phillips, president of the Minneapolis Central Labor Union, and Robert Wishart backed MacLean's selection. Thus, the new police chief was boldly stamped with the union "bug," a factor that would work to labor's advantage, even if it would not necessarily advance the welfare of the city at large.

Though the process of "clearing" the police chief with organized labor appears highly unorthodox, Humphrey and his biographers are prone to boasting about Humphrey's accomplishments in the field of law enforcement. Humphrey himself has repeatedly stressed that he had a clear-cut responsibility. Yet it is far from clear just what his achievements were. Under his reign, in fact, union mobs were actively encouraged to *defy* the law, the crime rate soared, and the police department at times operated in a manner bordering on scandal. While Ryan may have been an excellent police chief, even Mintener acknowl-

*Ryan was still sheriff when interviewed for this book.

edges that his successor, MacLean, was "weak" and had policemen working for him who were "too close to the rackets."

A little over a year after Humphrey had been in office, the Minneapolis *Morning Tribune* ran a story which tends to cast a cloud over his self-proclaimed reputation as a "crime-buster." The headline read: "City's Crime Up 66.8 per cent." The article said:

> Crime in Minneapolis for the first eight months of this year is 66.8 per cent above the corresponding period last year, Police Chief Glenn MacLean reported Tuesday.
>
> Up to August 26, Minneapolis police had investigated reports of 2,838 crimes of all kinds, compared with 1,700 in 1945 to the same date.
>
> MacLean said much of the increase, especially in petty thefts, can be attributed to improved police bookkeeping, but he acknowledged there has been a strong 'tendency toward an increase in crime. . . .'
>
> Greatest increase in the city was noted in robberies, burglaries, larcenies, forgeries and auto thefts while crimes involving violent death have actually decreased.
>
> Sex crimes increased sharply on a percentage basis. . . .[2]

Mayor Humphrey was quick to insist the figures meant only that law enforcement was more efficient than in previous years. MacLean said there was bound to be an increase during the post-war period of adjustment, but the *Tribune* also reported that "The Minneapolis figures far surpass the 13 per cent increase reported by J. Edgar Hoover, director of the FBI, for the entire nation during the first six months of this year."

There were other areas of law enforcement which did not particularly reflect credit on Humphrey's police department. The Rev. Henry J. Soltau, a respected resident of Minneapolis, repeatedly contended that vice conditions in Minneapolis were "making a joke out of the police department." (Indeed, during 1948, when Humphrey was running for the Senate, the state liquor control commission, apparently feeling Humphrey and his police were unable to cope with vice conditions, dispatched one of its own agents to Minneapolis to sign complaints charging ten taverns with maintaining gambling devices. The action was taken without notifying either Humphrey or Minneapolis law authorities. Humphrey roared that it was a "political trick" to embarrass him, but he didn't deny that the taverns had been engaged in illegal activities.)

More serious, however, was an incident involving the Minneapolis police with the notorious Kid Cann in December, 1946. Isadore Blumenfeld, alias Kid Cann, alias Fergie the Bull, was reputedly boss of the Minneapolis underworld. Squat and swarthy, he controlled bootlegging operations during prohibition. He had been arrested more than a dozen times on charges ranging from picking pockets to murder, but by 1947 he had been convicted only twice—in 1932, when he was fined $1500 for operating an alcohol still, and in 1934, when he served in the Minneapolis workhouse on another liquor charge.

In the fall of 1935, Walter Liggett, editor of *The Mid-West American*, a Minneapolis weekly, complained to police he'd been beaten up by Kid Cann and six henchmen after publishing an article charging Cann with "muscling into" Minneapolis night clubs and establishing a gang-owned liquor store. Police blandly reported that Cann "told a different story." Though no arrest was made, Liggett nevertheless continued his crusade. And on December 9, just as he stepped out of his car behind the modest apartment house where he lived, he was machine-gunned to death by a killer in a car waiting in the alley.

Liggett's wife, who had been with him, and a bystander both swore they had instantly recognized the killer as Kid Cann. "As he shot," Mrs. Liggett told police, "he had a snarling smile on his face I'll never forget." And though Kid Cann produced an elaborate alibi, public clamor forced his arrest and indictment for murder. During his trial, sensational charges were made that jurors had been threatened with violence if they failed to vote for acquittal. Kid Cann was acquitted.

During the 1940's and 1950's, Cann was still the subject of attention by law officials, not only in Minneapolis but in Chicago and other cities. Appearing on July 6, 1950, before crime hearings conducted by the late Senator Estes Kefauver, Virgil W. Peterson—Operating Director of the Chicago Crime

Commission—testified that "in Minneapolis, Minn., perhaps the outstanding racketeer has been Isadore Blumenfield, alias Kidd Cann." Peterson related that Cann, "a suspect in a number of unsolved murders," had tried to move in on the police in Minneapolis and that there "have been charges that he owns night clubs in the vicinity of Minneapolis. Although this has not been proved in court, there is good reason to believe that he has financial interests in some of these night clubs."

Nevertheless, Humphrey's police department displayed an amazing partiality toward Cann when he became involved in trouble. On December 31, 1946, Kid Cann and three of his friends in the lobby of the Nicollet Hotel in Minneapolis began to beat up one Rudolph Parapovich for reasons which are still obscure. Observers agreed, however, that Parapovich was more than a match for Cann and his allies and dished out far more than he received.

Two uniformed police squads were called to the hotel at one in the morning, but apparently arrived just as the fight was about over. Instead of taking everyone into custody, the policemen, lo and behold, singled out only Parapovich for arrest. They did not even make out a report on his assailants. Furthermore, the police decided to give Cann a royal escort to the General Hospital, where he was treated for the pummelling given him by Parapovich.

Cann had given his name as "J. B. Davis" to both the police and the hospital, but newspaper accounts at the time reveal that the police were well aware that Davis was actually Cann, a fact confirmed by MacLean, detective inspector Eugene Bernath and even Humphrey. (Cann, typically, had originally lied about the affair, claiming the police must have been "confused" about his involvement and that he had been in Florida when the ruckus occurred.)

In view of Cann's notorious record as a key underworld figure, the incident stirred up something of a storm, but the police appeared eager to cover up the entire affair. Reporters who plowed into the case were given little information. The attitude of the police was reflected in a series of responses Police Chief Glenn MacLean gave to a *Tribune* reporter:

Reporter: "Just what was this all about?"

MacLean: "It was just a fight."

Reporter: "Did you know it was 'Kid Cann' who was beat up?"

MacLean: "I was told who it was, unofficially, the next day."

Reporter: "Did that information make any difference in your attitude when you discovered there was no report on what really took place?"

MacLean: "No, I turned it over to Bernath. . . ."

Reporter: "Isn't it customary for uniformed squads to make out a report of a serious fight in a leading hotel when prominently known characters are involved?"

MacLean: "It is not necessary in the case of a little fight when no complaints are made."

Reporter: "Well, in this case a man known about town was badly hurt. I should think that the police would have made an exception in such a case and reported immediately. Don't you think it might have led to more serious trouble?"

MacLean: "No. I didn't pay much attention to it, and I didn't know just what took place except that four men decided to beat up one man and got taken themselves."

Reporter: "Then you wouldn't want to make an investigation of this?"

MacLean: "No."[3]

Detective inspector Eugene Bernath took an even more surprising view of the Cann episode. Not only was he opposed to any further police investigation of the matter, but he lashed out at the newspapers that were interested in the affair. In a speech before the Commonwealth Club, he was quoted as saying the town's citizens should "go after those dirty newspapers who [*sic*] are digging up skeletons."[4]

In spite of the police department's preferences, fresh aspects of the Cann episode continued to make news in those "dirty newspapers." Rudolph Parapovich, the man who had clobbered Cann in the Nicollet brawl, suddenly found himself jailed on another charge on January 15. There was speculation that this was another "favor" for Cann from Humphrey's police department. Still later in the month, Bernath was quoted as saying at a luncheon meeting at the Commonwealth Club that Kid Cann was running the Happy Hour Cafe. Bernath's reported statement—which he later denied—aroused immediate controversy, for if Cann actually did run the Happy Hour he was operating it in flagrant violation of a law which prohibited liquor licenses to those convicted of a felony. Informed of the published statement attributed to Bernath, Alderman Harold Kauth, chairman of the committee issuing liquor licenses, appeared flabbergasted. ". . . The police department just cleared the place for a license renewal," snapped Kauth. "If Kid Cann is interested in it [the Happy Hour], nobody ever reported it to us."

Events surrounding this latest development of the Cann affair continued to grow more curious. After Bernath's statement appeared in the press, Bernath denied that he had linked Cann to the Happy Hour. He now insisted that as far as he knew Cann was not the owner and he had no idea if he had an interest in it. Yet while Bernath was stressing his ignorance of any link be tween the Happy Hour and Cann, just three days earlier Mayor Humphrey had said that bills for the treatment of Cann were being paid by the manager of a cafe—the Happy Hour. "This is just some of this mystery that is inherent in the system of liquor around this town," Humphrey had exclaimed.[5]

The more one looked into the affair, the fishier it became. As public clamor arose over the incident, Mayor Humphrey himself became discontented with the performance of his police department. Whereas he had initially commended the department's handling of the case,* he now decided to dispatch a vigorous letter to Police Chief MacLean. Said the mayor:

> . . . I am cognizant of the fact that where disorderly conduct is so readily ascertainable as in the case in question, apprehension and arrest could have and should have been made.
>
> I wish to state this as a future policy and one to which I require rigid adherence—that whenever there is manifest evidence of disorderly conduct in a public place or a public street, and where those who are involved in such disorderly conduct are present when the officer arrives, the participants be immediately taken to police headquarters where they may be examined, testimony taken, and, if need be, those involved in the incident be placed in the custody of the jailer and held on charges of disorderly conduct or contributing to a public nuisance in the streets and public places of Minneapolis.

*The Minneapolis *Morning Tribune* reported on January 14, 1947, that Mayor Humphrey said the police had "properly handled" the Cann case. Humphrey likened it to "any other drunken brawl."

The officers involved in the case of J. B. Davis or Isadore Blumenfeld and party should be severely reprimanded for inefficient police work and the captain on duty at the time should be informed that in similar incidents he will be held strictly accountable for the most efficient handling of such a case. . . .[6]

Two days later, Humphrey's tough stance had turned to marshmallow. The Minneapolis *Morning Tribune* told the story:

Police Chief Glenn MacLean Thursday had weathered one of the stormiest periods in his tenure of office, an offshoot of an incident made public concerning a fight involving Isadore (Kid Cann) Blumenfeld.

And MacLean, who has had many administrative troubles since he succeeded Ed Ryan nine months ago, apparently emerged stronger than ever. MacLean's position became critical Tuesday when he received a letter from Mayor Hubert H. Humphrey in which the mayor said officers who investigated the fight should be reprimanded.

Yesterday MacLean flatly refused to reprimand the policemen, adding that he intended to run the department as chief "not only in name but in fact."

The situation was tense. If Humphrey's letter could be interpreted as an order, it meant that the police chief was declining to follow the order. . . .

Humphrey was in Washington on a two-week trip. . . . When MacLean took his firm stand yesterday, after reviewing a formal statement submitted by William R. McCormick, captain in charge of uniformed policemen the night of the fight, and stated definitely there would be no reprimand for the policemen involved, the mayor was called by long distance telephone by his secretary, Arthur Naftalin.

MacLean conferred with the mayor by telephone. Then he stated that his decision not to reprimand the officers who handled the incident was "in no sense a defiance of the mayor's orders."

He stated that following receipt of the mayor's letter of Tuesday, he had questioned the officers again and was satisfied that no reprimand was in order, that the policemen had properly discharged their responsibilities.

Mayor Humphrey dictated a statement over the telephone to Naftalin.

"I want it clearly understood that I have complete confidence in Chief MacLean," he said. "And statements which suggest disagreement between us on policies or matters of administration are erroneous.

"My administration has followed the single policy of fair and strict law enforcement, and Chief MacLean has adhered to this policy in every detail.

"The decision as to the final disposition of this case is in his hands, and, if Chief MacLean is convinced that the officers acted properly in this case, I support his judgment. . . ."

MacLean's stand, and the mayor's statement backing him up, were seen by city hall observers as a signal victory for MacLean in his determination to be police chief "in fact" as well as in name.[7]

Thus ended *l'affaire* Cann. From beginning to end, the Cann case had been treated in a highly disturbing fashion by the city's law enforcement officials. To recapitulate: With three of his friends, Cann, a known hoodlum, jumped a man in a prominent hotel for the purpose of giving him a beating; the victim, it turned out, was the only person arrested; the police didn't even make out reports on the known assailants; Cann, moreover, received a royal escort by the police to the hospital, but was not booked; Cann later told the public a lie when he claimed he was not involved in the brawl; a fortnight later Cann's intended victim was again locked up by the police; the newspapers reported that a top law official said that Cann owned the Happy Hour cafe, even though that would have been illegal under the law; the official later denied he made the statement or knew of any link between Cann and the Happy Hour, but the mayor himself had revealed that the Happy Hour management was mysteriously picking up Cann's hospital tab; and, finally, the mayor initially insisted that the police officers who handled the case "should be severely reprimanded for inefficient police work"—and then immediately retracted his stand when the police chief said no reprimand would be forthcoming. The police, moreover, not only approved of the way the case was handled, but the detective inspector exhorted the town's citizens to go after "those dirty newspapers" that were delving into the controversial affair. Whatever else might be said about the episode, it could hardly have enhanced confidence in the police department or embellished whatever reputation Mayor Humphrey may have held as a crusading zealot for law enforcement.

This was not the first time Humphrey's police department had come in for stiff criticism. Only six months before the department had been under fire for the way in which it had handled a situation involving Gerald L. K. Smith. A former lieutenant to Huey Long, Smith was then—and is today—a rabble rouser who spouts anti-Semitic and anti-Negro venom. Not only has he consistently taken a demagogic stance on these issues, but some of his ex-supporters have publicly accused him of cultivating the support of Nazi sympathizers.

In August of 1946, Smith had made arrangements to speak in Minneapolis, but Smith was prevented from doing so by a gang of union-led pickets who managed to cow Police Chief MacLean.

The CIO's publication, *Minnesota Labor*, which vigorously upheld the right of free speech for out-and-out Communists, gloated over the fact that Smith was stopped from speaking. A headline in its August 23 issue read:

GERALD L. K. SMITH SILENCED.

The story under the headline happily noted that "Gerald L. K. Smith, self-styled rabble rouser and America's No. 1 fascist, was stopped cold here Wednesday night. He was prevented from holding a meeting and spewing his racial and religious hatred by a picket line. . . ."[8]

Smith was originally scheduled to speak at the Hennepin County Republican Club headquarters. Picketing started there two hours before Smith was expected to arrive. As a result of pressures, the managers finally refused Smith permission to use the building. The Smith followers were then told by Renata Legant, Smith's secretary, that Smith could speak at the Leamington Hotél, three blocks away.

The pickets then zeroed in on the Leamington. The Minneapolis *Star* reported:

> By the time pickets got to the hotel [Leamington], Smith forces, listed on the hotel bulletin board as the "Northwest Pioneers," were in the ballroom, had a score of guards holding the double doors and admitting only those holding invitation letters.
>
> A chant, "Down with Smith!" began in the outer lobby.
>
> Shortly after 8 p.m. the doors at the left side of the hall, against

which chairs had been stacked, buckled and the pickets burst into the hall bearing placards denouncing fascism, racial hate and Smith. Chains were raised as weapons or shields during the first hectic minutes. . . . As the pickets surged forward, the Smith followers, who had filled perhaps 350 of 450 chairs in orderly rows, faded back to the opposite side of the room. Some slipped out a door. William Mauseth, CIO-PAC director, pushed rapidly forward through the advancing pickets, shouting to the assemblage, "Get out or we'll put you out."[9]

Reporting on the same episode, *Minnesota Labor* said:

A hurried consultation between Walter Frank of the AFL, picket captain, William Mauseth, state CIO-PAC director, and Chief of Police Glenn MacLean, resulted in an agreement that pickets would withdraw if assurances were received that Smith would not speak. The pickets then marched to the mayor's reception room at the City Hall for a previously arranged meeting. There they discussed the events of the evening and overwhelmingly expressed themselves that they would keep inciters of hate against labor and minority groups out of Minneapolis. When Smith attempted to enter the ballroom after the pickets had left, he was barred by the police and the Smith followers left.[10]

The Smith incident set off a steady stream of letters to Mayor Humphrey asking him for an explanation. While the newspapers reported that the anti-Smith pickets were to blame for the disorder at the Leamington, Humphrey condemned "radical and militant minorities on both the Left and the Right." In addition, he chose to praise the police for the way in which they handled the situation.[11]

Yet the police had obviously not handled the situation well at all. Smith had received advance assurances from the city that he would not only be permitted to speak but would have police protection as well. But Humphrey's police department obviously did nothing to protect Smith and uphold law and order. The police did nothing to prevent an unruly mob from storming the Leamington and physically threatening Smith's followers. The police flatly refused to take into custody elements of the anti-Smith forces who engaged in violent and disruptive tactics.

The police did nothing to see to it that Smith had a chance to speak. Indeed, the police, at the behest of a gang of labor toughs headed by Stalinist William Mauseth, forced Smith into silence. Only a handful of people would defend Smith's views. But Humphrey's police department had hardly acted properly by bowing to mob rule and suppressing that cardinal tenet of liberalism, free speech.

Humphrey and MacLean championed union-led mobs on other occasions as well. Biographer Michael Amrine credits Humphrey with never using the police to break a strike, leaving the impression that Humphrey was an enlightened mayor who refused to employ repressive police measures to prevent workers from picketing. But the mayor and his police chief went much further than this in favoring unions over management, even to the extent of permitting massive and illegal picketing so management would knuckle under to "reason." Humphrey did not only refuse to break strikes by employing the police, but he used police powers actively to aid the unions.

In August, 1945, for example, Humphrey repeatedly declared he would use police powers to "seize" Northern States Power Company when a strike threatened. That such a move would undoubtedly have violated the rights of private property and have been ruled illegal by the courts at that time didn't seem to bother the mayor.

The threat, of course, was aimed foursquare at the company owners, not the potential strikers. If Humphrey had actually been able to "seize" the company, the union members, upon whom he depended so much for political support, would hardly have been likely to suffer. Once having taken over the company, the mayor, by his very political commitments, would probably have felt compelled to give them a salary in line with what they desired. Humphrey, it must be noted, did not put the heat on the *strikers* by declaring that he might have to "draft" workers or obtain a possible court injunction against their striking. Instead, as his Populist and political instincts told him, he should threaten the capitalists—much as he would do several years later when he sided with President Truman when Truman attempted to seize the steel companies at the time of the Korean conflict.

In October of the same year, Mayor Humphrey rushed to the aid of union pickets who protested the fact that office employees of the Hart Carter Company were escorted through picket lines so they could continue working.

The plant had been struck by 71 employees of Local 1139, United Electrical Radio and Machine Workers. The strikers had originally permitted office workers into the plant but had subsequently thrown up a barrier around entrances to the company and physically threatened those who wished to work. The strikers' actions clearly violated Section 13 of the Minnesota Labor Relations Act of 1939, which made it unlawful for persons to obstruct "ingress to and egress from any place of business or employment." Yet Humphrey and the police bowed to the union mob. *Minnesota Labor* reported:

> AFL leaders joined the CIO here [Minneapolis] this week in protest to Mayor Hubert Humphrey against the police breaking a CIO picket line and the protest bore fruit immediately.
>
> Picket lines of strikers at the Hart Carter Company here were broken Tuesday morning when office workers, who had been asked to stay out of the plant, went through the picket lines with the aid of the police. They gathered in front of the plant office again Wednesday but lacking police interference, after union leaders' protest to the police, they did not try to crash the picket line. . . .
>
> The [labor] committee that went to see Mayor Humphrey was assured that police subordinates had acted without instructions Tuesday morning and that the police would cooperate in the future. The promise was kept 12 hours later.[12]

Once again, Humphrey and his police had clearly thrown their weight behind the unions, even though the pickets by blocking entrances and threatening workers had unquestionably acted in violation of both state and local law.

Humphrey's refusal to abide by the law when the unions were involved was dramatically demonstrated in April, 1947, when the Northwestern Bell Telephone Company strike spread across five states, including Minnesota. The main company building in downtown Minneapolis was hit hard by the labor-management dispute. The company's cables were cut, other damage was inflicted on company property and even emergency telephone service was sabotaged by the strikers. As usual in these hectic postwar years, the strikers resorted to massive picketing, barring employees who wished to work from getting inside the Minneapolis plant.

Hardly a day went by during the strike when newspapers didn't refer to the impenetrable barriers the strikers had erected at company entrances. Both Mayor Humphrey and Sheriff Ed Ryan, the former Minneapolis Police Chief, recognized that the mass picketing was illegal, but only when the protests rose to a white heat did they finally issue a low-key warning to the unions. Ryan, though biased in favor of the strikers, addressed them at a mass rally, saying, "There is a law which requires you to permit free ingress and egress . . . and we are pledged to uphold that. We are your friends but please don't put us in the middle."[13]

The Minneapolis *Star* reported on April 21 just how the pickets were putting Humphrey and his police in the "middle."

Emergency telephone service, said the *Star*, was crippled when

> massed pickets at the main exchange of Northwestern Bell Telephone Company in Minneapolis prevented nearly 200 relief operators from getting to work. . . .
>
> The lines were tight at the employees' entrance on Third Avenue S. at 6:30 a.m. There were 60 pickets shuffling on the sidewalk as in a prison gang step—nearly body-to-body.
>
> A group of non-striking employees stood on the walk. One man tried to get through the line. As he walked from the curb toward the circling pickets, a dozen other pickets joined the tight circle. The pickets placed their elbows on their hips and created a barrier similar to a conga dance. Pickets elbowed and bumped the worker. He stepped back, turned on heel and went across the street to the city hall.
>
> By mid-morning there were more than 100 telephone workers waiting either in the municipal building corridors or on the sidewalks across from the scene. The parade of pickets continued while a policeman on the corner of Fifth Street and Third Avenue South stood by. Another was in the alley of Third Avenue, where a dozen pickets were crowded together before a rear entrance.[14]

As the strike wore on, the Minneapolis *Morning Tribune* wrote in an editorial more than two weeks later,

> picketing of the telephone building became more militant. Failure to reach an agreement on terms for settlement at one point resulted in a statement by a union official that picketing would become more militant. Consequently, it can be assumed that the increased militance of the pickets was directed and not spontaneous.
>
> Pickets were massed at the building entrances. At the direction of leaders they formed impenetrable lock-step formations. Persons seeking to enter the building, either to work or conduct business with the company, were jostled and forced back.
>
> Such tactics are in violation of the law. Whether the union members or their leaders think it is a bad law is beside the point. The law is there. It should be observed. If it is not observed, it must be enforced.[15]

Humphrey's reaction to all this was to side with the strikers. In spite of the fact that he knew such actions were against the law, the *Star* reported Humphrey as saying "We will not use police to break a strike." Translated, this meant that the mayor was declaring he would not use the police to uphold the state labor code which forbid blocking of entrances to buildings. Humphrey's partisan streak in this matter was just beginning to show.

The *Star* reported on April 30 that a jammed line of pickets had blocked passage to all but a few "top management personnel. . . . One girl was bumped and jostled onto the street when she tried to enter. Pairs of pickets in an endless belt jammed men employees between them. . . ." When company officials initially protested to Police Captain George Hillstrom, Hillstrom replied that "his orders were to 'prevent violence and be neutral.' "[16] Those "orders" could only have come from Police Chief Glenn MacLean and/or Humphrey.

Humphrey's union bias became even more transparent at a meeting of assembled strikers at the Minneapolis Labor Temple. Speaking to the gathering, the mayor proudly boasted of the fact that he "did not enforce the law against mass picketing" because, he said, he had tried to compel Northwestern Bell Telephone Company to come to grips with the true processes of collective bargaining.[17] "I think by our action this week [that is, not using the law against mass picketing] we have precipitated real bargaining—at least they're talking," Humphrey declared.[18]

That astounding statement was even too much for the Cowles publications, which appeared to have a schizoid personality by always lavishing praise on Humphrey but consistently criticizing Humphrey's policies and political allies. Ripping into Humphrey's declaration, the Minneapolis *Star* stated:

> Monday's Minneapolis *Star* printed a news story on the telephone strike situation which quoted Mayor Hubert Humphrey as saying, "I did not enforce the law against mass picketing last Monday because that was part of my plan to force the telephone company to come to grips with true collective bargaining."
>
> *Star* readers know well that this newspaper has been generous in its editorial support and praise of Mayor Humphrey whenever it has felt, as it frequently has, that his position has been right.
>
> If yesterday's *Star* quoted the mayor accurately, as we assume to be the case, then we hope that the mayor's statement was an ill-considered extemporaneous remark which does not represent his sober conviction.
>
> The mayor of Minneapolis is pledged by solemn oath to enforce the laws, all of them, impartially. Whether the telephone company has or has not come to grips with what Mayor Humphrey believes to be true collective bargaining is completely beside the point. As the official charged with the administration of the police department the mayor has the function of enforcing the laws, not acting as a judge.
>
> The *Star* trusts that Mr. Humphrey regrets his unfortunate statement as much as do those Minneapolitans who have heretofore had confidence in the mayor's intellectual honesty and political courage.[19]

Humphrey never did regret his statement, certainly not in public. But as the criticism against him intensified, Humphrey tentatively decided to abandon his position of not upholding the law. Part of the pressure causing Humphrey to reverse his field had been applied by Bradshaw Mintener. Mintener threatened to resign from Humphrey's law enforcement commission unless the picket lines were opened.

The day following the Minneapolis *Star*'s stinging editorial, Humphrey, with a dramatic flourish, visited the picket lines himself. With the *Star*'s words still ringing in his ears, he boomed out to the pickets and available reporters: "Those picket lines will be opened. There will be free ingress and egress at the buildings."

Under pressure, Humphrey had shifted his course 180 degrees, but he was soon to return to his pro-union course. After ordering the police to keep the picket lines open for an hour or so, he decided to use the occasion to bawl out company officials. Turning to the Bell Company's vice president in Minneapolis, Humphrey barked out: "If you will sincerely live by the spirit of the law on collective bargaining, there will be no trouble." The mayor then demanded that the firm stop telling customers in recorded messages that only emergency service was possible because of the strike—even though this was an obvious truth.

"As long as there is ingress and egress," Humphrey declared, "there can be no emergency. Unless you stop those messages about 'emergency' and 'strike,' you better be ready with lawyers because I'll show you it is against the law.

"*I* say there is no emergency. You just can't get enough people to work for you" (emphasis added).[20]

Humphrey's public flareup at the company was no doubt his way of trying to soothe the pickets whose "trust" he had just violated by upholding the law, but his statements were absurd on their face. It was patently obvious—contrary to whatever Humphrey chose to say—that the company could not handle normal telephone service because of the strike. Not only was normal service curtailed, but even emergency service had been crippled because of the action of the strikers. And despite Humphrey's claim, the company had a perfect right to record messages explaining why its operations had been sharply reduced. For Humphrey to demand that the company stop relaying information to its customers could be considered an effort to stifle freedom of speech. And what sort of standard of justice was he trying to impose when he demanded silence from the company but not from the union and its pickets?

Incredible, too, was Humphrey's assertion that the company was so unpopular that it just couldn't get enough people to work for it. That some workers didn't care to work for the company was clear, but it was difficult to tell how many since the strikers, acting in opposition to a law which Humphrey, himself, had refused to enforce, had physically prevented employees from going inside the company's doors. Yet somehow Mayor Humphrey felt impelled to preach to the company about living up to the spirit of collective bargaining. Clearly, Humphrey had turned the world upside down.

Humphrey's little drama at the picket lines was actually nothing more than a staged show for the benefit of the newspapers and the public that had been roasting him for failure to open the company's entrances. For a short time, it is true, Humphrey had seen to it that the picket lines were open, but the papers reported that the pickets quickly closed them after Humphrey left. A little over a week after Humphrey's performance, the Hennepin County District Court felt compelled to issue a restraining order against the pickets. Even following this, the pickets continued to close up entrances to the company.

There is an interesting postscript to the telephone strike. In early May, while the strike was still on, a disagreement occurred between Mayor Humphrey and *Minnesota Labor*, the weekly publication of the state CIO council, over the "progressive" program Humphrey had previously endorsed. The CIO organ maintained that the program, drafted and adopted at a February 23 convention of labor, liberal and DFL forces, contained a clause which stated:

> Law Enforcement: Fair and Impartial Enforcement. Oppose Use of Minneapolis Law Enforcement Agencies Against Organized Labor.[21]

When apprised of *Minnesota Labor*'s claim, Humphrey responded: "That's not true and that's not in it and I don't subscribe to that." He added: "I wrote that program." The correct version, Humphrey explained, read like this:

"We stand for fair and impartial enforcement of all existing laws without fear or favor to any group or combination of interests and with guaranteed protection of civil liberties and human rights."

"That is the statement I stand for and none other," Humphrey declared.[22]

The mayor may have been right about the wording of the clause, but he received no help in substantiating his claim from George P. Phillips, the Central Labor Union president who possessed the original program adopted at the February 23 convention. When told that the press wanted to reproduce his official copy of the program, Phillips said: "You'd better quit looking because you're not going to get it."[23]

The fact is, of course, that whatever the platform's wording, Humphrey did not use the city's legal machinery in any vigorous fashion to prevent union violations of the law. He might deny it, but it was all too obvious that, as far as Mayor Humphrey was concerned, the unions had the run of the town.

8

Humphrey's Leftist Coalition

In creating the Democratic-Farmer-Labor Party, Humphrey had permitted Communists and extreme leftists to gain control of the party's nerve center. In winning the mayorship in 1945, he vigorously courted the pro-Communist elements that virtually controlled the state's CIO labor federation. For nearly two more years Mayor Humphrey cultivated the backing of pro-Communist radicals until events impelled him to take them on in a political life-and-death struggle.

The evidence does not suggest that Humphrey was a dedicated partisan of the extreme Left movement in the United States. Indeed, his own predilections, though radical, were not pro-Communist in orientation. He had revealed he was opposed to the "totalitarian doctrines proposed by communism" in his Master's thesis at Louisiana State University. When he took on Mayor Marvin Kline in 1943, he publicly repudiated the support of Vincent Dunne, a Marxist revolutionary. One of his first acts as mayor was to appoint Ed Ryan—a 1943 supporter of Humphrey—as police chief. The CIO considered Ryan an anti-Communist and fought his selection.

But Humphrey's desire to cooperate with the extreme Left—at least until 1947, and even beyond, as we shall see—more often than not overcame his anti-Communist inclinations. Having created a base of support lopsided with leftists, Humphrey was not inspired to move against those he hoped would propel him to even greater political heights. In his Master's thesis he had related, approvingly, how FDR had compromised with "democratic collectivists" and the strident leftist elements in the CIO. Mayor Humphrey, father of the DFL, was not about to reject the path of his political idol—until circumstances forced his hand.

Following his election in 1945, he was quick to ingratiate himself with the radical elements that controlled the state's CIO. The CIO's pro-Communist *Minnesota Labor*, for example, reported that close to 700 progressives and liberals of Minnesota "packed the main ballroom of the [Radisson] hotel to honor" the fellow-travelling Elmer Benson at a testimonial dinner in August, 1945. Among those at the head table: Mayor Hubert Humphrey.[1]

In November, Mayor Humphrey, attending the annual CIO convention in Minneapolis, addressed the CIO's Political Action Committee along with Benson and Stalinist William Mauseth, then CIO-PAC director. The resolutions and rhetoric that flowed from the gathering could have been scripted in the Kremlin.

The convention passed a resolution urging all unions to wage an "unrelenting struggle against the evils and dangers of Catholic-baiting, Jew-baiting, Negro-baiting, alien-baiting and other group discrimination that go hand in hand with labor-baiting." Such heavy-handed epithets, of course, were usually hurled by Communists and leftist propagandists at anyone who opposed the progressive paradise in the Soviet Union and/or the excessive demands of Communist-dominated unions in the United States.

In passing an eight-point domestic program, the CIO called for, among other things, increasing wage rates nationwide by at least $2 a day; establishing a guaranteed annual wage; enactment of a permanent Fair Employment Practices Committee; and the establishment of TVAs around the country. It also demanded that Congress "eliminate the Rankin un-American committee, which is the successor of the notorious Dies committee."[2]

The chief activity of the "Rankin un-American committee"—a choice invective hurled by leftists against the House Committee on Un-American Activities—was to probe Communist subversion in the United States.

Minnesota Labor reported Humphrey as "strongly endorsing" the CIO's eight-point program before Congress, though it is not absolutely clear whether he embraced it entirely. To be sure, Humphrey's support of the CIO's *domestic* program did not necessarily reveal his willingness to curry favor with the extreme left-wing in the United States, for liberals, radicals and Communists have historically found themselves pushing for similar domestic programs. The acid test of whether a person cultivated the Communist line was whether he also endorsed a foreign policy which coincided with the aims of the Soviet Union. Humphrey did.

Since Roosevelt's death, the United States was dimly becoming aware of Stalin's aggressive designs. Angered and frustrated by Soviet duplicity in Europe, President Truman began to feel the war-time agreements with the Soviet Union had been a "one-way street."

In the famous conference at Yalta, a resort in Russian Crimea, Roosevelt and Churchill had been more than generous in feeding Stalin's aggressive appetite. Based on Soviet demands, the final Yalta agreement transferred a large chunk of pre-war Poland to the Soviets; ceded, in effect, half of Germany to Russian control; recognized Soviet control of Outer Mongolia; approved the transfer of Japan's Kurile Islands to the Soviet Union; and acquiesced in Soviet control of key ports and railroads in China. The Soviets had not only requested—and received—Allied approval for this land grab, but had begun, without Allied consent, to erect Communist puppet governments in Soviet-occupied Eastern Europe. On June 23, 1945, Maynard B. Barnes, U.S. representative in Bulgaria, telegraphed Washington that the moment had come to resist Russian imperialism. Similar warnings at about the same time came from U.S. representatives in Rumania.

Undaunted by Soviet skulduggery, the CIO adopted the Communist line that American foreign policy was to blame for the post-war tensions between the Soviet Union and the United

States. Benson and others rushed to the defense of Moscow and tore into American diplomacy. Claiming that Soviet Russia was non-aggressive, Benson charged that it was the American "militarists" who talk about "building ships and guns" who were disturbing the peace. CIO delegates heard the secretary of the Wisconsin State CIO score American support of Chiang Kai-shek, who would soon be in the midst of a full-scale war with the Chinese Communists—aided by the Soviets—over the control of China. Secretary of State James Byrnes was sarcastically referred to as a man "who talks of free elections in Rumania and Bulgaria" but is "himself from a southern poll-tax state."[3]

A policy plank adopted viewed with "genuine alarm the course of American foreign policy in recent months. The present Administration appears to have departed substantially from the foreign policy outlined by the late President Roosevelt. . . . We see American foreign policy intervening in the internal affairs of liberated countries, too frequently in behalf of reactionary groups who were three months ago numbered among our enemies. . . . We see our foreign policy protecting, and in some cases encouraging, the establishment of fascist dictatorships in South America. We see a retreat from the strong Potsdam declaration for imposing a hard peace on Germany and Japan, and the encouragement of reactionary groups within both countries to continue their plot for world conquest at some future time. . . ."[4]

The Soviet Union was not conspicuous in any CIO resolution. But in its own Aesopian language, the CIO was clearly accusing the United States of having created whatever breach now existed in U.S.-Soviet relations. It was not the Soviets, but the Americans, who were supporting "reactionary" groups in Germany and Japan, and thus, inferentially, worsening American-Soviet co-operation. It was not the Soviets, but the Americans, who were violating war-time agreements such as the Potsdam declaration. In the view of the CIO, the post-war tensions between the United States and the Soviet Union would vanish if Truman would return to the policies of FDR—i.e., surrender to Stalin's demands.

The public record does not reveal whether Mayor Humphrey

found himself in exact accord with these particular pronouncements, but neither does it reflect his opposition. His presence at the convention and his cordiality toward the CIO leaders hardly indicate disagreement. And it is quite likely that he sympathized with CIO policy, judging from his pro-Soviet foreign policy speech in January before Minneapolis' First Congregational Church. At that time, it will be remembered, Humphrey approved of the Soviet conquest of the Baltic states, endorsed the thought that Stalin should ensure the establishment of "friendly" governments on the Soviet Union's borders, and justified Russia's "absorption" of its neighboring states. Furthermore, it is quite clear that Humphrey found himself in agreement with another resolution adopted by the convention: having America withdraw its support from Chiang Kai-shek.

Whether Humphrey was aware of it or not, the Communists and their sympathizers, both here and abroad, had begun launching a frenzied campaign to get the United States to ditch this leader of Nationalist China. For four long years, the United States had been Chiang's strong ally, aiding and encouraging him to defeat the imperialist designs of Japan. The blood and treasure that Nationalist China lost in the Second World War—largely as a result of United States encouragement to stay in the fight—was enormous. But the Communists and their leftist supporters had entered into a grand design to remove the head of the Nationalist government from power. The Communists reviled Chiang because he was pro-West and militantly anti-Communist. His demise would create a power vacuum and permit the conquest of China by a rebellious Communist Chinese faction led by Mao Tse-tung.

The Soviet Union aided Mao extensively. Immediately after its declaration of war on Japan in August, 1945, 700,000 Russian troops marched into Manchuria, and, in clear violation of the Sino-Soviet Treaty of August, began restoring this area to the control of the Chinese Communists rather than to the Nationalists as they had promised. When the Nationalists tried to enter Manchuria in October, 1945, the Soviets blocked them from entering the Manchurian port of Dairen which—thanks to Yalta

—was now under Russian control. As Anthony Kubek relates in his authoritative *How the Far East Was Lost:*

> The Red Army's refusal to allow the Chinese Nationalists to use Dairen constituted a violation of the Sino-Soviet Treaty of August, 1945, according to which Dairen was supposed to be an international port. Thus Chinese Nationalist forces could not be transported by sea to Manchuria and were landed instead in North China. Thence they marched north, overland, being also denied the use of railways by the Russians. As they reached Manchuria, they were met by the Chinese Communist forces armed by Russia and in prepared positions.[5]

In the face of such Soviet aid to the Chinese Communists, it was apparent that for the United States to withdraw its support of Chiang would mean the eventual domination of China by the Communists.

The evidence of Soviet treachery was already becoming clear by November, when the CIO convention adopted a resolution calling on the U.S. government to stop military and financial aid to Chiang Kai-shek and his pro-Western government.[6] But it was even more obvious by December when Humphrey, curiously enough, began assuming leadership in this blatant left-wing campaign to have the United States pull the rug out from Chiang. *Minnesota Labor* in its December 7, 1945, issue reported:

> The demand for recall of American troops from China and revision of the State Department's policy of armed intervention in the domestic affairs of that country have almost reached the proportions of public clamor.
>
> Led by Mayor Hubert H. Humphrey and County Attorney Michael J. Dillon, 32 Minneapolitans last Sunday dispatched President Harry S. Truman a telegram on the subject. The message read:
>
> "The use of troops in China, deeply resented by the Chinese people, is creating suspicion throughout the world as to the foreign policies of our government.
>
> "A policy of armed intervention in the domestic affairs of nations can only lead to another, more devastating war than the one just concluded.
>
> "Therefore we respectfully and earnestly urge you to recall our troops from China and to carry forward a policy that will ensure

peace, greater democracy and security for all the peoples of the world."[7]

The diplomacy that Humphrey was advocating in his "Quit China" telegram could only have benefitted the Communists. Neither Humphrey nor his fellow signers appeared to be bothered by the fact that they were demanding that the United States remove its troops while Soviet soldiers were having a free hand in Manchuria. Indeed, though the Soviet government had announced on October 17 that their armies would be evacuated by November, it was not until the spring of 1946 that they would pack up their bags—staying just long enough to loot the country of $1 billion in industrial equipment and to ensure that the control of Manchuria—the key to the domination of China—was firmly in Communist Chinese hands. Furthermore, there was no valid reason why the United States should withdraw its troops as long as Soviet troops remained and as long as Chiang, the legitimate ruler of China and recognized as such by the Soviets in their 1945 treaty with China, wanted them to remain.

In vigorously urging the United States to take steps which would mean the abandonment of China to the Communists, Humphrey was doing the bidding of the pro-Communist CIO-PAC in Minnesota. The move to send the telegram, in fact, had been inspired by the state CIO-PAC office, whose director William Mauseth was a known Stalinist. Signers comprised some of Minnesota's more "progressive" citizens, including Robert Wishart, state CIO counsel Douglas Hall, Mrs. Marion LeSueur of the Farmer-Labor Association and Mauseth himself.[8]

The Democratic-Farmer-Labor Party, comprising elements of the old Democratic Party plus the Farmer-Laborites, could have been labeled the house that Humphrey built. Its construction, however, had been far too hasty. Long before the merger plans had been consummated, there had been dark forebodings that any new party consisting of an amalgam of Democrats and Farmer-Laborites would soon be dominated by leftists. Such prophecies turned out to be all too true. Though Elmer Benson and his followers had permitted the Communists to capture the Farmer-Labor Party, the Benson crowd had received important positions of control in the newly-formed DFL. Bit by bit it managed to gain ascendancy in the party.

August, 1946, marked the month and year when the leftists took control. In a roaring dispute at the DFL executive committee in early August, Orville Olson emerged as state campaign manager. Political onlookers declared his victory revealed that Benson and his followers were now in the saddle of the DFL. Olson, who later became state manager for the Wallace For President movement, was already known to be "very, very far to the Left"—as he was described by the Minneapolis *Morning Tribune*. He had been closely identified with the Benson administration in the late 1930's. As personnel man at the highway department, Olson was favorable to employees and applicants who shared his pro-Communist leanings. Connected with the national administration in Washington following Benson's term in office, he came back to Minnesota in the spring of 1946 as representative of the National Citizens Political Action Committee (NC-PAC), of which Benson was the national head. He then organized the far-Left Independent Voters of Minnesota, the state affiliate of the NC-PAC.[9]

Olson's emergence in the strategic post of DFL campaign manager was not the only sign that the Benson crowd was in command, but it was the most convincing. The DFL had also managed to nominate candidates who were considered close to Benson or, at least, echoed his political opinions.

Harold Barker, the DFL candidate for governor, received enthusiastic support from *Minnesota Labor*. The official CIO organ found the convention had "made an excellent choice by endorsing Harold Barker," noting further that he had been "speaker of the House during the administration of Elmer A. Benson."[10] Barker, however, was not nearly so radical as other DFL candidates. State Senator John Blatnik became the DFL candidate for Congress from the 8th district. Blatnik, at this time, was ardently wooing pro-Communist elements in the party and surrounded himself with leftist advisers. In 1946 he was enthusiastically portraying Marshal Tito of Yugoslavia as the "George Washington" of his country.[11]

Douglas Hall, state CIO counsel, became the DFL's congressional candidate for the fifth district in Minnesota. Running against Rep. Walter Judd, he assailed American foreign policy, defended Soviet absorption of the Baltic states and seriously asserted that the Soviet Union had not engaged in aggression. He pictured U.S. foreign policy as being in the clutches of anti-Semites and "cartel" attorneys.[12] Though he vigorously denied the charge, Hall was so far to the Left that he was openly branded a Communist, even by members of the DFL.

For Senator, the DFL nominated Prof. Theodore Jorgenson, a frenetic Soviet apologist who became a tool of the Benson claque. When Winston Churchill charged in Fulton, Missouri, in March of 1946 that the Soviets had erected an "iron curtain" in Europe, Jorgenson promptly tagged the British leader as an "ardent imperialist." He consistently defended Soviet aggression and stubbornly sought to show that Russia was being unjustly vilified by the West. Jorgenson agreed with those who felt the United States was chiefly to blame in its post-war disputes with the Soviet Union.[13]

The DFL leaders offered further evidence of their radicalism in their reaction to a sensational speech delivered September 12, 1946, by Henry Wallace in Madison Square Garden. The ex-Vice President, now Secretary of Commerce, ripped into current American diplomacy, pinning the major responsibility for East-West troubles on the United States.

Sponsored by Benson's National Citizens Political Action Committee and the Independent Citizens Committee of the Arts, Sciences and Professions, a Communist-front organization, Wallace had originally intended to direct some criticism at the Soviet Union as well. As he began to talk, however, he was met with a chorus of hisses and boos at every unfavorable mention of the Soviet Union. Believing that discretion was the better part of valor, he then eliminated most of his remarks which could be interpreted as being anti-Soviet. The total impact of his speech was to lay the lion's share of the blame for the Cold War upon the Western powers and the United States.

Said Wallace: "Make no mistake about it. The British imperialistic policy in the Near East, combined with Russian retaliation, would lead the United States straight to war. . . .

"We are reckoning with a force which cannot be handled successfully by a 'Get tough with Russia' policy. . . . Throughout the world there are numerous reactionary elements which had hoped for Axis victory . . . [and] continually try to provoke war."

We want cooperation with Russia, Wallace stressed, "and I believe that we can get cooperation once Russia understands that our primary objective is neither saving the British Empire nor purchasing oil in the Near East with the lives of American soldiers. . . ."

Equating Soviet aggression in Eastern Europe with legitimate American global diplomacy, Wallace exclaimed: ". . . We have no more business in the political affairs of Eastern Europe than Russia has in the political affairs . . . of the United States. . . . We are striving to democratize Japan and our area of control in Germany while Russia strives to socialize eastern Germany. . . ." Lending further credence to Soviet propaganda, he charged that "the U.S. and Britain have encircled the world" with air bases which, he claimed, should be put under control of the United Nations. He declared the United Nations must become a world federation. But, he added, "we cannot expect Russia to become part of such a federation until the United States has demonstrated her ability to eliminate the excesses of the post-war business cycle." At still another point: "I realize that the danger of war is much less from communism than it is from imperialism" —imperialism being a word that Wallace and his audience identified with Western powers.[14]

The Wallace speech caused a furor in the top echelons of the State Department. Shocked and angered, Secretary of State James Byrnes insisted that Truman fire Wallace, which Truman did. Byrnes had been carefully making it clear that the United States was out to check Soviet aggression in Europe and elsewhere, and Wallace's speech had dramatically undercut his policy.

Humphrey's DFL, however, immediately rallied to Wallace's side. So did the state CIO, whose influence pervaded the DFL leadership. *Minnesota Labor* ran such news stories as: WORKERS-FARMERS CONFERENCE SUPPORTS WALLACE FIGHT FOR PEACE; DISTRICT CONVENTION BACKS WALLACE, PEPPER; IRON RANGES CIO-PAC INVITE WALLACE AND PEPPER TO SPEAK; HENNEPIN CIO COUNCIL PRAISES WALLACE.

The DFL leadership also invited both Wallace and Sen. Claude Pepper (D.-Fla.)—who had shared the same platform with Wallace in the Garden—to campaign for the DFL slate. Dr. Jorgenson, John Blatnik, Douglas Hall and other DFL candidates either supported Wallace outright or asked for his aid in the campaign.

Humphrey's own attitude toward the Wallace affair and the left-wing dominance of the DFL was curiously ambivalent. Humphrey had begun, it appeared, gingerly to oppose some of the pro-Communist radicals in the DFL in 1946, but he was unwilling to antagonize them for fear of losing their backing. Diligently trying not to offend a single soul, Humphrey oscillated between the non-Communist and pro-Communist factions in the DFL. His seesawing on the Wallace speech sharply illustrated his tendency to court both sides simultaneously.

Humphrey is reported to have at first supported Byrnes over Wallace, but his support was lukewarm at best. Indeed, Humphrey began to soft-pedal his support for Byrnes at a banquet held in Minneapolis by the Northwest Farmers and Workers Educational Conference just nine days following Wallace's speech. *Minnesota Labor* reported that "Mayor Humphrey had been 'dismayed' by the criticism that had been directed against him for a statement credited to him by the newspapers, in which he declared himself in favor of the Byrnes-Truman course being pursued at Paris. Without directly denying that he had made such an assertion, Mayor Humphrey went on to state that there was only one section of the Wallace speech that he objected to and that was the section in which Wallace 'speaks of two spheres of influence—one in the East and one in the West, and that we have no right to interfere,' adding, 'We have got to learn how to get along with the Soviet Union.' "[15]

Humphrey still appeared to be making amends to his left-wing supporters at a political rally in the Radisson Hotel in Minneapolis in early October. There Humphrey lavished praise on Dr. Jorgenson and Sen. Claude Pepper (D.-Fla.), a featured speaker who had been imported to aid a sagging DFL campaign.

Humphrey's singling out Jorgenson and Pepper for special praise hardly jibed with his initial pro-Byrnes statement. In his campaign, Jorgenson had ostentatiously embraced Wallace, proclaiming his Madison Square Garden speech "a great service" to the public. Wallace, said Jorgenson, "has done a courageous deed in pointing out to the American people the dangers of the present foreign policy."

He classified Wallace's critics as being "found mainly in the camp of those who also oppose progressive policies in America."[16] But the laurels Humphrey handed to Pepper were even more astounding in view of the fact that Pepper had not only embraced Wallace's views, but had gone even further.

Since Wallace's speech and his subsequent dismissal by Truman, Sen. Pepper had ardently sought to take over the left-wing leadership of the Democratic Party. His views on foreign and domestic policy, actually, were far more extreme than those expressed by Wallace.

In the furor over Wallace's speech, it had been largely overlooked that Pepper had made statements similar to those of Wallace and from the same platform. Yet where Wallace had been booed on occasion for derogatory remarks regarding Soviet Russia, Pepper, who said nothing unkind about Moscow's rulers, had been greeted with wild and raucous cheering. Pepper brought the Madison Square Garden crowd to frenzied applause with such statements as, "We have not only a right but a duty to say to our President: 'You have let yourself be captured generally by men who in many cases never in their hearts believed in either the New Deal or the Good Neighbor policy of Franklin D. Roosevelt.

" 'And if we go on as we are now going, appeasing the imperialists in the Republican Party and a handful of revenging Democrats, there can be no end but war.' " Pepper had also called upon the United States to take its troops out of every country except enemy-occupied territory, supply Russia with loans, and permit Russia to have a free hand in the Dardanelles.[17]

Reporting on Pepper's remarks, *Time* magazine had said:

> Russophile Senator Claude Pepper had brought down the house when he cried: "With conservative Democrats and reactionary Republicans making our foreign policy . . . it is all we can do to keep foolish people from having us . . . drop our atomic bombs on the Russian people" (his speech was much more fully reported in Moscow than Wallace's).[18]

Pepper, in fact, repeated this theme on September 18 when he told the Brotherhood of Railway Trainmen in Florida that President Truman's advice on foreign policy comes "from the same men who would cut labor's wages, lengthen hours and deprive you and your families of the necessities of life."[19]

Nevertheless, Humphrey chose to shower Pepper with high praise at the Radisson rally, proudly proclaiming him as "one of the stalwart champions of progressive leadership in the nation."[20]

Nor had this been the first time Humphrey had paid his respects to Pepper, who had long been known as a strong supporter of Joseph Stalin. Earlier in the campaign, Humphrey had attended a dinner in honor of Pepper thrown by Orville Olson's pro-Soviet Independent Voters of Minnesota, the state affiliate of Elmer Benson's National Citizens Political Action Committee. Sitting at the head table, Humphrey had heard Pepper slyly accuse the United States of embracing the "fool's gold of imperialism."[21] There is no public record of Humphrey's having disassociated himself from Pepper's remarks at this time.

Having embraced Pepper in early October, Humphrey began to switch signals again toward the end of the month, when he made it known he would try to avoid Wallace when he came to Minneapolis to campaign for the DFL ticket.[22] Why support Pepper and avoid Wallace? Unkind commentators remark that the reasons had little to do with principle, but a lot to do with the fact that Wallace had received far more unfavorable publicity in the press than had Pepper.

But Humphrey's inconsistencies during 1946 did not end here.

Humphrey, for example, had sided with the non- or anti-Communist DFL faction in some of the intra-party fights in 1946. But he quickly snuggled up to the radicals when he saw power shift to their side. In order to smooth over one fight, in fact, Humphrey went so far as to say that his thinking paralleled that of Mrs. Marian LeSueur, a pro-Soviet radical who was vice chairwoman of the DFL.[23]

During the campaign, moreover, he barnstormed for the DFL ticket, urging voters to cast their ballots for such radicals as Dr. Jorgenson and Douglas Hall. He paid tribute to Dr. Jorgenson—in spite of his well-established pro-Soviet views—for "carrying the fight to the opposition" and as one "who knows the problems of the worker and the farmer from bitter experience" and who will make a "senator of whom Minnesota can be proud."[24]

"The candidates of the Democratic-Farmer-Labor Party," he declared in a Minneapolis speech, "which is the party of the people of Minnesota, merits the support of every progressive individual. That includes the candidates for state office, for Congress, for the United States Senate. Each and everyone of us, between now and Election Day, must do his or her part, to see that every voter goes to the polls. That is the surest guarantee that Barker, Jorgenson, Wier, Hall, Blatnik and the other state and congressional candidates will receive the kind of vote that will reflect the great progressive sentiments of our state."[25]

Vigorously defending the DFL from charges of pro-communism, Humphrey declared: "The last dirty trick of our Republican opponents is to smear with communism such men as Barker and Jorgenson; they arouse the resentment of every honest voter in Minnesota."[26]

And again: "Red-baiting" of DFL candidates "simply indicates the bankruptcy and desperate situation of the opposition that they must resort to name calling."[27]

The DFL did poorly in 1946. In the major political offices, only John Blatnik—the vociferous supporter of Tito—won, with Humphrey dutifully hailing the victory. As in the old Farmer-Labor Party, the new Democratic-Farmer-Labor Party was losing support because of Communist infiltration. As the DFL began falling off in popularity, Humphrey, too, began teetering away from his left-wing friends just four months after the November election. On March 18, 1947, he would declare what the Republicans and even many members of the DFL had known to be the case for some time. "Communists and their supporters," Humphrey proclaimed, had taken over the DFL in Minnesota. "If I have to choose between being called a Red-baiter and a traitor," he said, "I'll be a Red-baiter."[28] Finally, Humphrey was to come to grips with the very problem he had largely helped to create.

9

The Honeymoon Ends

Hubert Humphrey won a second term as chief executive of Minneapolis by a nearly two-to-one margin on June 9, 1947, polling 97,000 votes to Frank J. Collins' 49,600. The results immediately propelled him forward as the DFL's most promising candidate to run against Senator Joe Ball in 1948. Humphrey was excited about the prospect of getting a crack at Ball's Senate seat, but he must have possessed nagging doubts as to just how valuable a DFL nomination would be. Minnesota was now a Republican state. It had a Republican governor, two GOP Senators, a lopsided Republican delegation in the House and a predominantly Republican legislature. It would be almost impossible to dislodge Ball from the Senate without a united DFL Party behind him. And while a strong DFL organization was precisely what Humphrey needed the most to venture into the political arena against Ball, the DFL was coming apart at the seams. Just as the old Farmer-Labor Party had lost support because the Communists had captured control, so was the new DFL group faltering because Communists and left-wing extremists had managed to work their way into prominent positions of power.

Humphrey had himself to blame for this state of affairs. The Farmer-Labor Party had been taken over by the Communists under the pro-Communist Benson. Yet Humphrey had worked closely with Benson to form the DFL. Nor had Humphrey opposed Benson and his crowd from acquiring key posts in the DFL hierarchy. Humphrey may not always have gone along with the DFL's most radical members, but he stoutly defended them, campaigned for them and lent his own considerable prestige to many of their causes.

By 1947, however, he had become alert to the possibility that the radicals and their dupes posed a distinct threat to the DFL's survival. The control they wielded in the party had already caused massive DFL defections, and there would no doubt be a continuing exodus from the party unless the Communists and the fellow travelers were rooted out.

The burgeoning conflict between liberal and Left factions in the DFL mirrored a larger dispute that was bitterly dividing the entire liberal-Left spectrum throughout the nation. Since the advent of the New Deal and the charismatic FDR, a broad coalition of liberal and radical elements had appeared almost solid in their support of the Democratic Party. They found it easy to join with FDR to fight for militant unionism and "reform" of the capitalistic system in the 1930's, and the wartime alliance against the fascist powers knitted these elements even closer together. With FDR's death and the succession of Truman to the Presidency, this coalition, for a variety of reasons, began to fragment seriously. The war was over and FDR was no longer at the helm of the Democratic Party. Weaned and bred by Kansas City's bosses, Truman would not wash down with many liberals, and early in his regime the big names in liberalism —Bowles, Wallace, Ickes, Morgenthau, etc.—had exited from government.

When the Republicans swept both houses of Congress in 1946, the liberals, who had previously figured they had won a permanent lock on the legislative branch, set to tearing each other apart in assessing blame for the losses they had sustained.

But the biggest single issue upon which the liberal-radical coalition was splintering was the issue of communism. Though most liberals had initially been sympathetic to the Soviet economic and political "experiment," many had been gradually disillusioned as they watched Stalin impose upon Russia a terror apparatus which literally liquidated millions of human beings, enter into a pact with Adolph Hitler and begin imperialist ventures in Eastern and Central Europe both before and after World War II.

Others, however, retained their illusions. In the immediate post-war years, this pro-Communist element deserted the leadership in the Democratic Party to rally around a new leftist folk hero: Henry Wallace. An Iowa farmer of Republican ancestry, a former Vice President and an ex-U.S. cabinet official, Wallace nevertheless chose to become a pawn of the American Left. Following his dismissal by Truman over his foreign policy pronouncements at Madison Square Garden in September, 1946, Wallace steered even more determinedly toward a pro-Soviet course. He continually eulogized Soviet communism and selected to pin the blame for Soviet aggression on alleged American "provocations." Wallace had devoted and powerful supporters. The CIO, while seriously divided, was generally in the Wallace camp. It employed as general counsel Lee Pressman, who quit his job in February of 1948 to take a position of leadership in the Wallace movement. Pressman, who joined the Communist Party in the 1930's, by his own admission didn't break with the party ideologically until 1950. The CIO-PAC, the political action arm of the CIO, supported Wallace in his dispute with Truman and Byrnes over foreign policy. The National Citizens Political Action Committee, a CIO-spawned organization whose aim was to attract non-labor support for labor and liberal causes, vigorously backed Wallace. Ditto the Independent Citizens Committee of the Arts, Sciences and Professions, a pro-Communist group composed of liberal "intellectuals."

By the end of 1946, Wallace had turned into a highly troublesome figure for the Democratic Party. A liberal "martyr," sacrificed by the Truman Administration, he had acquired the job of editor of the *New Republic*, the chief house organ of American liberalism. In addition to having a vehicle whose views influenced an important segment of the Democratic Party, Wallace became the compelling force in the newly formed Progressive

Citizens of America, the result of a merger between the NCPAC and the ICCASP at a Chicago conference in late December.

The PCA, as many had predicted, was to become the fulcrum for a third-party movement led by Wallace. When Wallace returned from a well-publicized European tour in the spring of 1947, he barnstormed the country under PCA's auspices, preaching the gospel of "peace with Russia" and a revived New Deal. On December 29, a not exactly unexpected announcement came from America's most prominent pro-Soviet apologist: Wallace, permitting his other shoe to drop, revealed he would be a third-party candidate in 1948.

As the Wallace movement gathered momentum, the anti-Communist and non-Communist liberals became determined to set up an opposition force. Their concern for creating a powerful, non-Communist liberal organization—one that would work within the framework of the Democratic Party—stemmed partly from the realization that Communist manipulation of the Wallace movement and control of various liberal causes had blackened liberalism's image around the country. There was still another reason for establishing a group that would vigorously oppose the Wallace forces: to persuade as many liberals as possible to line up with the Democratic Party.

Though not necessarily enamored of Truman, many prominent liberals in the country still felt comfortable enough parked under the big Democratic tent, even though it harbored persons with such diverse views as the conservative Sen. Harry Byrd of Virginia and the radical Sen. Claude Pepper of Florida. They also believed it would be virtually impossible to create a thriving third party, and that the best the Wallace effort could hope to achieve was to drain enough votes away from the Democratic Party so the "reactionary" Republicans would regain the White House. In their view, the creation of a vigorous liberal organization that would lock horns with Wallace would be the best way to minimize the impact of Wallace's defection.

Thus, on January 3, 1947, more than 400 persons gathered in Washington's Willard Hotel to form a new group, one that would work to "reform" and "mold" the Democratic Party in a more liberal pattern. The meeting had actually been called by the Union for Democratic Action, an organization of dissident socialists and liberals. Noted theologian Reinhold Niebuhr, chairman of the UDA, presided at the conference as Chester Bowles called for the conferees to form a progressive front—free of Communist influence—"to establish liberal control of the Democratic Party."[1] The conference drew up plans for an organization called the Americans for Democratic Action, though it was not until March that ADA would emerge fully born.

Included among the founders were such prominent liberals as Walter Reuther, head of the United Auto Workers; Mrs. Eleanor Roosevelt; columnist Marquis Childs; James Carey, secretary of the CIO; David Dubinsky, head of the International Ladies Garment Workers Union; and James Loeb, executive secretary of the UDA and the driving force behind ADA's birth. The three top officers were Wilson W. Wyatt, national chairman; Leon Henderson, chairman of the executive committee; and pollster Louis Harris, national treasurer. Franklin D. Roosevelt, Jr., and Mayor Hubert Humphrey were each selected to be a national vice chairman.

Highly liberal in its domestic policies—the first issue of the *ADA World* called for "public acquisition of monopolies"—ADA was less radical in its foreign policy. Albeit cautious, ADA nevertheless supported a policy of blocking communism in Europe, including Truman's program of military aid to Greece and Turkey and the Marshall Plan.

During the three-month gestation period that it took to become a full-fledged organization, ADA activity attained large-scale proportions. Moving swiftly in response to its first gathering, ADA staged regional meetings to launch chapters throughout the United States. Conferences were held in such cities as Chicago, Seattle, Los Angeles, Louisville, Minneapolis, and Baltimore. Keynoting the regional, state and local meetings were such headline speakers as Arthur Schlesinger, Jr., Franklin Roosevelt, Jr., and Hollywood actor Ronald Reagan.

Mayor Humphrey played a highly influential role. Humphrey

helped organize ADA chapters outside his own state, but he paid particular attention to forming an ADA chapter in Minnesota for the purpose of combatting the Communist and left-wing elements attempting to subvert the DFL. Organization plans for the Minnesota chapter had been given the green light at the ADA regional nine-state conference held in early March of 1947 in Chicago, where delegates stressed the importance of using ADA as a means to lick the Communists politically. Subsequently, a group of Humphrey advisers became the nucleus of the ADA in Minnesota. Among its influential members: Humphrey's secretary, Arthur Naftalin; his former professor and campaign adviser, Dr. Evron Kirkpatrick; Orville Freeman, who had met Humphrey as a student at the University of Minnesota and had become an influential part of his administration; Eugene McCarthy (now a Minnesota Senator); Eugenie Anderson, who became an Ambassador to Denmark; and Max Kampelman, a close Humphrey friend and adviser.

Kampelman says that ADA "was the vehicle to kick out the Communists in Minnesota." And despite the later soft-on-communism policies of the national ADA, the Minnesota chapter played a major role in drumming the Reds out of the DFL. Dr. Kirkpatrick, now head of the American Political Science Association in Washington, had long been an active opponent of the Communists. Naftalin, who later wrote his Ph.D. thesis on the Communists in the Farmer-Labor Party, vigorously opposed their policies. Though a World War II pacifist and economic socialist, Kampelman was no friend of the Communists, and earnestly fought them in Minnesota. Since the DFL fight, Kampelman has authored valuable books and articles shedding much light on the Communist conspiracy. And Kirkpatrick recalls that Orville Freeman, a salty ex-Marine, energetically battled the Communists in the DFL and, indeed, proved to be a most effective in-fighter by scrapping with the leftists while holding on to his elected post of secretary of the left-wing dominated state executive committee. Many, in fact, believe that the right-wing might not have won without him.

Freeman says the fight for control of the DFL was the "most

vicious" political battle he's ever been in, and frankly admits having used something less than Marquis of Queensbury rules in that savage contest. Several times he nearly came to blows with key radicals, and he stood ready to slug it out with Elmer Benson when Benson referred to Freeman as a "fascist."

While Humphrey had apparently cultivated the gardens in both the pro-Communist and anti-Communist camps from 1944 through 1946, he ferociously fought the pro-Soviet element in the DFL in 1947-48 as if his life depended on it. Actually, his political life did hang precariously in the balance. The pro-Communist influence over the DFL was already proving disastrous to the party's popularity. If the radical element retained the party's reins, the DFL would almost certainly lose additional support in the state and from the national Democratic Party. If the Communists were kicked out, on the other hand, the DFL would probably survive as the legitimate Democratic Party in Minnesota with close national ties. Yet, unless Humphrey were willing to put his own prestige on the line, the Communists were quite likely to capture the DFL permanently. Humphrey was willing to stick his chin out, all right, but even so he managed to make fewer political enemies in this life-and-death struggle than some of his supporters. As Freeman himself explains it, Humphrey was just "more adroit."

On March 18, 1947, Humphrey sounded the tocsin that would commit him to a fight to the finish with the DFL's left-wing faction. Speaking to an ADA-sponsored rally in Minneapolis, Humphrey unleashed the charge that "Communists and their supporters" had seized the reins of leadership in the DFL. Humphrey's proclamation was made to a meeting of 300 persons who had gathered at the Curtis Hotel to hear Leon Henderson, another ADA official, outline ADA's policies and political philosophy. To a cheering audience, Humphrey lashed out at Communist members and sympathizers "who are busy this week learning the party line which is to be announced next week."

In hurling his challenge at "true liberals, true Democrats and true Farmer-Laborites" to recapture the DFL, Mayor Humphrey declared that leftist activities in the DFL had driven thousands of the state's liberal citizens out of the party. Humphrey particularly singled out for criticism the DFL Association, a grassroots group with powerful influence over the DFL party structure. Over the previous weekend, the association had voted to condemn President Truman for advocating help to Greece and Turkey for the purpose of blocking Soviet expansion, and it had voted to send a copy of its resolution to Humphrey. Retorted the mayor: "I don't want any totalitarians of the Left telling me what I should think about the situation in Greece and Turkey, and I don't want them sending me any resolutions of what they think."

Humphrey stressed: "If I have to choose between being called a Red-baiter and a traitor, I'll be a Red-baiter."[2]

Humphrey's thunderbolt, the first statement of its kind made publicly by a leading DFL candidate, was a virtual declaration of war by the "right-wing" DFL faction against the leftists. Nor did Humphrey let up. Not long afterward he would say:

"These people headed by Elmer Benson are trying to wreck the party, and if they don't succeed one way they will try another. You must remember this is the same clique that tried to stab Floyd B. Olson and called President Roosevelt a warmonger back in 1940.

"I am among those who helped shape the Democratic-Farmer-Labor Party and I am interested only in seeing that it stimulates action toward good government."[3]

The left-wing faction swiftly retaliated. Ex-governor Elmer Benson, even before Humphrey's verbal assault on him, repeatedly assailed the mayor, as did Orville Olson, then executive secretary of the pro-Wallace Independent Voters of Minnesota. Olson, for example, accused Humphrey of betraying the "farmers and labor unions who [*sic*] are being attacked by the coalition of reactionary Democrats and Republicans."[4] Fence straddlers and long-time Communist apologists like Rep. John Blatnik cautiously rapped Humphrey for being "unfair" in his charges against the DFL.[5]

At the DFL's state executive committee meeting on June 29, the mayor was subjected to a series of attacks in the left-wing flavored sessions, including an intemperate assault by Benson. Much of the antagonism directed against Humphrey developed from his ties with the ADA, of which he had recently been elected state chairman. The executive committee grudgingly commended him on his re-election as mayor, but refused to add a proposed bouquet by Freeman, its right-wing secretary, for "his outstanding leadership to the progressive forces in Minnesota."

The day-long meeting at the Radisson Hotel also laid the groundwork for the 1948 campaign by naming a "political action committee" headed by Humphrey foe Benson.[6]

The left-wingers were just warming up. Humphrey soon became the target of a stinging attack by the *Minnesota Leader*, the pro-Wallace organ of the DFL Association. "Your association with the unsavory Americans for Democratic Action," the *Leader* heatedly observed, "created nationally to serve as liberal window dressing for the Wall Streeters and militarists behind Truman and created in Minnesota as a haven for reactionary elements in the Democratic and Farmer Labor parties, is another indication of the character of your associations. . . . By your associations and your record you have ruined any chance of your being an acceptable progressive candidate in the 1948 elections."[7] Humphrey was also accused of being a tool of the Cowles Press and General Mills.

The split in the DFL in Minnesota crystallized even more sharply following Wallace's famous declaration on December 29, 1947, in which he resigned from the Democratic Party to run as a third-party Presidential candidate. Speaking in Chicago, the former Vice President explained that the Democrats had rejected his plea for the Administration to "repudiate universal military training and rid itself of the Wall Street-military team that is leading us toward war," to curb "monopoly profits" and to preserve the living standards of the American people. Though he had originally hailed it as his own creation, he now came out against the Marshall Plan for helping divide Europe into "two warring camps."

The Wallace statement might have been expected to lessen

the burning conflict within the DFL. As in other states, it was believed by some that the Wallaceites in Minnesota would vacate the Democratic Party to form their own. Instead, they initially refused to go the third-party route, deciding it would be easy enough to take over the existing Democratic organization, which was already heavily saturated with pro-Communist radicals. At the second annual convention of the Progressive Citizens of America, former Minnesota governor Elmer Benson declared, "If we retain control of the Democratic-Farmer-Labor Party at the state convention, Wallace will be the nominee and we will present him at the national Democratic convention. . . . If President Truman runs in Minnesota, he'll have to run as an independent, or however he wants to label it."[8]

Thus, the Wallace proclamation coupled with the Benson strategy did not diminish but escalated the bitter civil war within the DFL. The war would rage on for yet another nine months on the stump, in the precinct caucuses, through county, district and state conventions and, finally, even in the rarefied atmosphere of the State Supreme Court.

The right-wingers executed several important maneuvers following Humphrey's battle cry against the Communists in March of 1947. Conservative union leaders in the AFL and the CIO actively aided the Humphrey partisans in the DFL. In November of 1947, the state CIO's less radical faction had actually scored a victory over the left wing, the results of which inordinately helped Humphrey supporters. The right wing also had help from outside the state. CIO president Phil Murray, who had been straddling the fence, pitched in on the side of the anti-Communists. Even radical labor leader Walter Reuther, an ADA founder, lent his prestige to the DFL's right wing. In addition to this, the anti-Communist wing had mobilized the Young DFL clubs against the Wallaceites.

According to Freeman, a key victory for the right-wing faction occurred at the DFL state central committee meeting on February 20, 1948, which was attended by 138 delegates. While the leftists controlled the executive committee and the "higher echelons," they were unable to dominate the more representative central committee. Asserting its will over the Benson faction at the February meeting, the Humphrey-led wing appointed exclusively from its own ranks a steering committee which, in effect, took control of the party from state chairman Harold Barker, a "soft-on-Wallace" type, who, Freeman says, was a "stooge" for the leftists. This steering committee was delegated powers to make vital decisions regarding arrangements for the precinct caucuses and the county and state conventions.

By the spring of 1948, the battle for the precinct caucuses was well under way. The fight here was crucial, for those elected in the precincts became delegates to the county conventions, which, in turn, selected delegates to the state conventions. The DFL left-wingers had managed to seize control of much of the DFL's party machinery in past years by capturing these caucuses.

According to Kampelman and Kirkpatrick, the right wing had to concentrate its energies here if it was going to defeat the pro-Communist wing of the party. As the fight for the precincts intensified, the pro-Humphrey faction stepped up its warfare against the leftists. The right-wingers, for example, set up in strategic Hennepin County a D-F-L Volunteer Committee, which distributed on a mass basis such literature as: "Will the D-F-L Party of Minnesota Be A Clean, Honest, Decent Progressive Party?—Or—Will It Be A Communist-Front Organization?"

The pamphlet clearly spelled out the Communist tactics to take over the DFL. "This year," the pamphlet stated, "there is a concerted, well-organized, well-financed movement under way to take over the D-F-L and make it a Communist-front organization. . . . The Communist Party of Minnesota—using the Henry Wallace third-party campaign—is engaged in precisely this movement. If we do not do our job, the party-liners will succeed in this undertaking. With its membership—estimated at 300 in Hennepin County—the Communists can do this job. They are now assigning each of their members, through the Communist Party's secret cell organization, to a precinct."[9]

To prevent a Communist takeover, the pamphlet included detailed instructions showing how the rank-and-file could take over an official precinct caucus. The appeal to the rank-and-file was not only ideological, but was practical. Describing what would happen if the Wallace forces won, the pamphlet warned: "The Minnesota D-F-L Party will adopt pro-Communist, pro-Soviet platform and resolutions. . . . Minnesota progressives will have no political party and no one to vote for. Our promising candidates for state and national office simply will not run on the ticket of a party that supports the pro-Soviet line that our United States is corrupt and vicious and that the Soviet Union is the spearhead of a great new world power. The D-F-L Party will be destroyed. There will be no chance of defeating the Republicans. We, as progressives, will perhaps suffer a defeat from which we will never be able to recover. . . ."[10]

Elections for control of the precinct caucuses were on April 30. According to volunteer committee literature, "These primaries will tell the story. These primaries will determine who is to have the party: either the third-party Wallaceites, who are trying to steal the party, or the DFL regulars, who want to build a strong party, in order to attract good candidates to run for office."[11]

On April 18, just 12 days before the voting, the newly-formed right-wing steering committee of the DFL's state central committee moved to bar third-party supporters of Henry Wallace from voting in the precinct caucuses. J. Howard McGrath, Democratic National Chairman, threw his weight behind the maneuver a bare 48 hours before the vote. In a telegram to Freeman, still the right-wing secretary of the DFL party, McGrath said the national policy favored limiting the caucuses to Democratic Party members and considered it perfectly proper to disqualify the Wallaceites on the grounds they were not loyal Democrats but third-party supporters. DFL state chairman Harold Barker and others insisted such a move was illegal. Disputing Barker's stand, Freeman contended that to forbid disqualification would mean that the highest official party authority, in this instance the steering committee of the state central committee, is powerless to prevent its capture from within by a new independent third party."[12]

The Humphrey faction scored a major victory on April 30, winning a clear numerical majority of the precincts throughout the state. The McGrath-Freeman ruling to disbar avowed Wallaceites from the precinct caucuses facilitated the Humphreyites, but even without resorting to such tactics—which weren't vigorously employed anyway because of lack of enforcement machinery—the Humphrey wing won a resounding triumph. Wallace supporters were all but blanked in two outright tests of major dimensions.

In St. Paul, the scene of a crucial test between the two factions, right-wing DFL forces elected 462 county convention delegates to 60 Wallace-pledged delegates. And in Duluth, believed to be a Wallace stronghold, right-wingers won in 64 of the 75 precincts. In Minneapolis and other areas the Humphrey forces marshalled separate caucuses, but over all the conservative DFLers had triumphed. The Wallace-Benson crowd cried "foul" at the right-wing tactics and Mrs. Marian LeSueur, state DFL vice chairman, resigned her position in the party with a blast at "the disgraceful performance of the Humphrey-Orville Freeman group in the precinct caucuses."[13]

In spite of a serious defeat, however, the Wallace forces were not yet ready to capitulate, since it was their hope that through the help of state chairman Barker or the courts, they could get the county and state conventions to permit participation of disputed delegations chosen by the Wallaceites. In the April 30 precinct caucuses, for example, the left-wingers—charging that the party machinery was operating illegally—set up their own caucuses in many areas and elected delegates pledged to Wallace. But the left-wingers were doomed to be disappointed.

When the right wing won an overwhelming victory in the May 14 county conventions, the Wallace-Benson faction was forced to resort to tactics born of desperation. It contacted Harold Barker, state chairman of the DFL, demanding that Wallace delegates be allowed to participate in the state convention called for June 12 and 13 at Brainerd. If this demand were turned down, the Wallaceites vowed to call their own convention and repudiate the Brainerd gathering as illegal.

As the DFL regulars were assembling at Brainerd, a pre-convention credentials committee virtually smashed the hopes of the Wallace faction. It not only recommended the seating of the anti-Wallace delegations from St. Paul and Duluth counties, two of Minnesota's three big delegations, but it threw the dispute over whether the right-wing or left-wing delegation in Minneapolis should be seated to the heavily-loaded anti-Wallace rural county delegates.

The left-wingers then tried to take their case to the convention floor. But when the convention formally met in Brainerd on June 12, the Wallaceites received a rude reception. Orville Olson, state Wallace campaign manager, sparked the approximately 800 delegates into cries of "throw him out" when he argued for the seating of the Hennepin County (Minneapolis) delegation headed by an open Wallace supporter. Swinging into a political speech and avoiding an argument on the seating contest, Olson declared: "I believe you people in the Minneapolis DFL realize it is time to join Wallace's fight for peace. . . ." At that point a roar of boos swelled up from the Brainerd auditorium floor, but they went unheeded by Olson. "Powerful forces within the Democratic Party," he continued, "have torn it apart from Franklin Delano Roosevelt's program. Some groups such as one led by Humphrey. . . ."

The mention of Mayor Hubert H. Humphrey—strangely the first of the convention—brought the delegates to their feet. For more than two minutes they stood to cheer their candidate for the United States Senate. State DFL chairman Harold L. Barker attempted to restore order immediately, but when Olson renewed his pro-Wallace speech, delegates screamed: "Throw him out." Olson retired.

Arthur Naftalin, a leader of the anti-Wallaceites in Hennepin County, then took to the microphone. Charging that the Wallace faction in Hennepin County was "of a revolutionary character," he moved the seating of the right-wing delegates. By a voice vote, the convention approved the motion.[14] Greeted by jeers and catcalls, five of the Wallaceites bolted to the sidewalk in front of the convention hall to hold a "meeting," with Francis M. Smith, the Wallaceites' legal counsel, acting as chairman. He appointed a secretary to keep minutes, declared in session the meeting of a rump convention of the DFL and then adjourned to the American Federation of Labor Temple in Minneapolis, where a gathering of the left-wing faction was already in session. Writes Mitau:

> According to leaders of this group, five hundred delegates from fifty-one counties assembled for the Minneapolis convention. They listened eagerly as Benson termed the "program of Marshall, Forrestal, Dulles, Vandenberg and Company the most gigantic international swindle of all time . . . intended to suppress common people in every part of the world."[15]

The convention then organized itself into the Progressive Democratic Farmer Labor League, and endorsed candidates for senator and governor. In addition, five nominees were named to run for Congress—the Bensonites actually endorsed DFL Rep. John Blatnik*—and 11 Presidential electors were pledged to Wallace.

Though seemingly down and out, the progressives still had a last-minute trick up their collectivist sleeves. Rushing to the secretary of state's office before the DFL regulars, the Wallaceites submitted on June 14 a list of Wallace-pledged Presidential electors under the DFL party label. The secretary of state accepted it. Since he could only accept one list of electors under a party label, the regular DFL convention at Brainerd was blocked from filing Presidential electors pledged to Truman. Thus, the DFL regulars had to petition the state Supreme Court for an order to oust the Wallace electors.

On September 2, 1948, the Supreme Court handed the Wallaceites a crushing defeat. In a 4-0 decision written by Chief Justice Charles Loring, Mike Holm, the secretary of state, was ordered to reject the list of Presidential electors filed under the

*Blatnik, though hardly an enemy of the Wallaceites, did later repudiate their endorsement.

DFL's party tag by the Wallace wing, and to accept the right-wing electors supporting President Harry S. Truman. Associate Justices Harry Peterson, Thomas Gallagher and Frank Gallagher, elected on a non-partisan basis but with Democratic and Farmer-Labor Party political backgrounds, did not participate in the decision, which was reached on briefs and without oral argument.

The court based its decision on a finding that "The Democratic-Farmer-Labor convention held at Brainerd was the duly called and legally organized convention of that party. . . ." Progressives conceded that, but argued that the regulars "arbitrarily, capriciously, oppressively and unlawfully excluded them from the session."[16]

The Supreme Court decided that "the rule with regard to judicial review of the actions of political conventions is that in factional controversies within the party . . . the court will not assume jurisdiction but will leave the matter for determination within the party organization." In effect, the court ruled that a convention is its own master "and those withdrawing cannot claim to be the legal party convention."[17] Predictably, the Wallaceites loudly protested and their legal counsel Francis Smith branded the decision the "brass knuckles rule," but the war was essentially over.

Orville Freeman, now DFL state chairman, went back to Holm's office—from which he had been turned away in mid-June—and again filed the list of 11 DFL electors pledged to Truman. This time they were accepted.

With the court's decision, some 160 key Wallaceites, headed by former Governor Benson, set up plans for formally creating the Progressive Party in Minnesota. Humphrey, the conservative DFLers, and the Minnesota ADA had finally achieved what they had set out to do: expel the Communists from the DFL in Minnesota.

10

The '48 Convention

President Harry S. Truman was not exactly a happy man when the Democratic National Convention met in Philadelphia in mid-July of 1948. His chances for winning the November elections were far from encouraging. Though Wallace's third party was as yet untested, it was bound to pull votes away from the Democrats. Moreover, the polls revealed that Truman would probably lose to almost any candidate the Republicans decided to run. So unpopular was Truman thought to be, in fact, that until about a week before the convention it looked as if he would be unhorsed from the Democratic ticket by a combination of liberals, northern Democratic bosses and southern conservatives.

Sparking the move to jettison Truman was none other than Humphrey's Americans for Democratic Action. Opposed to the Wallace third-party maneuver, the ADA was, nevertheless, disenchanted with Truman's brand of liberalism, though it was not so much a question of ideology as of "style." The product of Missouri's Pendergast machine, Truman, in the eyes of the ADA, just didn't have the grace or the charisma of an FDR. Even more important, he was considered a dead duck with the voters. Serious murmurings of a Truman mutiny were initially heard at the first annual ADA convention which gathered in Philadelphia in February of 1948. In March, Franklin D. Roosevelt, Jr., an ADA vice-chairman, dramatically called upon the forthcoming Democratic National Convention to "draft General Dwight D. Eisenhower." Having commanded the victorious Allied armies in Europe in World War II, Eisenhower seemed the perfect candidate to bolster the Democratic Party's sagging fortunes. Although Ike's political views were not really known, ADA felt it could turn the general, who had risen to his current prominence through FDR and other liberal New Dealers, into its own man.

With plans obviously drawn up well in advance, ADA, on both a national and local level, readily responded to Roosevelt's call. Surprisingly, the ADA campaign also struck a responsive chord among groups normally opposed to the ADA wing of the Democratic Party. Certain that Truman would lose, Jake Arvey, boss of the Democratic political machine in Chicago and a frequent ADA target, joined in the ADA drive to draft Ike, as did Boss Frank Hague of New Jersey. Conservative southern senators like Virginia's Harry Byrd, who vigorously opposed Truman's New Deal policies and civil rights stand, also allied themselves with the pro-Ike campaign.

Minnesota's Hubert Humphrey, an ADA spokesman and head of the state delegation to the Democratic nominating convention, had done a number of curious flip-flops on Truman, but wound up leaning heavily against him. In July of 1947, Humphrey insisted he would support Truman as the Democrats' Presidential candidate,[1] and by November, Truman publicly hoped Humphrey would become a senatorial candidate against Joseph Ball.[2] But as Truman's popularity plummeted and as the ADA began plumping for Ike, Humphrey lined up with the effort to purge Truman from the national ticket. The Minneapolis *Morning Tribune* of March 25, 1948, reported that Mayor Humphrey readily admitted his participation in a nationwide effort to "dump Truman" in order to find a candidate to "woo back" third-party votes to the regular Democratic ticket. Humphrey said his own personal choices for the job were, "No. 1, Eisenhower, and No. 2, Douglas [Supreme Court Justice William O. Douglas]."[3]

Humphrey not only began talking up Ike and Douglas, but led a successful fight to keep the DFL delegation to the Democratic convention unpledged to the President's nomination. The DFL state chairman and others had called for a vigorous endorsement of Truman, but Humphrey and his forces sabotaged the effort. The refusal of the DFL to pledge its national convention delegation to Truman "clearly was a victory for Humphrey," according to the Minneapolis *Morning Tribune*.[4]

In early July—a little over a week before the Democratic convention formally met on July 12—Humphrey signed a telegraphic appeal by state Democratic leaders calling upon the delegates to achieve "an open convention" and pick the "ablest and strongest man available" for the Presidential nomination. Among those who co-signed the telegram were such leaders of the pro-Ike drive as Jimmy Roosevelt, Sen. Lister Hill of Alabama and Gov. Strom Thurmond of South Carolina.

The drive to put over Ike actually came within an eyelash of success. As the Democratic convention drew near, recalls Clifton Brock in his *Americans for Democratic Action*, Leon Henderson, ADA's chairman, called attention to the fact that only 310 out of 1,234 delegates were pledged to Truman. Furthermore, 110 of the delegates were from the ranks of the ADA. With just a week to go before the convention opened, the ADA national office began mailing a series of daily leaflets to all delegates urging them to rally behind the American war hero.[5]

By this time all that seemed necessary to launch Ike into Presidential orbit was a nod from the general himself. But Eisenhower had different ideas. Though he had delayed any announcement for some time, on July 5 he publicly took himself out of the race. The ADA balloon had been rudely punctured. A day later, Humphrey was claiming, "I've said all along that I didn't think General Eisenhower would go for any draft movement," but he had by no means switched to Truman. Leon Henderson, ADA's national chairman, had talked of plans to enter the nomination of Supreme Court Justice William O. Douglas, who had been born in northern Minnesota. Humphrey, while not repudiating Truman, consequently began promoting the idea of a Douglas nomination. "I've been yelling only for an open convention," said Humphrey. "I think we'll get it. The name of Douglas will be entered in nomination. The delegates will have an opportunity to vote for him."[6]

In truth, however, there was no chance for the Supreme Court Justice. Unlike Ike, he was no military hero whose reputation could dazzle the electorate. Furthermore, the southerners and even many northern liberal bosses found Douglas too much of a radical for their particular tastes. By the eve of the convention, both the Ike and Douglas booms were dead, though some ADA delegates were still hoping that Ike would relent or that a new candidate would miraculously emerge from the political wilderness.

At this point, the Humphrey forces rapidly shifted gears. Realizing that Truman now would probably be nominated on the first ballot, Orville Freeman, the new DFL state chairman who had also fought to keep the Minnesota delegation unpledged to Truman, frantically called a caucus meeting of the state delegation to maneuver it into giving him wholehearted support. So sudden was the attempt to switch the unpledged delegates that it caused a jolt within the Minnesota delegation, even to such Humphrey confidants as Minnesota ADA chairman Arthur Naftalin.[7]

Freeman had called the pre-convention meeting just one hour ahead of a caucus called by Thomas W. Walsh, a St. Paul delegate-at-large and the strongest Truman booster in the Minnesota delegation. Walsh had tangled with the Humphrey forces in June when he lost his battle for a delegation pledged to the President. With the collapse of Ike's candidacy, Walsh now felt certain that he could generate full first-ballot support of the President. The Freeman move was clearly made in order to undercut Walsh and make it appear as if the new DFL leaders, not Walsh, were in command of the delegation and leading the move to get behind Truman's nomination.

Among other things, the DFL switch clearly signalled the fact that ADA had lost its bid to dump Truman from the ticket, but neither ADA nor Hubert Humphrey had yet finished harassing the President of the United States.

With Democratic Party unity appearing exceptionally fragile,

Truman was working hard to produce a platform on civil rights that would not stir up the convention. Fully aware that the Southerners were angered at his program announced earlier in the year, Truman had asked the platform committee to tone down the rights plank. Headed by Pennsylvania's Sen. Francis Myers, the platform committee came up with what it thought was the perfect compromise. It generally endorsed the full extension of civil rights and "called on Congress" to assure them within "constitutional limits."

This, noted New York *Times*' columnist Arthur Krock, "was to enable the Northern and Western politicians to go home and claim that the plank ratified the President's ten-point program for Congress on this reasoning: Mr. Truman obviously holds that his program is constitutional for Congress to legislate; otherwise he would not have 'called' on it to do so."[8] But Krock noted that the plank also had something for the Southerners as well. The authors of the plank, "acting by direction of the President," said Krock, had carefully excluded mention of *any* specific measures urged upon Congress by Truman. This, stressed Krock, was to enable the Southern politicians to go home and claim that Truman's program had definitely not been endorsed by the convention. *Time* magazine was to call the whole maneuver a "magnificent weasel."

But the platform makers had overlooked the determination of the Northerners, whose volatile ADA had drafted a militant minority report. Indeed, Humphrey, one of four ADA members on the platform committee, was personally directing ADA's civil rights strategy. On July 12, the subcommittee issued its draft of the plank. On the 13th Humphrey presented ADA's version to the full committee in the form of four amendments which called for "federal action" in a whole range of civil rights areas, including equal employment opportunity and voting. After an acrimonious debate, the committee rejected the amendments by a substantial voice vote. Undaunted, Humphrey then announced that ADA would slug it out on the convention floor. Sen. Scott Lucas of Illinois stormed out of the session, accusing ADA of "attempting to wreck the Democratic Party by insisting on its civil rights plank."[9]

In the unrelenting heat of the next day, the delegates settled soggily into their chairs while Senator Myers droned out the compromise platform. The instant he finished, Southerners jumped to their feet demanding to dilute the civil rights plank even further. At this point, ex-congressman Andrew J. Biemiller of Wisconsin, an ADA partisan and one-time Socialist who helped manage Norman Thomas' campaign in 1932, and a colleague of Humphrey on the platform committee, presented the Humphrey-Biemiller-ADA minority platform on civil rights. The debate was on.

Sitting at the rear of the speakers' platform as the controversy raged on, Humphrey drafted a 10-minute speech in support of the minority platform and had a stenographer type it out for him in capital letters. Then he made penciled notes, scratching out some parts and adding others. After some 35 minutes of Southern rhetoric, Humphrey stood up to make what has since become the most famous speech of his career:

I realize that I am dealing with a charged issue—with an issue which has been confused by emotionalism on all sides. I realize that there are those here—friends and colleagues of mine, many of them—who feel as deeply as I do about this issue and who are yet in complete disagreement with me. My respect and admiration for these men and their views was great when I came here. It is now far greater because of the sincerity, the courtesy and the forthrightness with which they have argued in our discussions.

Because of this very respect—because of my profound belief that we have a challenging task to do there—because good conscience demands it—I feel I must rise at this time to support this report—a report that spells out our democracy, a report that the people will understand and enthusiastically acclaim.

Let me say at the outset that this proposal is made with no single region, no single class, no single racial or religious group in mind.

All regions and all states have shared in the precious heritage of American freedom. All states and all regions have at least some infringements of that freedom—all people, all groups have been the victims of discrimination.

The masterly statement of our keynote speaker, the distinguished United States Senator from Kentucky, Alben Barkley, made that point with great force. Speaking of the founder of our party, Thomas Jefferson, he said:

"He did not proclaim that all white, or black, or red, or yellow men are equal; that all Christian or Jewish men are equal; that all Protestant and Catholic men are equal; that all rich or poor men are equal; that all good or bad men are equal.

"What he declared was that all men are equal; and the equality which he proclaimed was equality in the right to enjoy the blessings of free government in which they may participate and to which they have given their consent."

We are here as Democrats. But more important, as Americans—and I firmly believe that as men concerned with our country's future, we must specify in our platform the guarantees which I have mentioned.

Yes, this is far more than a party matter. Every citizen has a stake in the emergence of the United States as the leader of the free world. That world is being challenged by the world of slavery. For us to play our part effectively, we must be in a morally sound position.

We cannot use a double standard for measuring our own and other people's policies. Our demands for democratic practices in other lands will be no more effective than the guarantees of those practiced in our own country.

We are God-fearing men and women. We place our faith in the brotherhood of man under the fatherhood of God.

I do not believe that there can be any compromise of the guarantees of civil rights which I have mentioned.

In spite of my desire for unanimous agreement on the platform, there are some matters which I think must be stated without qualification. There can be no hedging—no watering down.

There are those who say to you—we are rushing this issue of civil rights. I say we are 172 years late.

There are those who say—this issue of civil rights is an infringement on state's rights. The time has arrived for the Democratic Party to get out of the shadow of state's rights and walk forthrightly into the bright sunshine of human rights. . . .

Frequently interrupted by applause, Humphrey received a tumultuous ovation when he had finished. Freeman, Humphrey's close friend, grabbed the state's standard and began marching down the center aisle, setting off a 10-minute demonstration on Humphrey's behalf. The Humphrey talk had become the one stirring note of the convention. The Southerners now seemed helpless in the wave of emotion let loose by Humphrey's oration. When Texas' Sam Rayburn called for a roll-call vote on a "state's rights" motion put forth by Texas, it was smashed by an overwhelming 925-to-309 vote. Two other Southern amendments were shouted down.

Then the Humphrey-Biemiller civil rights amendment was put to the gruelling roll-call vote. When the final tally was counted as 651½ to 582½ in favor, the pro-civil rights crowd roared in triumph.

The convention was chaos. Thirteen members of the Alabama delegation bolted. The full delegation from Mississippi followed them outdoors into a heavy rain. Defeated on the platform, the rest of the South then tried valiantly but vainly to rally its forces around Georgia's candidate for President, Sen. Richard Russell. But Truman won handily on the first ballot, 947½ to Russell's 263. The South had been routed.

Truman had won the nomination, but Hubert Horatio Humphrey was unquestionably the hero of the convention. Against heavy odds, Humphrey had managed to lead the drive to put over the ADA platform on civil rights—and it was done in opposition to Democratic Party leadership including the President. The ADA and Humphrey had forced the Democratic Party to accept their platform.

Humphrey had seriously risked party unity in his speech, and had gained prominence as a result, but his partisans insist that Humphrey was not thinking of himself. They say that Humphrey delivered his speech from the heart, that he reacts viscerally to the civil rights issue. As soon as he became mayor, his supporters point out, he established the first Fair Employment Practices Commission in any city in the United States. Max Kampelman says that "the first Negro to eat in the Senate Office Building was a Negro employee of Humphrey. I remember this because I was down here and the man's name is Cyril King, who since has become the government secretary for the Virgin Islands. When Cyril went down to eat with all the other employees, a waiter told Humphrey, 'you know this isn't done and you might get into trouble.' Humphrey replied, saying, 'Is this where the employees are supposed to be? He's an employee of mine.' " King—who confirms the story—stayed. That was all there was to it, Kampelman insists. Humphrey didn't flaunt it, Kampelman stresses, he just stuck up for Negro rights in a quiet way.

Though Humphrey may react instinctively to the civil rights issue, there can also be little doubt that his speech generated giant political benefits. In just 10 minutes, Hubert Humphrey, a relatively unknown political figure, had been catapulted onto the national scene in a massive way. Newspapers devoted their front pages to the "scrappy" mayor. More important, the speech had made Humphrey a hero where he needed to be a hero the most—in the state of Minnesota. The DFL had been wracked with bitter, internecine warfare between Left-Right factions, but Humphrey's talk undoubtedly appealed to the majority elements in both groups. The Left-Right factions could never get together on foreign policy, but on domestic issues they could—and often did—rally around a rousing issue like Negro rights.

When Humphrey returned to Minneapolis, a crowd of 2,000 cheering, applauding rooters greeted him at the Great Northern station. "The crowd . . . made the station's biggest wartime crowds look puny," claimed an article in the Minneapolis *Sunday Tribune.*[10] Bands played and more than 600 banners waved. Most of them read, HUMPHREY, CHAMPION OF HUMAN RIGHTS.

Other Humphrey fans, many of them University of Minnesota students, carried banners reading:

HUBERT H. HUMPHREY, MINNESOTA'S FAVORITE CITIZEN.

HUMPHREY FIGHTS FOR HUMAN RIGHTS.

WELCOME BACK HOME, HUMPHREY.

MINNESOTA'S PROUD OF HUMPHREY.

When Humphrey, his wife and two small sons, Hubert, 6, and Robert, 4, came into the station, the crowd burst into a shrieking version of "For He's a Jolly Good Fellow." Humphrey was hoisted to a table, grinning broadly. "I have a bad throat," he said hoarsely, "I just came back from a shouting in Philadelphia."

The mayor barely had time to tell the crowd, "This is the finest thing that ever happened to me," when five husky youths balanced him on their shoulders and carried him through the still-cheering crowd to the open car in which he and his wife led an 80-car parade down Nicollet Avenue. State Rep. George Murk, head of the musician's union, led group singing at the Nicollet Hotel reception. "First of all," said Murk, "let's sing 'Somebody Else is Taking My Place' . . . We are dedicating it to Joe Ball."[11]

Humphrey had clearly scored a stunning personal victory. But many felt that he had won at the expense of President Truman and the Democratic Party nationally. Typical of many reactions was that expressed by editor Scott Schoen of the Redwood Falls *Gazette.* Schoen said he thought that Humphrey no doubt counts on the publicity as "a boost in his campaign for the senatorship," but the move was "not one which achieved anything for the party or for national unity." The antipathy he caused among Southern Democrats, Schoen went on, would probably offset any liberal support the Democrats might take away from Wallace.[12]

Schoen was seemingly correct. Humphrey, while personally benefitting and helping to sow up votes in Minnesota, had split the Democratic Party wide open—again. Wallace had already formed a third party which was biting into the Democratic strength in the North. With Humphrey's civil rights triumph, the party could no longer count on the cushion of votes it always got from the Solid South. On July 17, just three days after Humphrey's famous speech and the adoption of his civil rights plank at Philadelphia, delegates from several Southern states met in Birmingham, Alabama, to found the States' Rights Party and nominate Governors Strom Thurmond of South Carolina and Fielding Wright of Mississippi for President and Vice President respectively. President Truman and old party-line Democrats were glum. Joining with his fellow ADA delegates, Humphrey had definitely advanced his own political fortunes, but in doing so it appeared that he had dug the Democratic Party's grave around the nation.

11

The Defeat of Joe Ball

Few political contests were more exciting or more furiously fought than the Humphrey-Ball race for the Senate in 1948. Fraught with high drama, a clash of ideologies and national significance, it was a battle that would rage right down to the wire. For more than a score of reasons it commanded national attention.

The outcome would determine the future course for the newly-born Americans for Democratic Action. It would determine whether the Democratic-Farmer-Labor Party would remain a power in Minnesota politics. And it would reveal the effectiveness of both the AFL and CIO, which were throwing in their massive resources to eliminate Senator Joe Ball from the political scene.

Both candidates, moreover, had captured the attention of the public. A political journalist for the St. Paul *Dispatch-Pioneer Press* in the 1930's, Ball, through diligent reporting, had exposed the sins of the old Farmer-Labor Party. He also did much to promote the candidacy of Harold Stassen, who whipped Gov. Elmer Benson in 1938. Stassen never forgot. When Sen. Ernest Lundeen was killed in an airplane crash in 1940, Stassen appointed Ball to fill the vacancy. Winning election in 1942 against former Governor Elmer Benson, Ball gradually became a crusader against excessive union power. He was a vigorous supporter of the Taft-Hartley labor law which passed over President Truman's veto in 1947. Indeed, his role in shaping this landmark measure aimed at curbing union power was nearly as important as Taft's—and brought down on him the unrelenting wrath of labor union leaders around the country. In 1948, the AFL and the CIO had singled out Ball as their number one political target.

Humphrey, too, had gained national attention. As a founder of the Democratic-Farmer-Labor Party and mayor of Minneapolis, he had received wide recognition. But his association with Americans for Democratic Action and his stirring performance at the Democratic National Convention had thrust him into the glare of national publicity.

Physically, politically and philosophically, Humphrey and Ball were strikingly dissimilar. Ball genuinely looked the role of Minnesota's senior Senator. He normally stood before the microphone in a slight slouch, his shock of graying hair blown down over his forehead. His tall, lanky frame and craggy features gave him a Lincolnesque appearance. Blunt and methodical, Ball gave off little in the way of oratorical fireworks.

Bubbling with energy, Humphrey appeared slight, dark and bouncy. Where Ball was slow and deliberate, Humphrey was impulsive and quick. Unlike Ball, Humphrey was eager to mix with the populace. Campaigning on the county fair grounds, he could be seen touring the midway, firing basketballs at the hoop at one concession, bantering with the operator of the shooting gallery at another. At informal gatherings, he frequently took time out to dance with several delighted old ladies. When he took to the platform, he pulled out all the stops. If Mrs. Humphrey was not along, he explained why: "We've got four little Humphreys, you know, and Mom had to get home to get Nancy off to Campfire Girls camp." Ball was humorless, but exuded a deep sincerity. Humphrey gave the folks a show, weaving in gags, mock tears and a general mugging that seemed to captivate the audience.

Humphrey was notorious for his political vacillation. He finally fought the Communists and some of the more extreme leftists inside the confines of the Democratic-Farmer-Labor Party, but he had wooed and coddled these elements over the years until inexorable forces had compelled him to choose sides.

When Henry Wallace had received a bad press for scoring American foreign policy in 1946, Humphrey was willing to disengage himself from Wallace, but not from Claude Pepper, who had received less unwelcome publicity while espousing even more extreme anti-American views from the same platform.

Humphrey was for law enforcement, but not when the labor unions raised a strenuous rumpus about a law they didn't like. He was for charter reform, but not if it antagonized anyone too much. He was for Truman one day, and against him the next. He seemed to want Ike to head the Democratic ticket, then apparently shifted to Douglas and then, lo and behold, wound up magically back on the Truman bandwagon. Like quicksilver, Humphrey was almost impossible to pin down, often giving off a stream of Yes's, No's and Maybe's to a single question in the space of a week.

The political arts of ducking and weaving were just not in Joe Ball. Plunging into the thick of controversial issues, Ball displayed lion-hearted courage. Some insisted he was unyielding and pig-headed, but no one could deny that he was at peace with his own conscience.

In the 1944 Presidential campaign, Ball revealed his flare for independence by suddenly switching from Dewey to Roosevelt, fearing that Dewey was incapable of handling foreign affairs. Politically, the move was disastrous, but that sort of thing didn't really bother Ball. Unlike Humphrey, Ball would not flatter an audience, but said what was frankly on his mind.

Evenly matched for the contest, both candidates were faced with major difficulties. Humphrey was breasting an apparently strong Republican tide in a normally Republican state. Gov. Thomas Dewey of New York was favored to beat Truman. The Republican governor, Luther Youngdahl, was a heavy favorite and the state's delegation in the Congress boasted of only a single Democrat.

The metropolitan newspapers, even the Cowles publications,

were supporting Ball, and the rural press was, more often than not, anti-Humphrey. Humphrey was also facing a two-front war. Not only did he have to battle the Republicans, but he was squaring off at Wallace-wing Democrats in his own party.

But Humphrey had many plusses on his side as well. The Cowles publications, while supporting Ball against Humphrey for Senator, had, to some degree, made Humphrey into a political figure. Over the years they had vigorously supported him for mayor, generally commending his attitude toward law enforcement and praising other aspects of his administration. When mistakes were made, the papers zealously sought to shield Humphrey from criticism, striking out instead at Humphrey's allies or labor supporters. Having built up Humphrey's reputation, the Cowles press could not have convincingly torn it down, nor did it really try. Thus, its opposition to Humphrey was not particularly strong or effective.

Ball, too, was knee-deep in trouble with his own party. By refusing to support Dewey in 1944, he had alienated scores of regular Republicans who demanded party loyalty. And his hammering away at the labor unions had not only aroused their leaders and members but had alienated powerful "soft-on-union" Republicans, including former Gov. Harold Stassen, who at that time wielded considerable weight in Minnesota Republican circles.

The 1948 Senatorial race in Minnesota became a classic conservative-liberal contest. Ball had started out in his political career as a liberal. A founder of the Minnesota Newspaper Guild, he finally quit when he discovered it had become Communist-dominated. He still spoke like a liberal when he supported FDR over Dewey in 1944, but after the war, his views became more markedly conservative in both foreign and domestic policies. Stalin's ruthless aggression abroad, big government at home, the Democrats' foreign policy and the power of America's labor unions became the major themes of his campaign. Humphrey, of course, was an ADA liberal who preached the gospel of "the bigger the government, the better."

They were at sword's point on virtually every vital issue of the day. Ball was vigorously opposed to the restoration of price-control legislation, labelling it a "totalitarian act when the country is at peace." To resurrect the Office of Price Administration, said Ball, "would mean the descent of an army of investigators upon private business."

As the ADA's star witness in January of 1948, Mayor Humphrey called for an extension of both price and rent controls in an appearance in Washington before a Senate Banking and Currency subcommittee.[1]

Humphrey was for large-scale foreign aid; Ball was opposed. Humphrey favored lavish subsidies to ex-GI's in college; Ball was not against subsidies, but snapped back at one questioner who asked why Ball didn't campaign for increased aid: "You've got to remember that you're not supposed to be getting a complete subsidy. Did it ever occur to you guys that you can go out and get a job to pad out your budget?"[2]

There were many issues that divided the two combatants, but nothing separated them more clearly than their respective stands in regard to labor.

Though he had started out in life himself as a militant labor union leader, Ball had become disillusioned with the labor movement over the years and became convinced that the government had to impose some limits on its awesome powers. For this reason he was a vigorous supporter of the Taft-Hartley law, and he fearlessly endorsed it during the 1948 campaign. Famed for his political courage, Ball took the case for Taft-Hartley to the labor unions themselves. Before the shop committee of Minneapolis local 1145, United Electrical Workers, with scores of outside union officials also in attendance, Ball staunchly defended his role in supporting the 1947 labor law. The audience was easily the most hostile he had faced in the Senate contest.

The workers had told Ball at the start that they intended to do a job on him, but for an hour after his speech he weathered a battery of fiery questions from unfriendly questioners. Ball opened up with an attack on the UEW's national leadership, declaring that it included several officers "who you know and I know are Communists."[3]

Of the Taft-Hartley law, he said it was not intended to outlaw strikes per se, although it was designed to deal with the problem of "industry-wide paralysis" strikes. He said it was aimed at "correcting certain abuses" like compelling someone to join a union before he could hold a job, secondary boycotts and wildcat strikes. He ridiculed labor's calling it a "slave labor" law and a "union buster." "You don't look like slaves to me," he boomed out. "Certainly your union hasn't been destroyed." Ball won few converts, but he did win the grudging respect of the union men who acknowledged that "the guy has guts."

Humphrey, of course, had always wooed the labor vote. Since the start of his re-election campaign in 1947, Mayor Humphrey, with his eye cast covetously on Joe Ball's job, began to embrace organized labor even more resolutely. He vigorously fought for repeal of Taft-Hartley; he supported labor's demands before Congress; he bowed down to its demands on charter reform; he refused to oppose the unions in labor disputes; and he became even more blatant in stacking the city government with labor-approved personnel. Even the Cowles papers began chiding him for his pro-labor stands.

Humphrey did not go unrewarded for his cordial treatment of the unions. Organized labor worked at fever pitch to put him into the Senate. Robert A. Olson, president of the Minnesota Federation of Labor, admitted that national AFL leaders had determined that the defeat of Ball was the top objective of labor's political efforts in 1948.[4] The federation would pour in the major part of a $300,000 kitty to defeat Ball. Labor leaders swarmed over Minneapolis in a frantic effort to rouse the voters against its number one enemy. Joseph Keenan, head of the AFL's Labor League for Political Education, breezed into the Minneapolis area to campaign for Humphrey. Walter Reuther, head of the United Auto Workers, planned to speak for the mayor until he was wounded by a mysterious shotgun blast; but Reuther sent in his political lieutenants anyway. Minnesota's major union of telephone workers, the Northwestern Union of Telephone Workers, endorsed Humphrey's candidacy. Affiliated with neither the AFL nor the CIO, the union had been befriended by Humphrey during the 1947 telephone strike. Phil Murray, president of the United Steelworkers and the CIO, publicly endorsed Humphrey. Toward the close of the campaign, William Green, president of the AFL, personally went to Minneapolis to whip up political winds against Minnesota's senior Senator. Green's October appearance for Humphrey, whom he had endorsed over a year ago, was regarded as the climax to labor's attempt to defeat Ball. The AFL leader told his listeners that Ball "went to the Senate as a liberal. He is now leaving it with the reputation of a hidebound reactionary." Item by item, Green raked the Senator over the coals. He attacked Ball for labelling some of the veteran organizations "gimme groups." Because he had voted against spending the taxpayers' money for a host of welfare measures, Green bitterly criticized Ball as one who had "doublecrossed the workers, the farmers, the veterans and his own party."[5] Reserving some of his bitterest words for the Senator's support of the Taft-Hartley law, Green declared that Ball "sold out whatever principles he originally had to the National Association of Manufacturers." Ball, he continued, tried desperately to make the Taft-Hartley law "even more drastic" than it is.

Humphrey, on the other hand, had had an "exceptional" record in public office; Green said Humphrey would protect the farmers' interests, back the veterans and would "work faithfully" for the repeal of the Taft-Hartley law. Humphrey, he exclaimed, "has made enemies—the kind of enemies a man in public life should be proud of, enemies among the reactionaries and the fascists. . . .

"Today these wealthy interests are pouring money into the state of Minnesota to defeat Mayor Humphrey for the Senate. The money is coming from the industrial barons of Wall Street and the oil barons of the South."

Green's speech was larded with the exaggerated oratorical flourishes for which he was famous, but he still uttered the most revealing words of the campaign. The AFL leader claimed that organized labor throughout the nation would celebrate Humphrey's election "as their victory."[6] Humphrey lived up to the prophecy.

Labor, however, was not the only major issue. Ball repeatedly assailed Humphrey's ties to the ADA and his connections with radical leftists. The ADA, Ball averred, was leading the country toward socialism. "There is no difference," he said at one point, "between the domestic program advocated by the *Daily Worker*, the Communist publication, and the one supported by the ADA. The ADA is led by such men as Leon Henderson, Chester Bowles and others who were in control of the Democratic administration. They are the men who advocate centralization of government control. The Democratic Party has been taken away from its original leaders by the ADA and others who do not believe in a free economy."[7]

Ball repeated this theme through the campaign. Humphrey, the CIO-PAC, the Wallaceites and the Communist Party, Ball charged a bit later, have a "startling similarity" in their domestic programs. The four are for complete repeal of Taft-Hartley, a return to OPA, higher expenditures and higher taxes, a program of socialized medicine, and "minimizing disclosures of Communist espionage in our government," Ball claimed.

Ball continued: "I think we are justified in wondering why this startling similarity in positions taken on domestic issues has developed. . . .

"The other curious development in this campaign is the way in which the apparently bitter fight here in Minnesota between the so-called right wing of the DFL party and the Wallaceites has evaporated since the primary election. Now they seem to be one big happy family, all together and united."[8]

Ball's charge would probably be branded as "McCarthyite" or some other epithet coined by today's news media, but the Senator had made a pertinent observation. Indeed, Humphrey in particular had appeared to take an extraordinary radical tack during his bid for Ball's Senate seat. With the DFL's right-wing faction in his hip pocket, Humphrey, especially after his swamping of a Wallaceite in the mid-September primary, seemed determined on taking stands that would win back at least some of the left-wingers who had deserted to the progressive wing of the DFL. Responding to Ball, in fact, Humphrey used words that were tuned to the radical wing of the party. He asserted that both the DFL and himself regarded communism as "evil," but he also added: ". . . we include in that same evil group your good friends of the Chicago *Tribune*, who so gallantly endorsed you, and also your friends of the National Association of Manufacturers, who have a record of being against everything that the people of this country have wanted."[9] In short, hard-core communism and the NAM were equally bad! In a score of other instances, Humphrey stood with the DFL progressives. Like them, for example, he had worked against Truman's nomination. During the Democratic convention, Humphrey had joined forces with the radicals to pass a strong civil rights platform that was certain to drive the Southerners away from the national ticket. He stood with the radicals on Taft-Hartley and the restoration of price controls. Though Humphrey, himself, had gloried in the role of "Red-baiter" when he had opened the first shot against the Communists in the DFL in 1947, he talked of "hysteria" about communism in his campaign against Ball. "In our hysteria," Humphrey said to students at the University of Minnesota, "we too often believe that someone who disagrees even a fraction with a member of the House Un-American Activities Committee is subversive and deserves to be investigated, hounded and persecuted."[10] Humphrey did not call for the committee's abolition, but he proposed a variety of measures which would have seriously hampered its activities.

More revealing than this was Humphrey's apparent reversal of his initial stand in support of Truman's foreign policy. In a joint appearance with Ball at an October meeting of the National Federation of Jewish Women, Humphrey lashed out at the Western policy of containing the Communists. "I don't believe in the policy of containment," Humphrey declared; America, he insisted, must search out "new means of negotiation."[11] Still later, Humphrey was quoted as proclaiming that containment against Russia or any country was "un-American."[12] According to another report, Humphrey had not only labelled "containment" as "un-American," but had urged the United States go on the "offensive" by offering American aid to Soviet satellites. (In fact, the Marshall Plan, America's foreign aid program, was first offered to the Communist countries, but they fortunately had turned it down.) In another Ball-Humphrey clash before the Minneapolis College Women's Club, Humphrey said he was opposed to appeasement of the Soviets, but he still stated he was opposed to containment. In connection with his remarks on containment, Humphrey also added that the United States should do nothing to "precipitate anything to drive Russia out of the United Nations. We should not drive her out by textual revision or a charter revision," a remark that apparently drew applause from Mrs. Lawrence D. Steefel, a Progressive Party spokesman.[13]

By denouncing containment, Humphrey was clearly pitching his remarks to the Wallaceites. The containment policy, as Humphrey was well aware, was essentially the policy adopted by Truman to prevent Communist expansion. It was, in Senator Ball's own words, "the keystone of the foreign policy on which the Democratic and Republican parties are united and which is the main target of Wallace's criticism."

Oddly enough, it was formulated by George F. Kennan, who has since forsaken this policy for one of conciliating the Soviets. A foreign service officer with a deep knowledge of Russia, Kennan had publicly presented the policy of containment for the first time under the pseudonym of "Mr. X" in the highly influential *Foreign Affairs* magazine of July, 1947. Outward "toughness" and single sporadic efforts to combat Soviet policy, he warned, were not enough. The main element of any policy, he stressed, "must be that of a long-term, patient but firm and vigilant containment of Russian expansive tendencies." The United States, he wrote, must apply counterforce "at a series of constantly shifting geographical and political points, corresponding to the shifts and maneuvers of Soviet policy." The policy of containment clearly represented a stiffening stance by the United States toward the Soviet Union and communism.

There were some critics who thought even "containment" was not enough, that the United States should try to liberate those under Communist tyranny through a broad array of tactics, not excluding military force. Yet these critics were a small minority.

The major thunderings against containment came from the Left, including the *Daily Worker* and, as Ball had noted, the Wallaceites. Columnist Walter Lippmann, an ardent advocate of Soviet appeasement, unleashed a frenetic series of articles condemning containment as anti-Communist extremism. Humphrey could hardly have doubted that his words, whatever he actually meant by them, would be construed as a basic criticism of the gradual hardening of our policies toward Moscow. His criticism of this Truman policy as "un-American" not only seemed a sharp departure from his previous pronouncements, but purposeful verbiage gauged to provoke a favorable reaction among the Wallaceites who also thought containment was "un-American."

Whether a conscious signal to the Wallaceites or not, Humphrey's fundamental positions and radical rhetoric did not go unrewarded. After Humphrey handily won his primary fight in mid-September, a number of progressives were willing to back him. In early October, in fact, Wallace himself said he hoped Mayor Humphrey would be elected to the United States Senate over Sen. Joseph Ball.[14] The Progressive Party's campaign manager, C. B. Baldwin, disclosed a day previously that the party favored Humphrey. Humphrey said he was surprised but "grateful for support on the basis of our program. . . . I do not expect nor do I want support of fascist-minded or Communist-minded people, however."[15] Some progressives in Minnesota tried to put a formal party ban on support of Humphrey, but the state unit of the Progressive Party recommended support of efforts to defeat Sen. Joseph Ball, adding: "The Progressive Party cannot assume responsibility for the candidacy and program of Humphrey nor does it, on the other hand, restrain individuals and groups who support our program from voting for Humphrey, if they see reason for so doing."[16]

This, obviously, was not an overwhelming endorsement, but it was far more than one might expect from a group that Humphrey had assailed when fighting its members for control of the DFL. Humphrey's policy of playing up to radicals paid off in late September when the Hennepin County CIO council voted 4-to-3 in favor of a resolution endorsing Humphrey against Sen. Ball.

Votes cast totalled about 20,000. The left-wing council had not been expected to give an open endorsement to Humphrey, but it got behind him after its executive board had recommended such action by a 5-to-4 vote. Robert I. Wishart, council president, had broken a 4-to-4 tie vote to back his old friend Humphrey.

The Wishart vote must have proved gratifying to Humphrey, who had courted him over the years despite his appalling pro-Soviet record. In spite of Wishart's views, Humphrey had placed him in his administration. On July 31, 1947, over four months after Humphrey had publicly warned of the dangers of Communists and left-wingers taking over the DFL, he paid tribute to Wishart at a testimonial given in his honor at the Nicollet Hotel. Humphrey, along with such left-wingers as Ernest de Maio, an actual Communist, sang Wishart's praises. Humphrey commended Wishart for his contribution as a member of the Minneapolis Board of Public Welfare and said this was not "only a testimonial to Bob Wishart, but the UE-CIO, the labor movement and a great company (Honeywell)."[17] Humphrey continued to play up to Wishart, even though through both 1947 and 1948 he was championing leftist causes. But the courtship had paid off.

Thus, while Humphrey did not go after the hard-core Communist vote in his 1948 campaign—indeed, he repudiated it—he did seek to reach those whose views were shaded considerably to the Left. Though the DFL had battled the Wallaceites, it was not completely free of their hold in the 1948 contest, either. Wallace-pledged candidates for Congress won DFL nominations in both the seventh and ninth districts. The DFL's Rep. John Blatnik, Tito's idolator, was endorsed by both the DFL and the Wallaceites, though Blatnik finally repudiated Progressive Party support.

On November 2, Minneapolis Mayor Hubert Humphrey beat Joe Ball by nearly 250,000 votes, winning 59.8 per cent of the vote. He had become the first Democrat in Minnesota to be elected to the U.S. Senate by the people. Minnesota had had two other Democratic senators, James Shields (1858) and Charles A. Towne (1900), but Shields had been chosen by the state legislature and Towne had been appointed by the governor to fill a vacancy.

Humphrey's victory was more than a personal triumph, for it had also been a victory for his Democratic-Farmer-Labor Party. The DFL, aside from giving President Truman a majority in the state, also elected three lawmakers to the Congress and almost toppled the state's popular GOP governor, Luther Youngdahl. In short, the DFL had become a powerful force in Minnesota.

The 1948 election must have dazzled the man who had been born in Wallace, South Dakota, only 37 years previously. Looking back, he must have felt more than a twinge of pride.

He had skyrocketed to political prominence since he first ran and was defeated for mayor just five short years before. Since that defeat, his accomplishments had been staggering: He had created the Democratic-Farmer-Labor Party; he had twice been elected mayor of Minneapolis; and he had fought—and whipped—the Communists in his own party. A founder of the Americans for Democratic Action, he had scored a sensational political victory at the 1948 Democratic National Convention, which adopted a Humphrey civil rights platform against the vigorous opposition of the party leaders. The Humphrey-ADA rights plank was considered the death knell for the party because it had caused the party's further fragmentation, but in fact the Democrats scored a major triumph in 1948. Indeed, the Republicans were to lose more seats in the Senate, the House and the state legislatures than they did in 1964 when Lyndon Johnson, with a united party behind him, beat Barry Goldwater.

Three days following his win, Senator-elect Humphrey appeared on the nationwide radio broadcast, *Meet the Press*. Asked if he believed that ADA was right in trying to ditch Truman in 1948, Humphrey replied: "We were dead wrong and I think confession is good for the soul." On the issue of communism, he remarked: "The best way to curb Communists is the kind of elections we had on November 2. They got so few votes that they are certainly not a menace in this country." On the subject of communism, however, this was definitely not the Senator-elect's last word.

12

Humphrey's Man on the FPC

Still flushed with his startling upset victory over Ball, Humphrey came to the Senate in 1949 eager to do battle against the bankers, the special interests, and conservative-minded Congressmen. In spite of the long standing custom that freshman Senators should be seen and not heard, Humphrey plunged into heated debate with his colleagues.

He introduced scores of bills—including a medicare proposal —but it was not until October that he became embroiled in a truly major controversy. The source of contention revolved around President Truman's desire to reappoint Leland Olds to the Federal Power Commission in 1949. Humphrey sided with Truman.

Olds was a complex personality who fancied himself as a champion of the consumer. Opposed by the oil and gas industry, he was a zealous promoter of public power and federal control over major industries.

First appointed to the FPC in 1939, without Senate hearings, he was reappointed in 1944—but opposition had developed in the interim because of some sensational last-minute revelations regarding Olds' previous radical activities.

In 1949, Colorado's Ed Johnson, chairman of the Senate Committee on Interstate and Foreign Commerce, named a seven-member subcommittee to examine the Olds case in detail.

Among the Senators on the subcommittee: John Bricker of Ohio, Herbert O'Conor of Maryland, Ernest McFarland of Arizona, Clyde Reed of Kansas, Homer Capehart of Indiana, and Ed Johnson. The chairman of the subcommittee was Lyndon B. Johnson, a freshman Senator from Texas.

The Olds controversy swept the nation by storm. It became a *cause célèbre* for most of the liberals. The ADA, the United Auto Workers and the National Farmers Union lined up solidly behind Olds. Indignant editorials poured forth from the New York *Times* and other leading newspapers, chastising Olds' opposition for allegedly toadying to the barons of the oil and gas industry. The President, thinking his own prestige was at stake, fought hard for Olds' renomination. William A. Boyle, Jr., chairman of the Democratic National Committee, flooded Democratic leaders all over the country with telegrams urging them to put the heat on any Democratic Senator who refused to confirm Olds' appointment. The Boyle telegram, which probably did more to anger Senators than to cow them, read in part:

> Federal Power Commissioner Olds has stood for what the Democratic Party has stood—the best interests of the general public in the public utility field. . . . I am asking every member of the Democratic National Committee and every state official of the Democratic Party to make it his personal responsibility to see that the Senators from his state are aware that the people want Olds confirmed and that their Senators' votes reflect this desire. Every resource of the Democratic National Committee headquarters has been turned to this goal at a special staff meeting held this morning, and I have personally discussed with Senate leaders the importance of this issue to the future of the Democratic Party. The issue is clear-cut. Let us resolve it into a victory for democratic liberalism.[1]

The Senators, however, were not to be intimidated. The Lyndon Johnson subcommittee held hearings over a four-day period and questioned 34 witnesses for and against Olds. Olds asked for three hours to respond to critics, and consumed four. Later, he requested additional time and testified for over two hours more. The subcommittee, composed of four Democrats and three Republicans, came up with a unanimous recommendation: The Senate should turn down Olds' appointment.

Supporters of Olds sizzled. Press reports hinted that the oil and gas interests had really dictated the recommendation, and there is no doubt they bore him much animosity. Olds had publicly declared his desire to regulate every aspect of the industry, even to the extent of determining how much individual gas producers could produce and sell, and to whom they could sell it. Nor was industry Olds' only enemy. Also opposing him were the state regulatory commissions, whose power Olds wished to reduce, and state officials who depended on the tax revenues from gas and oil producers to finance local and state government. But opposition from these sources didn't explain the *unanimous* recommendation against Olds by the Johnson subcommittee. Surely not everybody had sold out to the "interests." It couldn't explain either why Ed Johnson had voted for Olds in 1944, but had suddenly turned against him in 1949. Nor could it explain why New York's moderate Republican Senators, Irving Ives and John Foster Dulles, had told the Johnson subcommittee they were against Olds' renomination.

Indeed, as the hearings before the subcommittee unfolded, it became evident that the Senators, both on the subcommittee and off, were opposed to Olds primarily because of his life-long devotion to radicalism—not for his opinions regarding the oil and gas industry. Olds stirred up additional resentment by his refusal to renounce his previously published anti-American views and because of his slippery statements to subcommittee members.

The hearings produced some startling evidence concerning Olds' background. It was disclosed that Olds had been industrial editor of a Communist outfit called the Federated Press from 1922 to 1929, during which time he wrote five short articles a week. By his own testimony, Olds had contributed over 1800 articles to this news service, which served several Communist and leftist publications, including the *Daily Worker*, the official organ of the Communist Party.

The managing editor of the Federated Press was Carl Haeseler, a notorious member of the Communist Party who had served time in the federal prisons of Leavenworth and Alcatraz. The executive board included such active Communists as John W.

Edelman, Earl Browder and William Z. Foster. Both Browder and Foster were in turn to become head of the U.S. Communist Party. Its Washington representative was Laurence Todd, who also represented Tass, the official press organization of the Soviet Union. The Federated Press was largely financed by the Garland Fund, which was established in 1922 for the purpose of advancing Communist fronts. This Fund, which also fueled the *Daily Worker* and the *New Masses*, gave money to Olds personally.

The *American Labor Yearbook 1923-24* had this to say about the Federated Press: "The Federated Press lends itself continuously to the spreading of doctrines subversive of the best interests of the American working people as expressed in the bona fide trade-union movement."[2]

Advocates of Olds have suggested he was a youngster at the time of his association with the Federated Press. But he was 31 years old when he began work for it in 1922, and he continued to write for it until he was just shy of 40.

Rep. John Lyle of Texas, the major witness against Olds, entered into the hearing record over 50 photostats of Olds' writings during the 1922-1929 period. The writings reveal that Olds urged "comrades" to enroll in Communist "training" courses; that he hailed the "decay" of the church; that he advocated elimination of private property in productive enterprises; that he sneered at the Fourth of July as a holiday for "plundering capitalists"; that he hailed Lenin's slogan "All power to the Soviets"; and that he constantly compared Soviet Russia to the United States—with America coming off second best.

An article by Olds which appeared in the *Daily Worker* of July 28, 1924, read: "The Workers' School is giving a number of courses this summer which should prove of great value to the movement and the individual members of the party. . . . Comrades who have been too busy in the movement to follow the more general problems of communism will thus be able to clarify their ideas and equip themselves for greater usefulness in the movement."[3]

From the Federated Press *Labor Letter* of April 6, 1927: "The miners," said Olds, "have two alternatives: To develop along with the rest of organized labor, political power sufficient to put over nationalization, or to seek control by the workers themselves under a worker government."[4]

From a May 4, 1927 piece for the Federated Press: "So frequently does the electric light and power industry turn to its customers for new capital that we may well ask, why not operate the utilities as giant consumer cooperatives? . . . The only real customer ownership is by consumer cooperation. In the case of the giant utilities, this can only mean government ownership."[5]

Olds was constantly harping against the American system. "Now that the vacation season is about over, how about yours?" Olds asked in the October 15, 1925 *Daily Worker*. "Have you had your two weeks' fishing trip—with pay? This question is raised for every wage worker by a bulletin on vacation policies in manufacturing industries issued by the New York State Department of Labor. According to this report, the chances are 9 to 1 that you had your vacation with pay if you are an office worker, but 6 to 1 that you didn't if you engaged in actually producing the goods. . . . On this question Russia, where unions are a recognized part of the industrial order, presents a strong contrast. There the finest country estates are being developed as worker rest homes, and vacations with pay are a regular feature of union agreements."[6]

He assaulted the profit system in the Federated Press *Labor Letter* of April 12, 1928. "Unemployment," he averred, "could be practically eliminated if the country's vast supply of capital were administered for the people. . . . But as the development of the continent approaches its limit, the problem of unemployment and profitless industry will grow more ominous, the public projects will be increasingly nonessential, and a system of doles will be devised to sustain at a pauper level those workers rendered permanently unnecessary. Unless the profit system is superseded."[7]

The Federated Press *Labor Letter* of April 14, 1926 said: "Wanted—a goal that will restore dignity and quality to the life of the American worker. . . . Such promise," said Olds, "is not contained in the chief aims of the American labor movement today—high wages, pensions, and partial stability of jobs secured by cooperation with capitalism in the discipline enforced by its sordid aims. . . . A new age is being born which will succeed capitalist political democracy. The parliamentary systems which began in the Anglo-Saxon world with the Whig revolution in England, in Europe with the French revolution, are decadent. Under them political liberty meant the freedom of the commercial class to enforce sacrifices from the people." The new age, Olds had suggested earlier, would be a working-class revolution, a la Lenin or Mussolini.[8]

Olds' anti-Americanism included a denunciation of the Fourth of July. For Olds the Fourth had a new meaning. He expounded his philosophy in an article which appeared in the July 5, 1928 *Daily Worker:* "To millions of workers slaving throughout the world to provide the tribute exacted by the American dollar empire, Fourth of July will loom as anything but the birthday of liberty. They will view it as the day set apart by the world's greatest exploiters to glorify their rise to power. . . . The latest census of America's invading dollars shows $5,200,000,000 invested in Latin America. . . . The growth of imperial power over Latin America is evident in the increase in dollar investments in Cuba. . . . American dollars are boldly storming the economic defenses of other nations or filtering in as the situation requires. And behind the dollar are the American marines and the enormous potential war strength of the American people. All this is summed up in the celebration of Fourth of July 1928. It marks the development of empire worship."[9]

Most of the Senators were somewhat stunned at Olds' obviously Marxist sentiments, but they were not unkind to Olds during the hearings. After all, many thoughtful persons had held socialist and Communist views in the 1920's and early 1930's, but had renounced them when they had seen they were wrong. Olds too, it was believed, would frankly confess his association with leftists and then repudiate it. But Olds' testimony took a far different turn.

His testimony was marked with evasions. He couldn't recall such and such an event. No, he didn't think he had said that. He had never meant to promote the Soviet system, but was only interpreting events in an unbiased vein.

Sen. Lyndon Johnson asked Olds if he had ever spoken before the Trade Union Educational League. Maybe once, said Olds. But if he did speak, he couldn't recall who spoke with him.

Johnson asked: "You do not remember that you and Earl Browder were the principal speakers on that occasion?" Olds said that that might have been the case. Johnson was perplexed that Olds wouldn't remember, since Browder was a leading figure in the Communist Party and was an official of the Federated Press. Furthermore, the *Daily Worker* had advertised both Olds and Browder as key speakers. The *Worker*, in fact, followed with a report of the occasion and observed that Olds had "sketched in figures and statistics of the growing power of American imperialism. . . ."[10]

Johnson queried Olds: "When you accepted that engagement with the Trade Union Educational League, you did so with the full knowledge and purpose of that organization?"

Olds: "It was my understanding that the purposes of that organization were to develop the organization of the unskilled and semi-skilled workers in industry through the forming of unions on an industrial basis."

Sen. Johnson then educated Olds as to the real purpose of the TUEL. The *Daily Worker*, noted Johnson, had written: "The TUEL represents the left wing of the labor movement. Its purpose is to strengthen labor unions . . . by replacing reactionary and class collaboration policies with the unified program for the transformation of the unions into organs of revolutionary class struggle for the overthrow of capitalism and the establishment of a workers' and farmers' government."[12]

Olds evaded other questions as well. His writings clearly showed he was promoting the Soviet system, but Olds insisted, "I had no intention of boosting the Russian system. . . ."[13] Olds was obviously advocating something on the order of a "workers' government" based on some form of socialism, but he protested: "As far as my writings are concerned, my writings in the main were trying to show people just what the situation was. I was not advocating."[14]

Storming at Olds for his evasive tactics, Sen. Reed interjected:

"Mr. Olds, I have found in your own statement this language, that you did not advocate anything while you were acting for the Federated Press."

Olds: "That was my object, and that is as I recall my writing. . . ."

Sen. Reed: "You certainly do not mean to say, after the introduction of all this evidence, which is directly to the contrary, you do not still say that is true, do you?"

Olds: "I do. . . ."[15]

Olds had, of course, been advocating an economic system based on socialist and Communist concepts. But his insistence in 1949 that his writings in the 1920's only intended "to show people just what the situation was" indicated he still believed his articles had accurately portrayed America. That, in itself, was a revelation.

And when asked point blank to repudiate his writings, he refused to do so. Asked by Sen. Johnson whether he rejected the positions he had taken in these articles for the Federated Press, Olds said: "No sir; I do not." He conceded only that changes in conditions "would lead me to write some of those articles in a *somewhat* different way today."[16]

Supporters of Olds contended he had changed his mind since the 1920's. But the hearings revealed he continued to think in socialist terms and engaged in radical activities long after he had severed ties with the Federated Press. Olds himself volunteered the information that he had attempted to set up an organization in the United States "along the lines of the Fabian Society in England, with a view to laying the foundations for what later might be a labor party like the British Labor Party."[17]

Olds indicated at first that he had had only vague connections with the American Labor Party in 1938—a party whose upper echelons were infiltrated by Communists and which spawned the fellow-travelling Congressman, Vito Marcantonio. The second time Olds appeared before the subcommittee, however, Sen. Homer Capehart of Indiana probed Olds more thoroughly about his association with the ALP.

Capehart: "Were you chairman of the New York County American Labor Party in 1938?"

Olds: "Rockland County; yes I was."

Capehart: "And you were the temporary chairman and made the keynote speech to the American Labor Party at its national convention?"

Olds: "That is correct."

Olds admitted to Capehart that he had told the convention that the Labor Party was shaking the "old political machines," i.e., the Republican and Democratic parties. And these "old political machines," Olds said, "while giving lip service to the needs of the people, were in reality willing tools to the financial power that ruled America that made its democracy a sham."[18]

Asked what his philosophy was now, Olds admitted he was a public power advocate and that "the major developments of hydro-electric power in the river basins of the country should be made by the federal government."[19]

Did he still believe in nationalization of the coal industry, as he had indicated in his writings for the Federated Press? "I think," Olds responded, "it is going to depend a great deal on the coal industry itself whether or not nationalization is going to prove to be the only alternative. It did so prove in England."[20]

The hearings had dealt a fatal blow to Olds' chances. No longer seen as the champion of the consumer, he became in the eyes of the Senators a public power zealot with strong socialist leanings.

When the nomination came before the Senate, Lyndon Johnson, chairman of the subcommittee that had heard Olds, delivered a bitter attack against him. "In the twenties," said Johnson, "he scoffed at private property as just another myth; in the thirties he said our democracy had been made a sham; in the forties he has intimidated his staff [Olds had charged that the FPC staff was led by the nose by the industry], discredited his fellow Commissioners, fostered a smear on Congress, and taken the law into his own hands to substitute irresponsible confiscation for responsible regulation."[21]

Sen. Irving Ives remarked: "I oppose Mr. Olds for the very simple reason that I have no faith in him as an exponent of democratic government in a free society. His past record has revealed him to possess a personal political and economic philosophy which is utterly hostile to democratic government in a free society. . . . Any American who has denounced capitalism as decadent and the sanctity of private property as something to be discarded—and those are his words—and who has urged labor to seek to share in the new apportionment of authority through other than constitutional processes and who, when questioned on this expression of his philosophy, refuses to repudiate it or disavow it, is not only unsuited to hold public office in America, but holding such office, is a menace to America and to the free institutions of America. . . .

"Urging the 'elimination of competitive private capitalism,' he has condemned it 'as just another myth preached in the interest of a small class seeking to retain power and privilege'; and, mind you, Mr. President, he does not repudiate or deny that these are true expressions of his present-day philosophy. I have searched the hearings, and I cannot find any outright repudiation anywhere in the hearings or any denial along those lines."[22]

The evidence that had accumulated during the hearings regarding Olds' radical views did not, however, deter Hubert Humphrey from siding with Olds. Humphrey, in fact, lavished praise on the FPC Commissioner. On the day the Senate voted to confirm Olds, Humphrey filled the *Congressional Record* with six pages in his defense.

Humphrey's remarks were startling, to say the least. According to Humphrey, Olds was a "liberal," not a radical, and had served his country well. "There is evidence," Humphrey stated, "that he had the courage in the 1920's to stand up and say that he did not like the plundering of the stock market. He had the courage to say that he did not like the way the American enterprise system was refusing to recognize human rights.

"In the 1920's," Humphrey continued, "the American enterprise system should have been criticized, and anyone who conclusively criticized it should have a crown of diamonds. If there is any room in heaven for a politician, the politician who will be in heaven is the one who had the courage to stand up and condemn the exploiters of child labor and of adult labor, the exploiters of the widows who put their money into phony stocks.

"If Mr. Olds had the courage to stand up in the 1920's and say that he did not like that kind of rotten business practice, God bless him. Those who should be on trial tonight are those who sat serenely and did not raise a finger of protest when millions of people were robbed, families were broken, homes were destroyed, and businesses were bankrupted. All they did was to talk about some kind of business confidence, and prosperity around the corner, and split up the loot. If there is any divine justice those men will fry, and Mr. Olds will have a crown."[23]

These were strange words coming from a man who had proudly boasted that he had helped to defeat the Communists in the Democratic-Farmer-Labor Party in the 1947-48 period. Humphrey apparently found no difficulty in reconciling his brand of anti-communism with his praise for Olds' anti-American, pro-Soviet and anti-free enterprise articles—articles Olds had written when he was industrial editor of the Communist-controlled Federated Press. Olds had other supporters in the Senate such as Wayne Morse—then an Oregon Republican—but even Morse had conceded that Olds' criticism of American capitalism had been intemperate and extreme. Morse and other liberal Senators contended that what Olds had written had been written a long time ago, and that he should be judged by his performance as a member of the FPC. Only Humphrey was willing to go with Olds all the way.

Humphrey even defended the fact that Olds "had his name in the *Daily Worker*." "I submit," said Humphrey, "that some Senators had their names in the *Daily Worker* in the 1940's when the war was on. Senators had their speeches quoted in the *Daily Worker* during the years of the war. They did not exactly say they wanted it that way, but they got their names in the *Daily Worker* whether they wanted it or not."[24] Humphrey must have known, however, that this answer was less than candid. Olds, as any Senator who had followed the case knew, did not just have his name appear in the *Daily Worker*. He wrote anti-American diatribes for a Communist-controlled news service which catered to the *Daily Worker*—the official paper of the Communist Party.

Humphrey's defense of Olds, fortunately, was a losing cause. Fifty-three Senators voted against his nomination; only 15 voted for him. The issue had clearly marked Humphrey as a radical. But in a certain sense it had aided him politically. He had pleased the base of his support in Minnesota—the ADA, the DFL, the NFU, the public power advocates and even elements further to the Left. He had also banked some good will with President Truman, whom he had previously tried to dump from the Democratic Party ticket in 1948. Humphrey had gone to bat for the White House when it had desperately desired support and when other Senators refused to, something Humphrey would continue to do with ever increasing frequency. In 1951 when Humphrey asked Truman to help him in removing potentially powerful political opposition, Truman would come to Humphrey's aid. Humphrey's support for the President over the years was apparently not in vain.

13

A Strange Crusade

Taking aim in 1950 at Sen. Harry F. Byrd, a powerful Southern solon whose conservative economic philosophy was legendary even then, was not exactly the way for a freshman Senator to win friends and influence people. But brash Hubert Humphrey, who had made a big splash in the press in 1948 by assailing Dixiecrats, felt the time had come to take on the Virginian and his special Joint Committee on Reduction of Nonessential Federal Expenditures.

Far from serving as a useful check on wild government spending, blared Humphrey, the Byrd committee was a bust. On February 24, in a 2,000-word speech—short for Humphrey—the junior Senator from Minnesota ripped off a series of accusations. He contended the committee—conceived by FDR's Treasury Secretary, Henry Morgenthau, and operating since 1941—distorted the picture of federal employment. He charged that the monthly federal personnel statistics it produced were duplicated by other committees and were next to useless anyway. He said the committee used up valuable time—$375,000 worth—of the executive branch of government in acquiring its statistics. Indeed, he claimed the committee's very existence was contrary to the intention of Congress.

Piling up charge upon charge, he trumpeted: "It is my firm

conviction that this committee serves no useful purpose, and is merely used as a publicity medium. It deals only in generalities and violates the purpose for which it was created by wasting public funds rather than conserving them." It is, Humphrey insisted, the "No. 1 example of waste and extravagance" in the federal government.

"The continued existence of the Joint Committee on Reduction of Nonessential Federal Expenditures," he added, "is not conducive to the success of our efforts for the reduction of federal expenditures to which many members of this body are committed, and I cannot urge too strongly that this joint committee and its wasteful activities be abolished. . . .

"Let those who talk so much about economy and do so little about it make the first all-important move toward economy by abolishing a committee which has no right to exist, a committee which has merely existed because no one has spoken up to ask that it be dissolved. . . . I ask that it be done in the name of economy, so we can positively say we have really made a start on economy."[1]

The Humphrey assault was infinitely audacious, and not really in character with his basically cautious nature. The Minnesotan could always be found talking away on this subject or that, but he was not a person who normally rushed in to offend those who could hurt him. Yet Byrd had both prestige and power. The Senate was the citadel of the South, and Byrd, one of the Senate's most illustrious Southern patriarchs. It was true that Humphrey had not directly attacked Byrd by name. But by casting aspersions on his cherished committee, a symbol of Byrd's deeply ingrained conservative economic philosophy, Humphrey might just as well have slapped Byrd across the face with a wet towel.

Humphrey's brazenness consisted not only in daring to defy a Southern Lord, but in the way in which he chose to defy him. Disdainful of Senatorial courtesy, he had delivered his speech while Byrd was not in the Senate chamber. Even worse, Byrd was compelled to be away from the chamber in order to attend the bedside of his mother, who was seriously ill, a fact Humphrey apparently had not bothered to check. On top of all this, Humphrey—again contrary to Senate tradition—decided to impugn Byrd's motives by claiming he had turned the committee into a "publicity medium."

There was something of the absurd in Humphrey's intriguing assault, for it was the first time ever—to anyone's knowledge—that Humphrey had really cared a whit for economy in government. And he had launched this magnificent battle for economy by directing his fire at a committee whose *raison d'être* was to search out waste in government!

As a man who had scored so successfully against the Southerners in 1948, Humphrey undoubtedly felt he would score again. But he had dreadfully miscalculated. Senators and reporters, even those friendly to Humphrey, sensed that the Minnesotan's little drama was not about to win him the rave notices he had no doubt expected to receive.

Nettled by Humphrey's slings and arrows, Sen. Byrd rose to defend himself on March 2—nearly a week later. It was a day Humphrey would long remember. Byrd began his counterattack by tartly noting he had not been able to hear Humphrey's initial criticism "because of serious illness in my family." Then with devastating logic, he pointed out that Humphrey had committed at least nine major errors.

Humphrey had accused the committee of dealing only in generalities and claimed "the only reports" it issued were monthly personnel statistics. Refuting Humphrey, Byrd revealed that the committee had, in addition to the monthly committee reports pertaining to personnel statistics, issued no less than 26 fully documented and formal reports in regard to government waste. Far from dealing in generalities, these reports contained 75 specific recommendations for economy and efficiency in government. "These are documented," Byrd icily remarked, "in the public records of Congress which are available to all who would choose to have themselves advised as to the facts in this respect."

Even more important, as far as Byrd was concerned, the federal government had enacted 50 spending reforms recommended by the Byrd committee, reforms which saved the government

$2.4 billion. To support his claim, Byrd entered into the *Congressional Record* each and every reform suggested by his committee and subsequently adopted by the federal government.

Humphrey had insisted the committee's existence was in violation of the intent of Congress when Congress had passed the Legislative Reorganization Act of 1946. But Byrd reminded Humphrey that joint committees in existence prior to the Reorganization Act were not to be touched by the Act. Furthermore, said Byrd, if Congress didn't want his committee to exist it seemed very strange that it continued to appropriate funds so it could function.

Humphrey had contended that the Byrd committee had "indulged itself" in "persecution and prosecution," and "concealment, containment, evasion and misrepresentation."

"That is a pretty big charge," said Byrd; "it takes in a great deal of territory. I deny emphatically this allegation, and challenge the junior Senator from Minnesota to produce any evidence whatever that the committee has ever engaged in persecution or prosecution of anyone. . . . [Humphrey never did.] Members of the committee include some of the most highly esteemed Members of Congress, the Secretary of the Treasury, and the Director of the Budget. To say that these gentlemen who constitute the committee would engage in or tolerate any of these practices is an irresponsible statement which imputes unworthy conduct and motives on the part of the committee members. Every formal report of this committee has been agreed to by a majority of the members."[2]

One of Humphrey's most astounding claims was that the committee stands as "the No. 1 example of waste and extravagance" in the federal government. Byrd retorted: "This is not only a misstatement; even in this atomic era of superlatives, it must go down as a super-exaggeration. During the committee's existence [since 1941], federal expenditure budgets have totaled more than half a trillion dollars. Of this total, $127,500* has

*Humphrey, in his original attack, indicated the cost of the committee's operations was closer to $375,000. He charged that one had to figure as the true cost its appropriations plus $250,000, which Humphrey claimed was the sum of money it cost the federal departments to search out the information Byrd wanted for his committee.

been appropriated to the Joint Committee on Reduction of Nonessential Federal Expenditures, and I deny that any of it has been squandered. But even if there had been no return from the committee's work, to say that the loss of something over $100,000 in nine years would constitute the No. 1 example of waste and extravagance in the federal government is absolutely theatrical, and requires no answer. But it does indicate that the junior Senator from Minnesota discussed this subject in a mood that cannot be regarded as unprejudiced.

"In passing . . . let me say that only yesterday the junior Senator from Minnesota submitted a resolution calling for the appropriation of $250,000 for the examination of the coal situation. . . . Yet while condemning the expenditure of $127,000 as 'the No. 1 waste and extravagance' . . . the junior Senator from Minnesota seeks for his committee—I assume he will wish to head the examination or investigation—an appropriation of $250,000, for what purpose I do not know. . . ."[3]

(Byrd's difficulty in knowing was for the simple reason that the Committee on Banking and Currency, without any special appropriation, had already spent a month and a half taking a thousand pages of testimony on every phase of the coal situation. When Humphrey, moreover, was asked what information he thought his proposed commission could gather that the Banking and Currency Committee had not already gathered, he confessed his ignorance.[4])

Byrd continued: "After years of effort I am fully aware that an economizer has a thankless task in this day, when the one panacea offered for all problems is more and more government spending. But as chairman of the committee, I take pride in the fact that in all of its many reports during nine years there has not been a single instance of a factual statement having been successfully contradicted. If the Senator from Minnesota can point to a single inaccurate statement of fact by the committee, he has not done so. It is because of the accuracy of the factual statements of the committee that it has a standing for reliability throughout the country. This may account for the publicity complained of by the Senator from Minnesota, which has been given to the committee's reports and recommendations."[5]

Fully aware of Humphrey's vulnerabilities, Byrd then began to harp on Humphrey's own publicity seeking and marathon speech-making. During his first years in the Senate, Humphrey had earned such choice names as "Flannelmouth," "Gabby," "Whip-persnapper," "Pipsqueak," and other assorted degrading appellations. A *Newsweek* item noted that Humphrey was losing popularity with his colleagues because of his seemingly incessant chatter. Byrd poured salt into an open wound. With biting sarcasm, Byrd asked: "Why does the Senator from Minnesota object to this publicity? Why should he be afraid of it? In his speech in the Senate he said the committee 'serves no useful purpose' and is mainly used as a 'publicity medium.' As the Senator from Minnesota is a publicity expert himself, his statement, although not intended as such, could be regarded as a compliment from one who welcomes, and has been signally successful in creating, publicity for himself and his objectives. I know of no Senator who has more generously used the *Congressional Record* and other governmental facilities to promote his publicity. If he has ever hidden his light under a bushel, I am unaware of it. If he has ever run away from publicity, I do not know of it, and no one else does. I am not impressed by anything I have observed indicating that he is the shrinking-violet type evading publicity.

"The Senator charges propaganda when the newspapers publish the reports of the committee in its efforts to promote sound fiscal policies. But he continually strives to propagandize himself and those things he advocates as being proper and worthy. If the Senator desires to pursue the question of propaganda further, it might be interesting to measure on a day-by-day basis the propaganda he has inserted into the *Congressional Record* since he came to the Senate."

The Virginian remarked further: "I have analyzed every statement about the committee, made on last Friday by the junior Senator from Minnesota . . . I could go on . . . but nine misstatements in 2,000 words on this one subject should be enough. This is an average of a misstatement in less than every 250 words; and the Senator from Minnesota speaks like the wind."[6]

Humphrey flushed when a ripple of friendly laughter greeted Byrd's comments.

In concluding his statement, Byrd pointed out he had on several occasions offered to resign the chairmanship, but others had urged him to stay on. When the Republicans won the election in 1946, they even accorded Byrd a significant honor by asking him to remain as chairman of the committee. "I am perfectly willing to resign at any time," Byrd said humbly. "It would be a great relief to me to be relieved of the responsibility. I have no desire to continue as chairman of the committee, and whenever the Senate wants to change the committee, or abolish it, or do whatever in its judgment it may think proper, it is at perfect liberty to do so, and whatever it did would be entirely satisfactory to me. But I do not want it done as a result of misinformation such as that which has been presented to the Senate."[7]

Humphrey had received a thorough tongue-lashing, but this was to be the least of his ordeal. What followed was to be far more humiliating. In an extraordinary event, Senators from both sides of the aisle—conservatives and moderates—rose, one after another, to lavish high praise on Byrd. The maneuver was an obvious attempt to teach Humphrey a lesson for his rash remarks.

Humphrey watched in frustration as George of Georgia, Cain of Washington, Bridges and Tobey of New Hampshire, Williams of Delaware and a host of other influential Senators handed accolades to Byrd. Tennessee's Kenneth McKellar remarked that Byrd's committee had "done wonderful work" and "that the principal work of the joint committee has been done by the distinguished Senator from Virginia."

Humphrey had argued that whatever work the Byrd committee was doing should be done by the Committee on Expenditures in the Executive Departments. But Karl Mundt (R., S.D.), a member of this committee, denied the Committee on Expenditures had the ability to do the job of the Byrd committee since it wasn't a joint committee and had no representatives from the executive department on it. John McClellan, chairman of the Committee on Expenditures, said he was emphatically opposed to taking over any of the work undertaken by the Byrd committee.

Furious at finding one Senator after another siding with Byrd, Humphrey rose to be recognized only to be ignored by the presiding officer, who instead recognized Byrd, who in turn yielded to Mundt. Growing angrier, Humphrey called for a parliamentary inquiry. Again, Humphrey was ignored. As Mundt continued, Humphrey interrupted with a point of order. Finally recognized, Humphrey heatedly asked the presiding officer if it wasn't against the rules for Byrd to yield his time to others for a purpose other than a question. The chair agreed, ruled that Byrd could yield only for a question and then recognized Byrd. Byrd then yielded to Mundt for a "question" which involved Mundt's showering more flowery comments on Byrd and his committee. Byrd then yielded to McClellan, Ferguson, Tobey and Bridges for "questions" which turned into more lavish praise for Byrd. When the Senators present had finished paying their tributes to the Virginian, Byrd, with a twinkle, asked: "Are there any more *questions?*" He was drowned out by a roar of laughter.

Finally obtaining the floor, Humphrey renewed his attacks against the committee, but he was far more irate with his Senate colleagues who had treated him with obvious contempt. Flushed with rage, he began to lash out at almost every member of the Senate—save for a few liberal friends. He criticized Senators for refusing to show up for what Humphrey claimed were momentous speeches. He spoke out sharply against the allegedly "reactionary coalition" which controlled Congress "en masse"—remarks aimed at those who sided with Byrd. In a caustic comment about the tributes paid to Byrd, Humphrey said: "It would seem that this was testimonial day. This pleases me, because I believe we should not wait until people pass to their heavenly reward before expressing our feelings about them. I think it is fine, although irrelevant to the issue, that the Senator from Virginia now knows how much some of his colleagues think of him and how much they appreciate him. It should give him a greater sense of warmth and security in his work."[8]

Oblivious to the tomb-like silence which greeted his remarks, Humphrey started to attack Byrd's voting record as not in keeping with the times—and then launched fresh assaults against Byrd's committee. But Humphrey's attack had no real defenders. Only Sen. Paul Douglas (D., Ill.), a socialist in his youth, tried to prevent Humphrey from being flayed alive by his fellow colleagues. Essentially, however, Humphrey was alone.

Recalling the episode, Sen. Karl Mundt remembers when a number of Senators stalked out of the chamber for the purpose of embarrassing the Minnesotan.

It was a day Humphrey wished had never occurred. He had been wounded and humiliated. Except for a few liberals, his colleagues had isolated him. Later, Humphrey met Byrd by chance in a Senate elevator and ruefully remarked: "I may be a country boy from Minnesota, but I know when I've been run over by a Mack truck."[9]

Although Humphrey had been hurt, he was not contrite. In later days, he still continued to criticize the Byrd committee—though far less strenuously—and there is some indication that he was egged on by dyed-in-the-wool liberals in the Administration. It was common knowledge that they feared the power of the Byrd committee, which focused unpleasant publicity on the number of payrollers in government agencies. In spite of the fact that Humphrey said he desired to abolish the committee for economic reasons, Humphrey's real reason for criticizing the committee appeared to be precisely because it was such an excellent weapon that could be used to rally public pressures against waste in the federal government. "I submit," said Humphrey, "that every monthly report of the committee gets good coverage in the country. I submit that not only does it get good coverage, but that after these monthly reports come out, every Congressman gets thousands of letters about the number of people on the federal payroll."[10]

In short, the committee's resounding effectiveness in bringing pressure upon federal agencies to cut down on the numbers of federal employees was what Humphrey really objected to. Yet he would pretend he wanted to abolish the committee in order to save the people money. To his detractors, Humphrey was playing the hypocrite.

Whatever his motive, the Humphrey campaign fell far short

of success and Byrd remained chairman of his committee until he retired from the Senate in 1964—15 years after Humphrey had taken him on. While Humphrey failed in his goal, he did manage to learn something of value in his quixotic crusade. The lesson took some time to sink in, but he learned it was not particularly wise to attack head-on the centers of power in the Senate—even when the power was in the hands of Dixiecrats. Humphrey desired influence, and his bitter experience at being humbled by his colleagues during the Byrd affair taught him this was not the way to get it. Indeed, within the year Humphrey was playing up to Southerners, and in a few years he would be following the cue of the Southerner who put Humphrey into the Vice Presidency, Lyndon Johnson.

14

"I Am Not a Socialist"

During his first term in the Senate, Humphrey had proved himself a remarkably resourceful politician. He had come into the Congress a flaming radical, the No. 1 enemy of Dixie and an opponent of the Democratic Party's chieftain, President Truman. These attributes may have been useful in gaining him a seat in the U.S. Senate, but they seemed hardly likely to promote his political career once he was there.

The "Southern bourbons" controlled the Democratic Party in the Senate, after all, and Truman could hardly be favorably disposed toward the man who had split his party asunder in 1948 and had worked against his own nomination. But unlike many of the Senate's most prominent liberals—such as Morse, Douglas and Clark—Humphrey was not to be left out in the cold when it came to shaping Democratic policy. He seriously coveted power and developed the knack of obtaining it.

Toward the close of his first term, this raw, inexperienced freshman had managed to contain Southern resentment—even after the Byrd affair—and had projected himself into an influential role within the Democratic Party and even found himself a Truman favorite. Humphrey's quickness and likeable personality helped him gain acceptance. But Humphrey also learned how to mend his political fences.

Though he had tried to unhorse Truman from the Democratic ticket in 1948, he became Truman's most fervent supporter and legislative ball carrier. To some he appeared excessively loyal. When Truman pushed for a bill, Humphrey could be found energetically hailing it as a great piece of social legislation; when Truman wanted a specific measure killed, Humphrey wanted the "little Humphreys" to know their "daddy" supported the President's veto. It is a curious fact of life that Humphrey—known for his deep liberal convictions—has never had a serious public dispute with a Democratic President since he came to the Senate.

Humphrey's loyalty to Truman was not without reward. Truman not only helped move Humphrey up the Senate hierarchy, but quite possibly saved his political career. In the spring of 1951, Humphrey learned that Minnesota's highly popular governor, Luther Youngdahl, a Republican liberal, was being pressured by Minnesota Republicans to run against Humphrey in 1954. A number of political professionals were certain Youngdahl could win. Humphrey, a friend of Youngdahl's brother, was unwilling to find out. With Max Kampelman advising, Humphrey called upon Truman and pleaded with him to "persuade" Youngdahl to take a federal judgeship.

Truman felt favorably disposed toward Youngdahl, for he had been one of the few Republicans who had written him a letter of support after he had fired Gen. Douglas MacArthur during the Korean War. But there was no federal vacancy he felt he could give Youngdahl at the time. When Humphrey learned of the death of a District of Columbia judge a few weeks later, he called Truman and got him to agree that Youngdahl could be the replacement. Humphrey quickly placed a call to Youngdahl at a northern Minnesota hunting lodge. Preferring a warm spot on a federal bench to a heated campaign, Youngdahl came to Washington to accept the judgeship. The appointment infuriated Minnesota Republicans, who felt Youngdahl had sold them out, and it undoubtedly set back GOP fortunes in the state for years to come. Humphrey had pulled off a sensational political coup, and ironically, he owed it to the man he had tried to manipulate out of office only three years before.

Humphrey's attempts at mending political fences paid off elsewhere as well. In 1948 at the Democratic convention he had pushed for a civil rights platform which inflamed the South. Perhaps recalling his success at "Dixie baiting," he had squared off against Sen. Byrd in 1950. Humphrey was badly bruised on that occasion, as we have seen, and a year later he was attempting a different tack. This time he was extending an olive branch to the South. In a soothing 2,000-word letter to approximately 20 prominent Southern editors, Humphrey stressed his "deep affection" for the states below the Mason-Dixon line. He fondly recalled having lived in the South for a while and claimed he possessed a deep understanding of its problems. He assured the Southern editors he did not wish to go too far or too fast with the civil rights issue.

"I know that we frequently place too much trust in the power of the federal government. I know the federal government is not the only government that can deal with the pressing issue of human rights," he said.

A sponsor of much civil rights legislation himself, Humphrey stressed that the federal government had a role in setting certain standards, but added, "My program for civil rights places its main emphasis on community activity, individual responsibility, education and moral values, supported by legislative standards."[1]

His Southern overtures, though carefully guarded, were considered a significant step in seeking a civil rights compromise to head off a revived Dixiecrat movement. Whatever Humphrey's intention, the Dixiecrat movement did not spring back to life. By 1954, moreover, he found himself receiving the plaudits of such Deep South Senators as Walter George, who had volunteered to campaign for Humphrey.

None of Humphrey's politicking, however, would have availed him much if it hadn't been for the power and influence of a Texas Senator named Lyndon Johnson.

To the casual observer, Hubert Horatio Humphrey and Lyndon Baines Johnson may have seemed poles apart. One came from Texas and was considered Southern in orientation on racial matters; the other from the Midwest and a civil rights crusader. Johnson came in as a supporter of big business interests, particularly Texas oil companies; Humphrey was steeped in Midwest Populism—and was an enemy of the "bankers." Johnson was a "states' righter" and Humphrey a champion of federal intervention. Few would have guessed they would one day be linked in a common political bond which would carry them to the two highest political offices in the land.

Yet there were underlying similarities in their makeup which may well have helped form this bond. Both had come to the Senate in 1949; both had been raised in rural middle class surroundings; both had been teachers; both had had experience with New Deal agencies; and both had an innate love of politics. Socially they suited each other, and only a few years separated them in age.

Politically, too, they were far closer than many realized, and many of their differences in voting stemmed from their constituents rather than a true division in political beliefs. They were both products of the depression and ardent followers of Franklin Delano Roosevelt. If Johnson voted "conservatively" on matters such as oil depletion allowances, civil rights and labor legislation, it was because he could do little else if he expected to survive as a Senator from Texas. But Johnson's "conservatism" on some issues did not prevent him from supporting a host of New Deal-Fair Deal spending programs. What is often forgotten, moreover, is that when LBJ first ran for Congress in 1937, he was elected by championing not only the New Deal and FDR, but even FDR's greatest political blunder, the packing of the Supreme Court.

Above all, both Humphrey and Johnson were and are ambitious and extraordinarily pragmatic politicians, willing to bend with the wind if the occasion calls for it—even if it means completely reversing a former position.

It was ambition and pragmatism that brought them together. But Humphrey may have gotten the better part of the deal. Initially an outsider, Humphrey found that the key to success and power was sticking close to Lyndon.

Humphrey learned much just by watching Johnson in action. The Texas Senator advanced rapidly in the Senate scheme of things. Using his legislative experience gained in the House and his ingenious political talents, he was promoted to Senate Majority Whip in three quick years. Along the way, Johnson became Humphrey's friend, advising him to round out his rough edges and introducing him at luncheons to various important Senators.

The most significant blossoming of the relationship developed after the 1952 elections, when Democratic Majority Leader Ernest McFarland was beaten by Barry Goldwater. At that point, Johnson began to round up support in a bid to become leader of the Senate Democrats. But the liberals were intent on electing one of their own—Sen. James Murray, a liberal from Montana. Because of their growing friendship, Johnson beckoned Humphrey to his office to ask him to intervene with the Senate liberals on Johnson's behalf. Humphrey reluctantly explained to LBJ that he had promised his support to Murray, and intimated that the liberals were not so much seeking victory over Johnson as a display of strength, so that Johnson would have to meet their terms. While Humphrey was prepared to say that Murray would get at least 16 votes, Johnson revealed to a shocked Humphrey that Murray would get less than eight votes. Humphrey was still disbelieving, and though he did not really want to oppose Johnson, he felt he had committed himself too strongly to Murray to back out now.

When the Democratic caucus met in January, 1953, Johnson humiliated Murray, who received less than five votes. Always ready to move toward, rather than against, the power center, Humphrey quickly moved that the vote for Johnson be made unanimous.

Within hours of Humphrey's conciliatory gesture, the new Senate leader of the Democrats made a surprise visit to Humphrey and offered him his first main role in shaping Democratic strategy. He asked Humphrey to name the man he wanted to sit on the Democratic Policy Committee. Johnson also assured Humphrey he would appoint him to a place on the prestigious Foreign Relations Committee, as President Truman had desired.

Humphrey wanted a seat on the committee not only for "prestige" and his interest in foreign policy, but for a hard political reason as well. Rep. Walter Judd, a popular Republican and a foreign affairs expert, might run against him in 1954, and he felt experience on the Foreign Relations Committee could protect his Senate seat. Humphrey also secured a promise from Johnson that he could get back on the Agriculture Committee if a vacancy occurred. Opportunity conveniently knocked in May, 1954, with the death of Sen. Clyde Hoey of North Carolina—and Johnson, true to his word, put Humphrey on the committee. Thus Humphrey, thanks to Johnson, could boast to his constituents in the 1954 elections that he had positions on two powerful Senate committees.

Such favors, however, incurred obligations as well, including extraordinary devotion to LBJ's legislative program. An example of what sort of loyalty LBJ expected could be viewed in 1954, when a public housing bill was due to come to the Senate floor on a Monday afternoon. Worried that the bill could be defeated, Johnson called Humphrey-aide Kampelman on the Friday before, demanding that Humphrey return from a Minnesota speaking tour to ensure the measure's passage. When Humphrey hadn't returned by Saturday night, Johnson awakened Kampelman on Sunday to give him an angry tongue-lashing: "Tell Hubert to get back here," Johnson bawled. "God damn you ADA liberals," he cursed into the phone. "You run around the country making pious speeches about helping the poor while I do all the work."

Kampelman assured Johnson that Humphrey would return in time for the vote, but when Monday morning came Humphrey phoned Kampelman frantically from New York, telling him he had been delayed because of bad weather and couldn't make it until three that afternoon. Kampelman dutifully notified Johnson of the delay. After heaping additional abuse on the ADA, Johnson sprang into action. He had the Civil Aeronautics Board place Humphrey's flight on top priority, and sent his personal limousine to the Washington airport with a police squadron large enough for a Presidential motorcade to await

Humphrey's arrival. He then finagled Sen. Homer Capehart, who was leading the opposition to the bill, into postponing the vote until 4 p.m. Thinking he had the votes, the Indiana Republican agreed. Meanwhile, Johnson was fighting off crippling amendments which would have drastically cut the bill's funding. As Johnson stalled for time, Kampelman finally slipped him a note that Humphrey would shortly arrive. He did. The vote came and Johnson managed to win by one vote.

Over the years, Humphrey and Johnson worked well together, and inevitably there were liberal murmurings that Humphrey was selling out. As the relationship grew, it was true that Humphrey tended to shake his crusading image, though his votes were down-the-line with the ADA, AFL, and CIO. But the "selling out" charge largely stemmed from Humphrey's agreement to rally as many liberals as he could behind much of Johnson's strategy and programs. To the confirmed Senate liberals who had always looked upon Johnson as a sort of conservative Southerner, this was proof enough that Humphrey was no longer the liberal he had once been. Though Humphrey's liberalism may have been less glossy than in previous years, he did manage to gain influence and power and backing for projects that would satisfy Minnesota's voters. He also managed to build a bridge to the man who would lead him within a heartbeat of the Presidency.

Humphrey's political resourcefulness was also reflected in his voting record. Always mindful of his constituents, he fought for high farm subsidies—the position of Minnesota's powerful National Farmer's Union—and battled to prevent oleomargarine producers from gaining a strong foothold in butter-producing Minnesota. (Former Rep. Walter Judd recalls that when Humphrey was mayor of consumer-oriented Minneapolis, he favored *cutting* taxes on oleo so it could compete with high-priced butter.) Humphrey also tried to secure loans for small business, and promoted plans for the government to ship surplus food abroad —a factor which did not go unnoticed by Minnesota grain dealers who profited from such foreign aid programs.

While Humphrey tended to please his constituents and shifted gears rapidly on certain issues, his voting record more often than not reflected the views of the radical Left. His overall voting pattern, that is, was fairly consistent—even though Humphrey tended to confuse the issues verbally.

Federal aid to education? Humphrey was for it. Government control over the arts? Humphrey backed it. He had favored price controls, rent controls, public power (more TVAs), public housing, federally controlled medicine, and guaranteed incomes to the farmer.

In Humphrey's ideal world not a single area of American life would escape unscathed from the federal bureaucrats. Indeed, he was far ahead of his time in that respect. In 1952, the Council of State Chambers of Commerce analyzed 20 roll calls in the Senate. Humphrey favored increased federal spending on 18. He did not favor economy the other two times—he was absent.

Humphrey had warned of his own proclivities for spending on a radio program in November, 1949. At that time, he said: "To those who have been calling me the greatest spender, I want to say you haven't seen anything yet."[2]

The Chicago *Tribune* would editorialize on November 27:

> Mr. Humphrey has never been deterred by such sordid details as the expenditure of the taxpayers' money. A compilation of measures he introduced in his first four months in the Senate totted up to 22 billion dollars. . . .[3]

He was not, to be sure, above switching signals when the situation called for it. Thus a year later, as mentioned previously, Humphrey was posing as the *champion* of the taxpayer by launching a towering assault on the Joint Committee on Reduction Nonessential Federal Expenditures for being the "No. 1 example of waste and extravagance" in the federal government. That the committee, whose duty it was to expose waste, spent less in nine years than Humphrey might propose to spend in one hour on any given day did not deter Humphrey's criticism.

Humphrey not only assured his constituents and colleagues that he was against "waste" from time to time, he assured them he was as much a free enterpriser as the next man. Humphrey for a controlled economy? Not at all. "I do not believe in socialism. I do not believe in any type of collectivism. I believe in free enterprise,"[4] Humphrey would say with a positive air. But Humphrey's disclaimers did not completely dispel the doubts of the skeptical.

He had surrounded himself with advisers who had a socialist outlook on a wide variety of things. Max Kampelman, who moved with Humphrey to Washington to become his legislative adviser, endorsed Norman Thomas, the Socialist Party candidate for President, in 1948.

The Americans for Democratic Action, of which Humphrey was a founder, clearly favored socialism—at least in other countries—and showed it by sponsoring in 1947 a three-week tour in America of Jennie Lee, wife of Aneurin Bevan, an extreme left-winger in Britain's socialist Labor government.[5]

Humphrey was elected ADA's national chairman in April, 1949, serving in that position for one year. In 1949 the ADA sponsored a summer trip for young people to study Britain's socialist government. Circulated among government employees and Senate pages, ADA literature promoting the trip read:

> ADA has a deep and sympathetic interest in the program of Britain's Labor Government. ADA has held that what Britain is accomplishing may be one answer to the challenge of communism. For here freedom and planning are essentials of a mature and vigorous democracy. Britain has lost none of her democratic practices with the planning she has had to do to rebuild. In fact, she has added new privileges of citizenship with the broadened participation required by her health, housing, town and country planning and other social welfare legislation. . . . The 8 weeks in England will be spent at summer sessions of the Labor Party, Fabian Society, Workers Education Association and Trade Unions Congress. . . . The project director attended summer schools in Britain last year. . . . She is particularly interested in the exchange of peoples between nations as a means of building international understanding, and as a member of ADA believes that there should be more exchange of *like-minded* liberals throughout the world. . . . [emphasis added].[6]

From the circular, it would be difficult to escape the conclusion that ADA members and British socialists were "like-minded" and that the word "liberal," according to the ADA, was interchangeable with the word "socialist." But ADA's national chairman insisted he was opposed to socialism.

Humphrey was still national chairman when the January 27, 1950, *ADA World* supported the socialists for re-election in England. "A Conservative victory," said the *World*, "would mean that British trade unions would have less confidence in their government. This would tend to increase strikes and social tension. . . . A Conservative victory in Britain would give an enormous boost to the continent's conservatives, most of whom lack the feeling of responsibility. . . . A Conservative victory furthermore probably would mean eventual incorporation of Franco Spain into all the political, economic and military arrangements of Western Europe. . . . The most passionate hope of our most stubborn reactionaries is for a smashing Conservative victory, with all its implications for our own election this year and in 1952."[7]

The Labor government of Britain had been nationalizing the steel, coal, transportation and banking industries over the years. Bureaucracy had reached an all-time peak. In some cases the laboring man was a near slave of the so-called Labor government, and was not allowed to quit his job except through special permission of the bureaucrats. Humphrey nonetheless apparently saw little contradiction in saying he was for free enterprise and in supporting the socialists of England. When Sen. Homer Capehart attacked the ADA for rooting for a Labor victory, Humphrey gladly admitted that the ADA definitely "is interested in other elections in the world. . . . The ADA does believe it is important for the Labor government of Great Britain to win the election. I am not apologizing for the Labor government."[8] But Humphrey still insisted on his disclaimer: "I am not a socialist and I never want to be one. I believe strongly in real private enterprise—free enterprise, not monopoly enterprise."[9]

While Humphrey may never have wanted to be a socialist, he was certainly intent upon spreading the seeds of socialism, not only in Western Europe, but in the United States as well. The receiver of an award from the socialist League for Industrial

Democracy in 1948, he enthusiastically praised the socialist Rand School for Social Science in its 1951 anniversary celebration. Alexander Trachtenberg, who became head of the Communist secret police in the United States in the thirties, once said the Rand School "was the primary national education institution of the socialist movement. . . ."[10]

This factor, however, did not prevent Humphrey from proclaiming at that 1951 celebration: "My only regret in this heartwarming anniversary celebration is that Rand Schools do not dot the land from New England to California. The sense of indignity that one feels in considering the near void in adult education in the United States is assuaged in part by the long and important history of the Rand School of Social Science."[11]

The *ADA World* of March 29, 1947, had called for "public acquisition of monopolies" (read: nationalization of American industries). In June, 1949, Humphrey had proclaimed he was against nationalization. ". . . I am not a socialist. I do not believe in the nationalization of American industry, not even for sixty days. . . . There may be those who like tyranny of government or who may like nationalization of industry, but the junior Senator from Minnesota believes in free enterprise and representative government."[12]

Not quite three years later, Humphrey was in the forefront of those liberals who championed President Truman's remarkable attempt to seize the steel mills. To understand the full import of the seizure, and Humphrey's supporting role, requires some background information.

In April, 1952, the Korean conflict was still raging. The steel industry and the United Steelworkers of America, led by dour Philip Murray, had been wrangling for five months over a new contract. The government's controversial Wage Stabilization Board (WSB), packed with union ideologues, had recommended in March a wage settlement costing 26.1 cents per man hour. The WSB recommended further that the company should impose compulsory union membership on its employees. The union joyously accepted the proposal; the companies rejected it. Defense Mobilizer Charles E. Wilson rushed to Key West,

Florida to tell the President that such a wage settlement would prove dangerously inflationary, and when the President later said he would stand by the WSB, Wilson resigned in a huff. Nevertheless, the steelworkers' union issued an ultimatum: unless the company agreed in full to the much-disputed recommendations of the WSB, it would unleash a strike at midnight, April 8.

With the strike deadline only 90 minutes away, President Truman made a nationwide television speech which set off one of the biggest constitutional crises of the century.

"My fellow Americans," he started, "tonight our country faces a grave danger. We are faced by the possibility that at midnight tonight our steel industry will be shut down. This must not happen. . . . We do not have a stockpile of the kinds of steel we need for defense. . . . If steel production stops, we will have to stop making the shells and bombs that are going directly to our soldiers at the front in Korea. . . . I am directing the Secretary of Commerce to take possession of the steel mills, and to keep them operating."

Truman then vented his full fury against the companies. He said the industry's demands to raise prices were "the most outrageous thing I ever heard of." He insisted the recommendations of the pro-union Wage Stabilization Board were "fair and reasonable." "The steel industry," he said, "has never been so profitable as it is today—at least not since the profiteering days of World War I. And yet . . . the steel companies . . . want to double their money. . . . They [the steel industry] want something special, something nobody else can get. . . . And they are apparently willing to stop steel production to get it."[13]

Boiled down to essentials, the President said he was seizing the mills because the companies had refused to absorb union demands without raising prices.

By the time the President had completed his talk, Commerce Secretary Charles Sawyer had begun taking over the job of running the mills. Up went the symbols of federal possession: the U.S. flag and seizure orders on the company bulletin boards. When U.S. Steel's Ben Fairless next met with Sawyer, he acknowledged the swift change of ownership with a sour, "Hello, boss."[14]

The President had made some conspicuous omissions in his highly partisan presentation. He did not mention that the profit figures he used were profits *before* taxes. He did not allude to the fact his Defense Mobilizer had resigned because he felt the WSB's recommendations were outrageously inflationary. He did not say that he himself had once felt that the steel companies should be allowed to increase their prices if the workers were to receive higher wages. He did not say that one demand the unions—and the government—were insisting upon and the companies were resisting was compulsory unionism. Nor did Truman cite any specific legislation that permitted his "Gestapo-style" take-over, as some later called it.

Truman could not cite any specific piece of legislation upon which to base his actions simply because there was none. In fact, Congress had repeatedly turned down such legislation. On June 28, 1951, for example, the Senate by a 57-to-25 vote had crushed a "seizure" amendment introduced to the Defense Production Act. The rejected amendment—voted on during the Korean War— would have given the President precisely the powers he now claimed he had.[15]

Nor was this all that militated against Truman's decision. While the President was saying he needed to take the extraordinary action—specifically denied to him by Congress—of seizing the steel mills to keep steel production going, the fact was that the President *had* been granted powers to prevent the steel strike, powers which he refused to use. The law the President bluntly refused to employ was the Taft-Hartley Act, which permitted the federal government to obtain a federal injunction against any major strike for at least 80 days.

Why had the President refused to use Taft-Hartley? The general consensus was that it was an election year and the unions were opposed to the law. By avoiding Taft-Hartley and using the method of seizing the mills, moreover, the government could easily impose the union-supported wage settlement on the industry. The government could do this by seizing the mills, granting the union what it wanted, and then telling industry officials it would return the mills to private ownership only if they agreed to the wage contract awarded to the union by the government.

The President's seizure convulsed the country. The *Christian Science Monitor,* the Cleveland *News,* the Cleveland *Plain Dealer,* the Detroit *Free Press* and the New York *Times* were among the hundreds of newspapers across the land that angrily denounced the action as a clear violation of the Constitution. In a typical reaction, the Washington *Post* commented:

> President Truman's seizure of the steel industry will probably go down in history as one of the most high-handed acts committed by an American President. . . . If pretense is laid aside, it must be admitted that in this instance the President exercised the prerogatives of a dictator. If he can seize the steel industry, without any law on the books for that purpose, in order to impose upon it the recommendations of a governmental board, he can likewise seize other industries and labor unions. Reckless use of such power could quickly destroy our constitutional system. . . . Indeed, the very concept that the President has authority 'to do whatever is required'—to use Mr. Truman's own words—is totalitarian in nature.[16]

Sen. Hubert Humphrey, who only three years before had equated nationalization to tyranny, was four-square behind the President. At every turn in the dispute, Humphrey would rush to the President's defense. He stuffed into the *Congressional Record* mountains of material attempting to uphold the President's position. The Minnesota lawmaker endorsed the view that the President had "inherent executive power" to take over the mills. He claimed that "great statesmen like Alexander Hamilton"—who less than a year before he had likened to some "defunct Bourbon"—were on Truman's side.

After upholding the President's right to seize the steel mills, Humphrey would claim it was not for Congress but the courts to decide. But when the courts struck down the constitutionality of the act, Humphrey called for legislation to seize the mills. Not once did he call for the President to prevent the strike through use of the Taft-Hartley law—the only law which Congress had approved to deal with strikes in a national emergency. Humphrey, like his union supporters, preferred seizure.

In his 4,500-word decision in early May, Federal District Judge David A. Pine brusquely set aside the Truman seizure.

"The fundamental issue," wrote Pine, "is whether the seizure is or is not authorized by law." Pine found nothing in the Constitution to support the Administration's claim of unlimited "inherent" or "residuum" executive power.

Pine said he had been told by government lawyers that the Taft-Hartley law would be ineffective, but he replied: "[That] presupposes that the Labor-Management Relations Act of 1947 [Taft-Hartley] is inadequate when it has not yet been tried, and is the statute provided by Congress to meet just such an emergency. And it further presupposes . . . that, this statute being inadequate, Congress will fail in its duties under the Constitution, to legislate immediately and appropriately to protect the nation from the threatened disaster. I am unwilling to indulge in that assumption, because I believe that our procedures under the Constitution can stand the stress and strains of an emergency today as they have in the past, and are adequate to meet the test of emergency and crisis."

Humphrey, however, still upheld the President. The Supreme Court on June 2, in a six-to-three opinion, struck down the President's seizure of the mills. Justice Hugo Black, considered one of the most liberal members of the Court, delivered the opinion. Black stated that the President's powers, if any, must stem "either from an act of Congress or from the Constitution itself. There is no statute that expressly authorizes the President to take possession of property as he did here. Nor is there any act of Congress to which our attention has been directed from which such a power can fairly be implied."

Furthermore, said Black, there is nothing in the Constitution which would give him such inherent powers. "The Founders of this nation," he wrote, "entrusted the lawmaking power to the Congress alone in both good and bad times. It would do no good to recall the historical events, the fears of power and the hopes for freedom that lay behind their choice. Such a review would but confirm our holding that this seizure order cannot stand."

After the Court decision, the steelworkers went on strike. President Truman still refused to use Taft-Hartley to get an injunction against the strike. On June 10 he asked Congress for a law to seize the steel mills. Humphrey remarked: "I think the President outlined the only plausible course of action."[17] Labor and management finally did come to a meeting of the minds and Congress never did authorize seizure, but Humphrey had left in doubt his claim that he opposed nationalization of American industry—"even for sixty days."

It was not to be the last time that Humphrey would say one thing and mean something else.

15

The Politics of Red-Baiting I

It was autumn of 1950. The cold war was, unhappily, no longer cold. It had burst into scorching flames in late June when the North Korean Communists, with vast quantities of Soviet aid and encouragement, stormed southward across the 38th parallel. At home, America's lawmakers, largely reflecting the concern of the public, were contemplating what action to take, if any, against domestic Reds.

With Communist aggression apparent to the entire world, the occasion was ripe for action. The American Communists obviously were potential spies and saboteurs, and it was firmly believed they would do all they could to aid their Korean comrades. Even those skeptical liberals who had previously denied or scoffed at the Red menace were ready to admit it now. Significant evidence had been piling up steadily over the years.

As far back as 1948, Elizabeth Bentley and Whittaker Chambers, both former Communists, revealed to a stunned public that Red spy cells had existed and continued to exist in the highest government echelons. Similar unravelings of Red infiltration followed.

The year 1950 saw additional proof of Communist activities. In January of that year Alger Hiss, a key adviser to President Roosevelt, was convicted in federal court for having lied before the House Committee on Un-American Activities when he denied Chambers' testimony that he had passed on top government secrets to the Soviets. The AFL and the CIO continued to find Communists in their midst, and Communist-dominated unions were found to have control over vital defense industries. In March the Senate began hearings on explosive charges by Sen. Joseph R. McCarthy (R.-Wis.) that Communists in government had shaped and were shaping our foreign policy. In August, Judge Learned Hand of the U.S. Court of Appeals in New York wrote a 23,000-word decision proclaiming American communism a "clear and present danger." The ruling upheld the conviction of the Communist Party's 11 top officials, who had been charged with teaching and advocating the overthrow of the U.S. government by force and violence.

In view of the clear and present danger, the House in August, by a 354-20 vote, passed a bill requiring Communists and Communist organizations to register with the Attorney General and barring members of Communist groups from government defense jobs.

The Senate was debating a similar measure in September. Introduced by Sen. Pat McCarran (D.-Nev.), the bill eventually consolidated no less than seven measures, including the major features of a bill originally drafted by Sen. Karl Mundt (R.-S.D.) and a young California GOP lawmaker, Rep. Richard Nixon. The theory behind the Senate measure was that by compelling Communist organizations and their members to register with the Attorney General, the Reds would be forced into the open. They would also be restricted in their activities because those registered were to be barred from security and defense-connected jobs. If the Communists refused to register, they would be subject to fines and imprisonment.

The McCarran bill ruled that memberships of Red groups and the sources of their funds had to be revealed publicly. Literature disseminated by Communist organizations had to be labeled as coming from Communist organizations. The McCarran measure also proposed to establish a Subversive Activities Control Board which, upon application of the Attorney General, would determine—through rigid criteria—whether any group was Communist-controlled. Such a finding was subject to court review.

While the need for anti-Communist legislation was pressing, there was much dissension over the McCarran bill. The New York *Times* and the Washington *Post* opposed its alleged restrictions on civil liberties. President Truman thought it entirely unworkable. Also opposed was a relatively small band of Senate liberals, including Hubert Horatio Humphrey.

Humphrey began his assault on the proposed legislation when it first came up for debate on September 5. He feared that it would scoop up both innocent and guilty alike. Communist officials, required under the bill to register members of Communist organizations, would, said Humphrey, probably register innocent and respectable people. Furthermore, he said that perfectly loyal Americans opposing the Marshall Plan, aid to Korea, NATO and the FEPC—issues which the Reds also opposed—could be accused of being Communists by the Subversive Activities Control Board.

On September 8, Humphrey unleashed a different type of assault. Again taking pot shots at the registration provisions, he now claimed the bill was too *ineffective* to capture any Communists. In an exchange with Sen. Paul Douglas (D.-Ill.), he asked a series of rhetorical questions:

Humphrey:

If I understand the Senator correctly it is his opinion—is it not—that before the Communist Party itself would have to register it could have the benefit of every single administrative legal process that we have under the entire law of this country?

Douglas:

This is absolutely true. From the time the charge would be made the steps would be that the Communist Party would be notified, the hearings would be held before the trial examiners of the Subversive Activities Control Board, reports would be made, the evidence would be reviewed, the Board would make its final decision, appeal could be taken to the circuit court, and from the circuit court to the Supreme Court, and all along the line there could be delaying actions so that years could go by before there was even a final order compelling the Communist Party to register.

Humphrey:

And is it not true that all during this time every single Communist, little and big, vicious and semi-vicious, would be at large?

Douglas:

Not only at loose and at large but unidentified.

Humphrey:

Running around the country and being motivated even more than ever to do his dirty work and his sabotage?[1]

"I believe," Humphrey continued, "the effect would not be as intended, but eventually would result in impressing the American people with the fact that it is a measure which is incompetent, ineffective, and does not provide any protection for our national security."[2]

The Minnesota Senator was just warming up to his subject. He felt, he said, the intent of those awful registration provisions would be to outlaw the Communist Party, but didn't everyone know that history reveals that Communists become even more powerful in countries where communism is outlawed?[3]

And still another point: "How do we expose this fraud and this hoax? This registration provision is nothing more nor less than some sort of a political palliative. It is a sort of political opium to put the American people into a sort of swoon."[4]

Four days later the McCarran bill came up for a vote. It zipped through the Senate 70-7,[5] with only a few liberals willing to buck the overwhelming sentiment of Congress and the country. Hubert Humphrey's name, however, does not appear among those who voted against this piece of legislation. Nor did he miss the roll call, as he has been known to do on important occasions. Amazing as it must have been to his colleagues, Humphrey cast his vote *for* the very bill he had so bitterly denounced as a "hoax."

The Humphrey reversal was truly dazzling. On the day of the vote he had taken time out to defend the National Farmers

Union—influential in Humphrey's home state—from earlier charges by GOP leader Styles Bridges (R.-N.H.) that the union was Communist infiltrated.[6] But Humphrey did not utter word one as to why he had suddenly shifted his sentiments in favor of the McCarran measure—a measure he had criticized because he felt that under it such "innocent" organizations as the National Farmers Union could be cited as subversive.

Between Humphrey's outburst against the McCarran bill on September 8 and the actual vote on September 12, not one amendment was added which would have obviated any of Humphrey's previous criticisms. Indeed, on September 11 the Senate, by a voice vote, had incorporated into the McCarran bill amendments which *strengthened* the registration provisions and which President Truman had claimed he would veto. Before the final vote, moreover, the Senate accepted the Kilgore "concentration camp" amendment which permitted the government to intern people suspected of espionage and sabotage in time of national emergency. Yet Humphrey supported the entire package.

His apparent turnabout, however, was not the most bizarre of Humphrey's maneuvers in regard to this bill.

The Senate-passed bill went to a conference committee set up to iron out the differences between the Senate- and House-passed versions. The conferees adopted the major provisions of the Senate bill, leaving the registration and Kilgore measures intact. On September 20, the bill agreed upon by the conferees came up for a vote in the Senate. The bill passed 51-7.[7]

This time Humphrey had decided not to vote at all. Though earlier in the day he had approved the nomination of Gen. George Catlett Marshall for Secretary of Defense, Humphrey could not find the time to vote on the conference version of the bill. It was assumed, however, that because he had voted for the McCarran bill on September 12 and afforded absolutely no opposition to the conference version of the McCarran bill, he now definitely supported it.

On September 22, President Truman vetoed the bill on the grounds that it was a bad piece of legislation. Humphrey was the first Senator to speak on the veto: "I rise to make comment upon the message of the President of the United States and his very courageous action in vetoing the McCarran bill, H.R. 9490, known as the Internal Security Act of 1950. . . ."[8]

Once again Humphrey had somersaulted. In just two weeks he had denounced the McCarran bill, voted for it, and upheld its veto by the President. It was a stunning acrobatic performance worthy of the Flying Wolandas.

This time Humphrey felt compelled to justify his tortuous voting record. He complained that the conference report—which he had not thought important enough to vote on—had seriously weakened the Kilgore provisions which called for herding suspected saboteurs into concentration camps during a time of national emergency.

Humphrey's complaint about the conference report is not borne out by the facts. The detention or concentration camp provisions, originally dreamed up by Sen. Harley Kilgore (D.-W.Va.), were virtually untouched by the conference. The reliable *Congressional Quarterly Almanac* of 1950 specifically notes that the "final compromise bill contained the principal provisions of the House Wood bill and the Senate McCarran bill plus the Kilgore modifications."[9]

But Humphrey objected to it on other grounds as well. Once more he used the curious argument that the bill was not only too weak but too strong.

The bill he had called a "hoax" and charged would have no effect whatsoever on the Communists, could, it now seemed, be used to "crush organizations which seemed a bit unorthodox."[10] "The worst thing that could happen in America," Humphrey intoned, "is to have any kind of a law that would put a lid upon creative thought."[11]

But Humphrey would also make a confession. He admitted that his original vote for the bill might have been wrong. With Truman's veto, the "President of the United States has said to Hubert Humphrey, and I think he has said to other people, 'This is your chance to come clean. This is your opportunity to vote your convictions. This is your opportunity not to be swallowed up by the hysteria and tension of this hour.'

"I say very frankly that, like many other Members of this body, I was swallowed up, and I am happy I can release myself, and I am happy I can stand here in the tradition of Thomas Jefferson, the tradition of Thomas Paine, the tradition of Daniel Webster, and the other great men who did not sacrifice liberty for politics, and I am going to vote for liberty."[12]

And later on: "I join the ranks of free men. I am going to rectify the miserable mistake I made."[13]

Yet Hubert Humphrey, as usual, wasn't through talking on the subject, and when on September 23 the Senate voted on whether or not to sustain the President's veto, Humphrey was more turbulent than ever: "It is because of my deep concern for intellectual freedom, because of my deep concern for personal liberty, that I rise again to urge upon the Senate to sustain the President's veto."[14] Humphrey dramatically declared that Congress had seldom been faced with such a crucial decision. "Oh, yes . . . there was one other time. . . . In 1798 the Congress of the United States passed the alien and sedition laws."[15]

By this time Humphrey had almost forgotten that he had portrayed the McCarran bill as an ineffective tool with which to catch subversives. It was, in fact, its potential effectiveness that seemed to terrify him now.

The bill, he warned, could be used to destroy its opponents. "A new technique in American politics," he observed darkly, "has come into our midst, a technique that was developed to its finest point by ruthless, bigoted, immoral Hitler—the technique of the big lie. Hitler's master propagandist, Mr. Goebbels, told the big lie again and again. Mr. Hitler destroyed his opposition with smear, with the big lie. He branded as subversives those who stood against him, and the full power of the state was brought to bear upon them."

"There are," Humphrey said pointedly, "would-be Hitlers in America, Mr. President."[16]

Humphrey's picture of what the bill would do became even gloomier: "I hope," Humphrey continued, "we shall never be cursed with such a ruthless, barbaric philosophy as that which is found in communism. But I submit that every time a state has tried to eradicate its opposition—and history is filled with examples—those who were to be eradicated and destroyed rose up to destroy those who planned their destruction. . . .[17] Every state, every nation that has ever tried to outlaw a political party, every state, every nation that has tried to submerge a political party, every state, every nation that has tried to outlaw thought groups, pressure groups, or pseudo-political groups, has lived to rue the day; it has lived to see its work destroyed.

"People may say, 'the Senator from Minnesota is talking in the realm of the doctrine of eventuality.' . . . I want to remind this honorable body that our forefathers who wrote the Declaration of Independence . . . saw some eventualities. They, too, saw the possibility of 'the man on horseback.'[18]

"I say that the bill, which I fear is going to become law, represents no contribution to mankind. It will go down in history with some of the edicts of the kings of old. It will go down with the alien and sedition laws. It will go down in the annals of American legislative history as the great mistake of this generation—the political tragedy of a mature people."[19]

The more Humphrey talked, the more his passions began to boil. On and on he went. He invoked Milton, Jefferson, Voltaire, Plato, Woodrow Wilson, John Hancock, the Statue of Liberty, and Socrates and his cup of hemlock. Even the Rotary Club became a reason why the bill should not be passed. Oblivious to his surroundings, he ignored the sarcastic "Amen" from a scornful colleague interrupting his monologue. Indeed, he appeared to be spurred on to new rhetorical flourishes: "Our people came from countries dominated by the theory of divine right of kings. Our people said, 'We do not believe in that kind of tommyrot. We believe that all men are created equal.' Does anyone think," Humphrey continued, "King George III liked that? They had been pulling the old hocus-pocus over their people for centuries. They had been going around keeping people ignorant. . . . Then to America came the lovers of freedom. Why did they come to America? They came because they were considered to be dangerous in Europe. That is right. Tom Paine said:

'Where freedom there is not, there is my home.
To do good is my religion.'

"Many people do not like Tom Paine. I do not know anything about his spiritual or religious attitude. I do know his literature. I know he said: 'These are times that try men's souls.' I know he said something about sunshine patriots."[20]

Humphrey was clearly out of hand, and he was groping for even more ways to persuade his colleagues to his cause. Abruptly switching from Tom Paine to a new thought, he remarked:

"Do Senators remember that old song: 'Give me some men who are stout-hearted men—'

"I do not remember how many men they were going to get, but it was something like 10—

'and I will give you 10,000 more.'

"That is what we need, Mr. President.

"We are asking, this little handful of us, those of us who have been trying to sustain the veto:

'Give us some men who are stout-hearted men
And we will give you ten thousand more.' "[21]

Humphrey continued his remarkable peroration: "How many Senators remember the Jacobeans (*sic*) after the French Revolution? How many remember the history of the eighteenth century? I remember it, because I had to teach it."*

"Frankly," he said, "had it not been for the Jacobean (*sic*) philosophy Alexander Hamilton† might have dominated the

*Humphrey, however, had not recalled his 18th century history as well as he had thought. The Jacobean period refers to the 17th century and to the era of James I of England. Humphrey undoubtedly was referring to the Jacobins, who were violent revolutionaries in France and had no respect for law, order or humanity. What the Jacobins had to do with the McCarran bill is for future historians to determine.

†On April 9, 1952, as recorded on page 3825 of the *Congressional Record*, Humphrey said: ". . . the history of Constitutional law in this country is replete with cases, with citations from such eminent justices as Chief Justice Marshall and from great statesmen like Alexander Hamilton, in his discussions of the powers of the Constitution. . . ."

country. How we ever escaped one of those old defunct Bourbons, I do not know."[22]

Humphrey introduced his own home-spun philosophy: "I should like to say that if there is anything I found out in Sunday school and in church it is that the greatest thing man can do is serve his fellow man. It is better to minister than to be ministered unto. He who would be first will be last. That is what has got some people into trouble, because some of these folks have been members of groups which under this bill would be called subversive. . . ."[23]

Though Alger Hiss and a number of spy rings had been uncovered by the House Committee on Un-American Activities, Humphrey proclaimed: "We cannot check the march of communism in Europe and Asia, or its growth in America, by merely legislating against it—and cursing it. I repeat there is yet to be found by any of the proponents of this proposed legislation one example in history—give me one scientific example in history where anyone has ever stopped communism by investigating it, legislating against it, or cursing it.[24]

"No Communist or Fascist should be permitted to serve in any position of public trust where his employment would jeopardize the security of this nation. . . . But, to dismiss Communists from government jobs or to prosecute them in the courts does not destroy communism nor check its growth. . . .[25]

"We cannot lick communism with communistic methods. We cannot lick communism with just a little bit of communistic method, either, because a little of that communistic method is just enough to make it a police method.[26]

"I want a vote on this measure. I want a vote on it, because I want to be proud of myself; I want my name down on the *Record;* I want to be able to point out to the little Humphreys that their daddy voted to sustain the President's veto. I do not want any voice vote. We are going to have a roll call vote on this measure. I want to be on the side of the angels on this one. I want to walk in the spirit, the tradition, and the heritage of the men who have died for liberty."[27]

Humphrey had unloosed quite a stemwinder against the Internal Security Act of 1950. Though it was not necessarily memorable for logic, precision or deftness, only a cynic could believe that Humphrey hadn't finally made up his mind that the internal security bill was a menace to the Republic.

In spite of his oratory, however, he persuaded only nine other Senators to vote to sustain Truman's veto.

One year later the Senator who had challenged anyone to find a "scientific example where anyone has ever stopped communism by investigating it, legislating against it or cursing it" began his own investigation of communism in the labor unions with the purpose of promoting legislation to deal with the problem. Three years later, Hubert Horatio Humphrey introduced anti-Communist legislation to increase the powers of the Internal Security Act of 1950. Indeed, on August 12, 1954, Hubert Humphrey proudly proclaimed that the Internal Security Act was passed by a Democratic Congress. Referring to that Act, he told Sen. John Butler, "I am delighted to hear the Senator from Maryland state that we [the Democratic Party] passed an effective law against communism."[28] Without batting an eyelash, Humphrey would go even further than the FBI director, the Attorney General and Joe McCarthy were willing to go in order to battle the Communists. He would propose an amendment to the Internal Security Act to outlaw the Communist Party, making membership a felony. Ten years later, the Senator who wanted to be able to "point out to the little Humphreys that their daddy voted to sustain the President's veto" against the Internal Security Act would write a constituent in Faribault, Minnesota: "Thank you for sharing with me a copy of your letter to Senator [Eugene] McCarthy dealing with Communist attempts to infiltrate the civil rights movement, and registration of Communists under the Internal Security Act. As you are probably aware, I voted for the Internal Security Act. . . ."

16

The Politics of Red-Baiting II

It was August, 1954, only a few months before the off-year elections. The Democrats were the minority in Congress and were hungrily eyeing a comeback in November. They faced several obstacles, including Ike's success in bringing the Korean War to a close. The Republicans, moreover, appeared to be reviving a campaign theme they had successfully used in 1952: the Democrats are soft on communism.

It was no time, GOP partisans insisted, to return the Democrats to power. FDR, they said, had paved the way at Yalta for communism to take over Eastern Europe and the Far East. Under the Democrats, Communists, including Alger Hiss, had penetrated the top echelons of government. And hadn't Dean Acheson, Truman's Secretary of State, "invited" the Reds to attack Korea when he publicly declared that country outside America's defense perimeter?

Republican Sen. Joseph McCarthy, the Red-hunting Irishman from Wisconsin, was still riding high and doing damage to the Democrats. It was not until December, with the aid of Ike, that the Senate would censure him and his influence would wane rapidly. While McCarthy was portrayed in the press as a radical demagogue, he could not be lightly dismissed. During 1953, the McCarthy Permanent Subcommittee on Investigations brought two Communist cells to light, both of which were still in existence when the hearings took place. One of these, noted James Burnham, "was in the Government Printing Office, where along with ordinary public documents, thousands of secret documents are printed for the intelligence and military agencies of the government."[1] Another cell "was discovered to have been operating in the critical and most secret experimental stations of the Army Signal Corps, in particular the radar and electronic research installations at Fort Monmouth, New Jersey."[2] The cell was apparently initiated by Julius Rosenberg, executed for his espionage activities for the Soviet Union. It seems also to have been linked to the Elitcher cell in the Naval Bureau of Ordnance. A number of employees with access to secret data refused to testify and were suspended. McCarthy had uncovered the cells under the Eisenhower Administration, but they had been planted under a Democratic regime and the public knew where to put the blame. Since 1953, moreover, the Eisenhower Administration had begun publicizing the number of security risks the Democrats had presumably failed to clean out. In short, the Communist issue was very much alive as the 1954 elections were heading into the home stretch.

Since early July the Senate had in fact been considering S. 3706, a bill supported by the Republican Administration, which would have amended and strengthened the Internal Security Act of 1950. As reported out of the Senate Judiciary Committee, the bill provided for a new category of organizations that were subject to penalties under the 1950 Act. The new category was the "Communist-infiltrated" organization. The previous classifications were "Communist-action" and "Communist-front."

The new wording was aimed at Communist-infiltrated labor unions. The bill would have denied such unions any standing before the National Labor Relations Board. The NLRB, of course, was established to secure union rights. Thus to deny the unions legal standing before the NLRB—unless they chucked out the Communists—would have been a powerful persuader in keeping the unions free from Red control.

American liberals, for the most part, did not like the idea. But some Senators in this era of "McCarthyism" felt it didn't strike a severe enough blow against the Reds. One of them was Hubert Humphrey, who would vote to censure McCarthy a few months later.

On August 12, Humphrey introduced a substitute amendment to S. 3706. The amendment was daring: Humphrey wanted to outlaw the Communist Party. He attached provisions to the bill making it a crime to belong to the CPUSA. Party members could be given up to five years in prison and fined $10,000 under the Humphrey proposal.

The Minnesota Senator was belligerent in tone. "The apparatus of the Communist Party works literally at two levels: one, the soapbox type of apparatus, namely the public pronouncements; second, the carefully planned conspiratorial apparatus which carries on infiltration into key government agencies, labor organizations, and cultural institutions.

"The purpose of this amendment is to 'come clean.' I, for one, am growing sick and tired of having bill after bill brought to the Congress that does not reflect a willingness and the courage to go to the center of the problem."[3]

He continued: "The issue is before Congress, and I am quite confident that some persons are a little surprised that the junior Senator from Minnesota has placed the issue before Congress. Let the record be clear. This Senator has been fighting the Communist movement ever since he entered public life, and before. I am tired of reading headlines about being 'soft' toward communism. I am tired of reading headlines about being a leftist, and about others being leftists. I am tired of having people play the Communist issue as though it were a great overture which has lasted for years. . . .

"This amendment would make the Communist Party, its membership, and its apparatus illegal. It would make membership in the Communist Party subject to criminal penalties. It would support the Department of Justice by all the law which any department would need. . . . I do not intend to be a half patriot. I will not be lukewarm. The issue is drawn. . . ."[4]

Humphrey was far from being a "half patriot" as far as this

issue was concerned. In the course of campaigning for his amendment, he reminded his colleagues that on May 14 he had offered another anti-subversive measure which would have provided the NLRB with extensive authority to withdraw privileges from any Communist-infiltrated union. (The Congress, however, had not acted on his bill.)

Humphrey was also singing praises to the Internal Security Act of 1950. Referring to that law in a response to Sen. John Butler (R.-Md.), Humphrey noted: "Finally, may I say to the Senator, it is wonderful to hear from the Republican side of this body that laws passed by a Democratic Congress were really effective on communism. My party has been branded as being 'soft on communism.' I am delighted to hear the Senator from Maryland state that *we* passed an effective law against communism" (emphasis added).

Butler reminded Humphrey that the "Internal Security Act was enacted over the veto of a Democratic President." But Humphrey quickly made the rejoinder: "May I say to the Senator from Maryland that it was passed by a Democratic Congress?"[5]

As usual, Humphrey's performance had a certain marvelous quality about it. He delivered his lines with such boldness and authority that one might have believed he had held these views in his mother's womb. There was no trace in his manner to suggest that here was a man who was repudiating almost every belief he had enunciated just four short years before. Humphrey appeared oblivious to the fact that he had sustained the President's veto of the Internal Security Act and that he had wanted all the little Humphreys to remember it. He did not recall that the "junior Senator from Minnesota," as he so often referred to himself, had defied his fellow lawmakers at that time to find a "scientific example in history where anyone has ever stopped communism by investigating it, legislating against it or cursing it. . . ."[6]

Nor did he remind anyone of his statement in reference to the Communist Party that "Every state, every nation that has ever tried to outlaw a political party . . . has lived to rue the day. . . ."[7]

The Humphrey amendment to outlaw the Communist Party was adopted by the Senate 84-0. Despite its overwhelming approval, however, there was no great enthusiasm for it. The actual vote belied the true feelings of most Senators. Many Senators endorsed it because it seemed politically inexpedient to vote against a "tough-on-communism" measure. Others were confused. Still others, rather than haggle with Humphrey, went along with it, feeling assured that the House would water it down. Indeed, the House did exactly that, diluting the key portion of Humphrey's bill which made mere membership in the Communist Party a crime. So did the Senate-House conferees.[8]

The final bill sent to the White House left virtually none of Humphrey's original amendment intact. There was a declaration that the Communist Party "should" be "outlawed," but this was a meaningless phrase with no force of law behind it. The teeth of the Humphrey bill—that part making membership a crime—had been pulled. But more important, as far as anti-Communist experts were concerned, were the bill's other provisions, such as those making it illegal for any Communist Party member to "hold office or employment with any labor organizations," denying standing before the NLRB to any "Communist-infiltrated" organization and vesting power to determine which organizations were Communist-infiltrated in the Subversive Activities Control Board (an agency Humphrey had previously compared to a thought control unit).

Though precious little that was important in the final measure could be called Humphrey's handiwork, Humphrey voted for the package with gusto, remarking: "Although it is not as strong a blow as Hubert Humphrey would like to have struck, it still outlaws the party by taking from it its rights and privileges."

Humphrey added: "These rats are not going to get out of this trap. We have slammed the door on them, and if this law is not strong enough to do the whole job, I will come back next year to help make it stronger, if I am re-elected. . . ."[9]

Whatever the intrinsic merits of the original Humphrey bill, it served the political purposes of getting Humphrey and his liberal supporters off the "pro-leftist" hook. It was tough, for example, to accuse a politician of being "soft on communism" when he had just fervently championed a bill to make mere party membership a severely punished crime. But while the Humphrey maneuver may have swung weight with the average voter, it was not to be his finest hour with the editorialists of the nation's press.

Friend and foe alike roasted Humphrey for what they viewed as a crass political act. Political observers did not blink so much because they abhorred the idea of abolishing the Communist Party—though President Eisenhower, Attorney General Brownell and FBI chief J. Edgar Hoover had registered objections to any such legislation (among other things, they thought the original Humphrey bill was unconstitutional, would drive the Communists underground, and would wreak havoc with previous anti-subversive laws). But those who had followed Humphrey's career thought it more than grotesque that one of America's leading "liberals" had served up this very anti-liberal piece of legislation. And some of Humphrey's most ardent supporters cringed that it turned out to be "witch hunting" Republicans like Sen. Joseph McCarthy who helped to pull the teeth from some of the harshest Humphrey provisions. The press was nearly unanimous in pouring out its wrath on Humphrey.

The New York *Daily News* opined: ". . . the Fair Dealers, in introducing the bill, obviously hoped to get themselves off the 'twenty years of treason' hook socked into their political hides by Sen. Joe McCarthy and his fellow anti-Communists. We doubt that they'll fool many voters."

The Boston *Herald:* ". . . It may be that Senators Humphrey and Kennedy, in promoting the amendment to outlaw the Communist Party, persuaded the voters that the Democratic Party is not soft on communism, but they, with Sen. Morse, added no luster to their liberalism thereby."

The Hartford *Courant:* "The politically inspired anti-Communist amendments of Sen. Humphrey have now been simmered down by conference compromise. . . . Senator Morse hailed this palpably political gesture as evidence of the fact that so-called liberals are not soft on Communists. Perhaps it proves that to Mr. Morse. To others, it merely adds additional proof to the fact that there are some strange creatures wandering around with the tag 'liberal' on them."

The Baltimore *Sun:* "Having marched with Senator Humphrey up the hill, the Congress has now marched Sen. Humphrey down the hill, and with some vigor. Bowing to the Pied Piper-like influence of Mr. Humphrey and a little band of left-wing colleagues, the Congress had whipped through a bill to outlaw membership in the Communist Party. The bill was probably unconstitutional, it was certainly disruptive of the effective anti-Communist program which the Eisenhower Administration is now running. The bill that Congress now has enacted will leave the Smith Act and the Internal Security Act of 1950 intact, barring defects which are not described in the early dispatches. This is a good end to a disturbing incident."

The New York *Post:* "Questionable whether Humphrey himself can avoid registration as a subversive. . . ."

The Minneapolis *Star:* "It is a strange political season indeed when 'liberal' politicians who have heretofore vociferously denounced McCarthyism now attempt to out-McCarthy McCarthy. For that is the essence of the Senate's ill-considered, pell-mell drive to 'outlaw' the Communist Party and party membership. . . . There are, of course, arguments for the sort of action into which the Senate 'liberals' have stampeded both houses. . . . But they are authoritarian arguments and not the sort of thing one should expect from those who profess to be liberals. Some time ago Senator Humphrey made an impressive appearance as guest on the 'Invitation to Learning' radio program. Given his choice of a world classic to discuss, he chose John Stuart Mill's great essay, 'On Liberty.' We earnestly urge the Senator to reread that essay and reconsider his present conduct."

The New York *Herald Tribune:* "A much larger measure of good sense than had previously been evident on Capitol Hill prompted Congress to send a compromise Communist control law to the President yesterday. Cooler heads among the election-conscious legislators succeeded in removing the politically-inspired Humphrey amendment that would have made Communist Party membership a felony."[10]

Arthur M. Schlesinger, Jr., the national co-chairman of ADA, sent an urgent telegram to the President requesting him to veto the new Communist Control Act. Sensitive to the fact that the ADA's vice-chairman had introduced the feature in the bill to outlaw the Communist Party, the politically-oriented Schlesinger commented: "ADA does not take a position on the question of outlawing the Communist Party, but urges that the bill be vetoed, for it contains a hodgepodge of other provisions so vague and indefinite as to constitute possible danger to individuals and organizations in no way involved in the Communist Party or any other arm of this worldwide conspiracy."[11] (Humphrey had voted for these "other provisions" as well.) Particularly irksome, said Schlesinger, was the power the bill granted to the Subversive Activities Control Board which, he said, could determine bargaining rights for unions.

The American Civil Liberties Union, a long-time Humphrey ally, rapped the Minnesotan for his anti-Communist proposal. In its analysis of the Communist control measure, the ACLU said Congress had a certain responsibility to protect America's freedoms. But it said this responsibility was "disregarded" by Humphrey and others in their surprise attempt to illegalize membership in the Communist Party.

"The nub of our whole theory of separation of powers," it contended, "is that Congress shall not pass bills of attainder, which is a legislative act inflicting punishment without judicial trial. . . ."[12]

The most stinging rebuke emanated from the acid pen of liberal columnist Murray Kempton in the Now York *Post,* a few months after Humphrey had introduced his bill. Kempton wrote: "Americans for Democratic Action would be a vastly improved organization if it would do two things. The first would be to unfrock the Hon. Hubert Humphrey as its vice chairman. . . . Humphrey continues to offend the sensitive by defending the disgraceful bill he introduced into the Senate last summer which would have saved us from communism by sending every pitiable old woman in the open party to prison for five years as a conspirator. You would think it was something a man would prefer to forget, but Humphrey glories in it."[13]

But Humphrey was not playing to sophisticated columnists and editorial writers, or groups which took a deep interest in civil liberties. He was trying to make hay with his Democratic constituents, who, he felt, just might believe Republican rhetoric that the Democrats were "soft on communism." The bill to ban the Communists, in fact, became one of Humphrey's trump cards when he returned to Minnesota to campaign for the fall elections.

Almost from his first moment in the Senate, Humphrey had been busily preparing for the 1954 campaign. He realized that defeat would probably crush his rising political career. He had eliminated his most probable opponent, Luther Youngdahl, by boosting him to a federal judgeship; and he had catered to such powerful voting blocs as the labor unions, the members of the National Farmers Union, and even certain business groups like General Mills. But Humphrey was also out on the hustings. He visited Minnesota almost every weekend during 1953, and when Congress adjourned in 1954, he hit the county fair and civic festival circuit, travelling over 15,000 miles and visiting 175 Minnesota communities.

Minnesota Republicans, deprived of Youngdahl, decided to oppose Humphrey with popular State Treasurer Val Bjornson, a proven vote-getter who was able to please Minnesota's largely Scandinavian population by speaking Swedish, Norwegian and Danish.

Also in the race was Frank P. Ryan, an independent liberal. A colorful Minneapolis lawyer, Ryan attracted much attention because of his unrelenting attacks against Humphrey. Ryan charged that Orville Freeman, Humphrey's protégé and a candidate for governor, had with Humphrey's backing obtained a $50,000 Reconstruction Finance Corporation loan for a Huron, South Dakota firm that went broke after one monthly payment. (Humphrey had been raised in Huron and still had roots there.) Freeman, Ryan went on, collected $1,890 as the firm's attorney. The promoter of the firm, Ryan added, said he intended to boil potatoes for hog feed. "They don't grow many potatoes around Huron," Ryan noted.

Freeman put up a rather peculiar defense. He said Ryan's

attacks on Humphrey and himself had been prepared by "taking parts of a picture and using only those parts which have unpleasant connotations." Freeman also claimed that Republicans in the RFC had obviously been "feeding" material to Ryan. In short, Freeman did not actually deny the charge—nor did Humphrey.

Freeman did claim the project was sound and that it would have succeeded if the fellow behind it hadn't been killed in an auto accident. That only one person knew how to make this project succeed was, in itself, an interesting commentary on the RFC's business judgment.*[14]

Ryan also charged that Humphrey and Freeman had resorted to influence-peddling in obtaining settlement of a tax case. The matter revolved around Frank W. Griswold, a Minneapolis businessman and a Humphrey constituent. Griswold and three companies, according to press reports, were in the late 'forties held to owe the government over $500,000 in unpaid taxes and penalties. Republican officials in Washington supposedly had information that Humphrey interceded with the tax office on behalf of Griswold. Whether through Humphrey's intervention or not, the Griswold case was allowed to drag on until the statute of limitations no longer allowed criminal prosecution. The IRS finally settled the case, but for much less than the original amount of tax and penalties.[15]

But Ryan was intrigued by another aspect of the case. Only a short while after the settlement, said Ryan, Humphrey and his family moved to a farm owned by Griswold and lived there for several months.[16]

Republican campaign strategists had sought to capitalize on

*Claude Efnor, a crusty Minnesotan who can't abide Humphrey, wrote the following in his *Northwest Industrial News* (September, 1964): "A couple of Huron promoters somehow heard of this brilliant young lawyer Orville Freeman. . . . So they retained him and told him they proposed to open this old brewery and fix it up to boil potatoes for hog feed. There was just one little hitch—they had no money . . . so an application was made to the Reconstruction Finance Corporation for a $76,000 loan. The loan was refused because the RFC did not regard it as a sound investment. . . . But, from somewhere there appeared a hand of influence and pressure . . . who induced the RFC to grant . . . the more modest sum of $50,000 to open and remodel the tottering old brewery to boil potatoes. . . . The government kissed the $50,000 goodbye as the potatoes never got to the boiling point. . . ."

the incident as early as August. GOP congressional leadership, with an eye toward blowing Humphrey out of his Senate seat, tried to launch an investigation into the potentially explosive episode, but the investigation never got off the ground because the Congress was about to adjourn and most members were beating the bushes back home for the upcoming election.

According to Humphrey's friend Charles Bailey, Humphrey said he did not know of the case until it was settled. As far as living on Griswold's farm, Bailey said: "He agreed that he had lived on Griswold's farm for several months in 1950—but added that he had a canceled $500 check bearing a notation that it was paid for rent of the place, plus a photostatic copy of the deposit slip made out by Griswold when he put the money in the farm's bank account."[17]

Humphrey's Republican opponent, Val Bjornson, took "the high road" in his assaults on Humphrey. Bjornson tried to make mileage out of Humphrey's passion for reversing himself. Humphrey told Minnesotans he was for high price supports, but Bjornson waved about a 1948 Humphrey campaign leaflet which depicted him as a flexible support man. Humphrey sizzled when anyone suggested he had ever been opposed to the oleo tax which protected butter-producing Minnesotans. But Bjornson quoted from the 1948 *Congressional Record* in which Humphrey and Sen. J. William Fulbright (D.-Ark.) had this colloquy regarding the oleo tax:

Mr. Fulbright:

> . . . Is the CIO for the repeal of the tax?

Mr. Humphrey:

> I understand the CIO is for repeal of the tax, and so is the Senator from Minnesota.[18]

Bjornson taunted Humphrey for his endless position-shifting in regard to the 1950 Internal Security Act. Throughout the campaign, Bjornson harped on Humphrey's tendency to somersault on various issues. "I hesitate," said Bjornson, "to quote

Humphrey on any subject. When I search the record, I find it so tempting to engage in a series of Humphrey versus Humphrey quotations. . . ."

But neither Humphrey's inconsistencies nor his possible link to allegedly malodorous deals seemed to stir the voters. As Humphrey had wisely foreseen, however, the Communist issue did become a central part of the campaign.

Time and again Republicans made the claim that they had cleansed the government of security risks and Reds. Time and again Bjornson tried to link Humphrey with the Democrats' alleged softness toward communism. But Humphrey had an easy comeback: he had always fought communism and who, after all, had sponsored a bill to outlaw the Communist Party?

When the votes were tallied on election day, Humphrey won by a thumping 118,000 votes. He had kept his hold on labor and slashed into Republican farm strength. He also helped to carry into the governor's chair his protégé, Orville Freeman. Indeed, Humphrey emerged from the 1954 battle as the undisputed kingpin in Democratic politics in Minnesota and the leader of a well-oiled political machine.

Did he need his "ban the Communist Party" measure to win? Maybe not. But columnists like William S. White thought it helped Humphrey.

Years later, Humphrey told Michael Amrine, a friend and biographer, that he felt his bill would somehow get the Communist issue into the courts instead of the headlines.

But Humphrey confessed that his motive was, basically, political in nature. "This writer," said Amrine, "asked Humphrey in the autumn of 1959. . . . 'Do you think the law has done any good?'

"Perhaps he was merely speaking for the record, but Humphrey said he felt that passing the bill had saved several liberal Senators who might have been defeated, 'certainly at least two.' " Adds Amrine: "The elements are mixed in this man . . . and idealists from time to time will have reason to cringe over some of his words and deeds."[19]

17

Minnesota Nominates a Vice President

Hubert Humphrey has always had soaring ambitions. Never one to rest on his laurels, he was reaching for the Senate the day he became mayor of Minneapolis. Having been elected to the Senate, he sought the Vice Presidency. Failing that twice, he tried for the Presidency—an attempt that also met with defeat. Through luck and Lyndon Johnson, Humphrey has finally attained the Vice Presidency, a position which has only whetted his burning desire for higher office.

Throughout his Senate years, the Minnesotan revealed a stubborn persistency in attempting to achieve his vaulting aspirations. With a knack for bombastic statements and grabbing headlines, he consistently managed to make himself visible to a national audience—the *sine qua non* for politicians who nurture Vice Presidential and Presidential hopes.

With a loftier goal in mind, Humphrey had made his presence keenly felt at the 1952 Democratic nominating convention, where he worked with unflagging zeal for Adlai Stevenson and saw his chance for a Vice Presidential nomination go by the boards.

Four years later Humphrey was once again energetically seeking the second spot on a ticket with Stevenson, whose nomination was a foregone conclusion, but this time he felt more confident of winning the prize.

Humphrey had come to the nominating convention with the Minnesota delegation prepared to back him for the Vice Presidency. In addition, he had set up a campaign organization—formed by Rep. (now Senator) Eugene McCarthy—to aid him in recruiting support at the Chicago gathering. Humphrey was also doing his own politicking and vigorously pushed his campaign for the VP spot by placating the Southerners.

The man who had sparked a walk-out of Southern delegates from the Democratic convention in 1948 because of his fiery civil rights stand, told a nationwide TV audience during the 1956 conclave that patience was the essential ingredient in the fight to wipe out racial prejudice. Appearing on the CBS program "Face the Nation," Humphrey remarked that "We know you're not going to kill it overnight no matter how many platforms you write."

While still insisting he was for a strong civil rights platform, Humphrey suggested he was for a rights plank that called for "observance" of the Supreme Court decision against public school segregation rather than "enforcement"—a term particularly odious to Southerners. Optimistic that a platform acceptable to the South would be forthcoming—indeed, such a platform *was* forged with Walter Reuther and other ADA leaders, sans Humphrey, in opposition—Humphrey accused the Republicans of playing politics with the racial issue because they had no substantial Southern support to appease.[1] (After the election, Humphrey was to claim that Ike had won his landslide victory in many Northern industrial cities because of the Negro vote, and to charge that Democrats "are digging their own graves by inaction in the field of civil rights."[2])

Humphrey's high hopes for second place, however, rested on more than just a careful cultivation of Southerners and a good organization. A few weeks before the convention, Humphrey had talked with Stevenson at length at a testimonial dinner for Sen. Walter George (D.-Ga.) in Washington, D.C., and had come away convinced that he was Adlai's personal choice for the Vice Presidency. "That is why we got into this campaign," Humphrey's wife Muriel said later; "That is why Hubert announced he is a candidate for second place. It was breaking with tradition to announce for the Vice Presidency, but that is why we did it."[3]

Since the unwritten convention code dictated that the Presidential nominee select his running mate, Humphrey was now hopeful of seeing his campaign for the Vice Presidency bear fruit. A feeling of wild anticipation took hold of him as he watched Adlai, after winning the Presidential nomination, advance to the speaker's rostrum at Chicago's International Amphitheater to tell the conventioners his thoughts on his Vice Presidential choice. This moment of exhilaration, however, quickly evaporated as Stevenson dropped a bombshell: contrary to tradition, he was not going to name his Vice Presidential choice. Instead, he would permit the Democratic nominee to be chosen by the convention assembled in a wide-open contest.

The announcement stunned most of the delegates. Important political figures like convention chairman Sam Rayburn and Senate Majority Leader Lyndon Johnson bristled at the prospects of a free-for-all race. Sharing the South's distrust of Tennessee's Estes Kefauver, they feared that Estes' strong showing in the primaries would result in his eventual selection by the convention. Earlier, both Rayburn and Johnson had pleaded with the man from Libertyville, Illinois, not to toss the Vice Presidency open to the delegates. Such a move, they stressed, would not only aid Kefauver but add to Stevenson's Hamlet-like image of indecisiveness. People might think, they observed, that Adlai would have an equally difficult time about "whether or not to use the Seventh Fleet some night."

Adlai, nevertheless, was adamant in his indecision, having been largely persuaded that to make a choice would create more enemies than to let the delegates make it for him.

Humphrey and his people were obviously unhappy, but not yet totally discouraged, for it was widely believed by many in the Humphrey camp that they had the organization and the following to nominate their man.

Following Stevenson's shocker, Humphrey's 60 or 70 dedicated volunteer workers rushed to his hospitality headquarters at the Conrad Hilton hotel, where Humphrey hurried in about midnight. The Senator took personal charge of the "intelligence network" which had been operating for the past fortnight under direction of Herbert J. Waters, his administrative assistant. He assigned his workers—many of them DFL party workers and University of Minnesota students and faculty—to various tasks. Humphrey, himself, made a grand tour of humming private workshops of influential conventioners like Sen. Lyndon Johnson, who was believed to have much of the South in his pocket. A public relations expert developed literature for Humphrey—and opposed to his rivals—that was quickly mimeographed and prepared for distribution to some 1,372 delegates. Rep. John Blatnik and Mitchel Perrizo, Jr., a former state official, went to work on Minnesota delegation members at the Congressional Hotel. The candidate dismissed his workers shortly after 4:30 a.m., for as one of them put it: "The feeling was that nobody would be worth anything for the big day if they didn't get some sleep."[4]

But neither energetic efforts nor sleep was enough to make Minnesota's senior Senator a winner. Before the first ballot was well under way it was perfectly apparent the race was between Kefauver and Massachusetts' Senator John Fitzgerald Kennedy. Humphrey was running a poor fifth. The final reading of the first ballot showed Kefauver with 483½ votes, Kennedy 304, Gore 178, Wagner 162½, and Humphrey 134½. Needed to win were 686½.

Even more disheartening for Humphrey was that he could barely hold on to his own delegation. During that first balloting, Humphrey had fallen so far behind that the Minnesota delegation caucused to see where its sympathies lay. Minnesota was not yet willing to desert its favorite son, but sentiment for Kefauver was obviously strong and rising. Kefauver was popular with the Minnesotans, for he had not only won the state Presidential primary against Adlai but he was favored by Democrats in the farm belt because of his high price support stand. Moreover, by deserting Humphrey and jumping on to the Kefauver bandwagon, Minnesota could probably stop Kennedy, whose

Catholicism and votes for a flexible price support system made him a liability with Democrats in the Gopher State.

As the caucus began, the delegates were clearly in a quandary about whether to stick with Humphrey or go with Kefauver. To dump their senior Senator and the man who had founded the DFL would seem callous, yet political realities suggested it was the better part of political valor to vote for the Tennessee Senator. Reflecting the emotional tug on the delegation, chairman Robert E. Short announced: "We are about to cross the bridge I thought we'd never have to cross." He cast his vote for Kefauver. The vice chairman voted for Humphrey. Rep. Coya Knutson broke down in tears as she cast her vote for the Minnesota Senator "in one of the most difficult decisions I've had to make in my life." Other delegates were near the breaking point and chairman Short explained later that "everybody in the room was crying." More tears were to come. The caucus tabulation showed 20½ votes for Humphrey, 8 for Kefauver. The remaining three delegates, owning 1½ votes, were absent, though they later alined themselves with Humphrey. But Minnesota passed when its turn came to announce its vote on the first convention ballot. When the roll-call ended and Minnesota was called on again, Short grabbed the microphone, shouting: "Sen. Kefauver, in the interest of party unity, asks me to cast Minnesota's full 30 votes for Sen. Humphrey."

Humphrey's supporters gasped. Short, they felt, had conveyed the impression to other delegates—listening closely to this report from Humphrey's home state—that Kefauver was in actual control of most of the Minnesota votes rather than a minority of them. Joseph Robbie, Jr., a Minneapolis delegate, remonstrated with Short: "That may have a bad effect on Humphrey's chances," he cried. "It sounded as if Kefauver handed us most of the 30." Yet the fact was that while the Tennessean did not have the majority of votes, sentiment for him pervaded the delegation and the majority of votes cast for Humphrey were cast with a marked reluctance. If nothing else, the first ballot had correctly revealed Humphrey's alarming weakness in his home state.

As the second ballot began, a fatigued and almost beaten Humphrey sat with close friends in Sam Rayburn's private room in back of the convention platform. Michigan Gov. G. Mennen (Soapy) Williams was pleading with Humphrey to throw his backing to a stop-Kennedy move. His argument was that Humphrey's friend Orville Freeman would most certainly fail of re-election as Minnesota's governor if Kennedy, whose farm and labor record were not in tune with the radical Democratic-Farmer-Labor Party, were on the ticket. While Kennedy kept gaining, others were begging Humphrey to stick it out for the third ballot. Eugenie Anderson was there shouting, "Leave Hubert alone. . . . He's got to make his own decisions, so leave him alone. . . ." Everyone was crying. As one participant later recounted the scene to Ralph Martin and Edward Plaut: "Eugenie was crying and I was crying and the tears were just pouring out of (Neil) Stabler. . . ." About the only thing TV commentator Martin Agronsky can still recall of the 1956 convention is that lachrymose scene. "Hubert was crying, really sobbing, and so were some of his friends." When Kefauver entered the tear-sogged room, according to author Victor Lasky, "Agronsky quickly got on the air to report exclusively that Minnesota would now throw its support behind Kefauver and that might mean the ball game. The report, actually, was somewhat premature.

"Kefauver had to do considerable pleading before it happened. 'Hubert,' he said, 'you've just got to help me . . . you've *got* to help me. . . . Please.' Now Kefauver had begun to cry. 'In fact,' a witness said, 'everyone was crying, grown men all crying. . . . I'll never forget the water gushing in that room.' "[5]

At the end of the first run through the second ballot, the score of the front runners stood this way: Kennedy 559½, Kefauver 478½, Gore 96, and Humphrey 67½. Despite the pleadings for Kefauver, Minnesota had cast 16½ for Humphrey, 13½ for Kefauver.

As the switching began at the end of the second ballot, Kennedy, sprawled on a bed in his room at the Stock Yard Inn, watched himself surge even higher above Kefauver. Up and up climbed the Kennedy totals until at their highest they reached an unofficial 648, barely two-score short of the nomination. Then Kefauver received the break which changed the roll of the dice. Asking convention chairman Rayburn for unanimous consent to address the convention, Sen. Albert Gore threw his delegates to fellow Senator and Tennessean Estes Kefauver. Humphrey, seeing that he had no chance, went up to the platform behind the dais. "All right Estes," said Humphrey, "I said I would get out if I didn't make a good showing. And we've got to save the farm vote." A few moments later Minnesota threw its entire 30 votes to Kefauver. That, say the Kefauver people, is what cinched the Keef's victory. Before the nomination was handed to Kefauver by acclamation, the second ballot totals stood this way: Kefauver 755½, Kennedy 589, Gore 13½, Wagner 6, and Humphrey 3½.

The blow had been most embarrassing to Humphrey, but more humiliation was to come. The Minneapolis *Morning Tribune* reported that "the Vice Presidential drive of Minnesota's favorite son Hubert Humphrey faltered and died Friday—but there was little sorrow in his delegation. There was a tear here and there, but not in the eyes of the pro-Kefauver majority which—although its loyalties were severely tested by the Humphrey candidacy—whooped and shouted and pounded one another on the back as the phlegmatic Tennessee Senator, Estes Kefauver, inched his way to victory over Humphrey, far in the rear, and Sen. John F. Kennedy of Massachusetts. Humphrey just didn't have what it takes in 1956. True, he was the favorite of many farm, labor and congressional leaders, but it quickly became apparent that he hadn't gotten across to the delegates themselves. . . ."

With the announcement that Kefauver was the winner, pandemonium reigned in the Minnesota section. Mrs. Knutson threw her arms around an alternate delegate. "We saved the farm vote," she cried, "thanks to Hubert's switching." Yelled another: "Minnesota nominated a Vice President."[6]

18

Mission to Moscow

Humphrey was dejected by the Vice Presidential fiasco, but his pain may have been somewhat eased when the Stevenson-Kefauver ticket was swamped by Eisenhower-Nixon in November. And even before the wounds of his own defeat were healed, Humphrey began setting his sights for a prize higher than the one he had bid for and lost in 1956.

In order to be considered a Democratic contender for the Presidency in 1960, especially if Humphrey decided to go the primary route, it was urgent that he make himself highly visible to the public at large. To accomplish this objective, he needed a major forum to acquire national attention. While he held no formal leadership position and commanded no committees, he did his best to make himself heard through his post as chairman of the Senate Foreign Relations disarmament subcommittee.

From this vantage point, Humphrey, aside from holding well-publicized hearings on conventional and nuclear disarmament, ceaselessly bombarded the nation with his own remedies on how to achieve a disarmed world. In early 1957, for example, Humphrey called upon the Eisenhower Administration to "take a good long look" at the possibility of pulling back United States forces confronting—or nearly confronting—Soviet troops in Europe, a proposal put forth before Humphrey's subcommittee by the former ambassador to Moscow, George Kennan. Humphrey proclaimed this was a necessary first step toward world disarmament, apparently agreeing with Kennan that such a move would "put the . . . Soviet Union on the defensive," diplomatically if not militarily.[1]

Humphrey was also a vigorous champion of a ban on nuclear testing, despite grave warnings from Lewis Strauss, chairman of the Atomic Energy Commission, and several scientists, among them Dr. Edward Teller, that any test ban would work in favor of the Soviets. Indeed, Humphrey, through pressures resulting from his subcommittee's hearings, largely shaped the Eisenhower Administration's negotiations on the test-ban issue. During 1957 the United States continued to put before the Soviets a disarmament proposal whose main features included the suspension of nuclear tests and the prevention of the production of nuclear weapons, coupled with a satisfactory inspection system. As chairman of the disarmament subcommittee, Humphrey urged Eisenhower to treat the nuclear test ban separately. Writing to Ike in November, 1957, Humphrey suggested that the U.S. declare its "willingness to negotiate separately on a ban on nuclear-weapons tests for a two-year period. . . ."[2] Humphrey, moreover, insisted that "We cannot challenge the intentions of the Soviet Union on inspection unless we are in a position to negotiate on a test ban irrespective of the other measures in the four-power proposal."[3]

By late 1958, Humphrey could claim a victory of sorts. In October of that year, President Eisenhower voluntarily announced a suspension of U.S. nuclear tests for a period of twelve months, a moratorium that eventually would be extended until August of 1961. The suspension was proclaimed with the understanding that the moratorium would end if the Soviets, who had also proclaimed a moratorium, renewed their testing program. The President's action had largely resulted from two factors. First, the Soviets, after completing a massive test series of their own, had announced their own suspension of tests—an announcement designed to improve their "peace image" and put the United States in an embarrassing position before the world.

Secondly, there had been rising pressures from the Congress, stimulated by Humphrey, for detaching the nuclear test-ban issue from the broader disarmament package.

In capitulating to this Soviet-Humphrey strategy of treating the test ban as a separate issue, however, Eisenhower had not pressed upon the Soviet Union any inspection system of any kind. The U.S. moratorium was proclaimed on just the hope the Soviets would also forego any more tests. But this arrangement was also championed by Humphrey, who hailed the President's moratorium proclamation as a step toward peace and later campaigned, successfully, for its lengthy extension.

Three years later the Soviets, after almost certainly having cheated on the moratorium by conducting underground tests, unilaterally and openly broke the ban with a massive atmospheric testing program. Expert opinion believed that the astonishingly thorough open-air tests, coupled with probable Soviet cheating during the moratorium and the killing off of America's testing program, had enabled the Soviets to catch up with—and in some cases probably surpass—U.S. knowledge about nuclear weapons. But the verdict on the test ban was not yet in when Humphrey was launching his campaign for the Presidency in the late 1950's. And far from being criticized, Humphrey saw his work in the field of disarmament hailed as a major effort toward an elusive world peace. At any rate, he was receiving some of that vital "visibility" needed for a 1960 Presidential bid.

Though Humphrey had become better known as a result of his chairmanship of the disarmament subcommittee, a more important opportunity opened for him to gain the national exposure he desired.

In the fall of 1958, Humphrey had arranged to go to Moscow and several European capitals, ostensibly for furthering international cooperation in medical research. He took along with him his wife, Dr. Michael Shimkin of the National Cancer Institute, and Julius Cahn, a Republican and project director of the Senate Committee on Government Operations. While Humphrey denied it vigorously, politicians spotted the tour as a warm-up for the Presidential campaign that was only a little over a year away.

Humphrey's trip was to prove far more eventful than he dared to hope, with his most newsworthy experience occurring in the Soviet Union. His arrival in Moscow began in an auspicious manner. Unlike the majority of visitors not directly part of the U.S. Administration, Humphrey was royally received. He managed to appear on Moscow television and tape a 25-minute program for radio. He also wrote a signed article for *Izvestia*, demonstrating America's desire for peace (though the Soviets eventually decided not to print it). Checking in at 2:30 p.m. on December 1 with one of the officials handling his appointments, he was suddenly told that "the first minister" expected to receive him at 3:00. Humphrey had asked to be permitted to see the Czar of all the Russias, Nikita Khrushchev, but he had never really counted on it. "In a matter of minutes," Humphrey recounted the story for *Life* magazine, "I was at the Kremlin with two official escorts and an Intourist photographer. We walked at least 150 feet down a tremendous, carpeted corridor on the second floor, then another 100 feet or so along a similar corridor to our right and entered the outer office of the Premier's suite.

"At three minutes to 3:00 I was ushered into Khrushchev's office."[4] After a few photographs were taken, Khrushchev motioned Humphrey to a chair at the side of a long conference table and then sat down opposite him. Oleg Troyanovsky, a skillful interpreter, took a seat between the two at the end of the table. Humphrey and Khrushchev then began the famous 8½-hour talking marathon which was to put Humphrey on the front pages of newspapers and magazines across the world.

For Humphrey the interview was predictably exhilarating. He remembers Khrushchev as a "powerful and dangerous man" of revealing moods, whose "eyes were damp when he spoke of a son who was killed in the last world war" and which "gleamed in sentimental remembrance when he recalled the poverty of his boyhood, his Christian upbringing and his turn to atheism."

Poltician Humphrey talked about the perils of farm politics in the Midwest; the supreme ruler of the U.S.S.R. gleefully reminisced about outmaneuvering Molotov, Malenkov and Bulganin in the Soviet hierarchy. They chatted about Khrushchev's kidney troubles and the superiority of American corn. Humphrey was amazed at Khrushchev's extraordinary understanding of U.S. political details, ranging from a deep knowledge of constitutional balances down to vote margins and information on such individual races as the victory of Nelson Rockefeller for governor of New York and the defeat of Republican leader William Knowland in California.

"Khrushchev began telling me about capitalism," Humphrey related later, "and how he began as a worker. I told him a great many people in our country started at the bottom . . . and on capitalism I told him he just didn't know what he was talking about."[5]

When the conversation turned to Red China, Khrushchev refused to be drawn into the subject, but he did acknowledge that he thought the "commune" system was "reactionary." At one point the stocky Premier nearly bowled Humphrey over when he stated the communes were based on the principle of " 'from each according to his abilities, to each according to his needs.' You know that won't work. You can't get production without incentive."

"I felt as if I were about to fall out of my chair," said Humphrey. "Here was the leader of world communism rejecting the very core of Marxist theory."[6]

Humphrey denied politicking, but he could not let pass the opportunity to tell Khrushchev: "Mr. Premier, you and your system have been living on borrowed time. You have just had it easy with Republicans. Just wait until the Democrats come in. You want economic competition? We'll run you right out of Gorki Park."[7]

In the late afternoon, Humphrey made motions toward leaving but each time Khrushchev waved him back to his chair. Progressing through cheese, crab meat, bologna, beef, ham, wild fowl and Armenian brandy, the two then explored more serious subjects. As the evening wore on, it became increasingly evident that Khrushchev had not engaged the Minnesotan for idle chatter. He had, in fact, a deadly serious aim: to make Humphrey a transmission belt for Soviet propaganda.

For historical perspective, it must be recalled that Humphrey had been granted his interview shortly after the Soviet Premier's fiery November demands that the allies clear out of West Berlin within a six-month period, and turn this pro-Western outpost deep in Communist East Germany into a demilitarized zone. There was also the thinly veiled threat in Khrushchev's oratory that East Germany would once again block the transport routes from West Germany to Berlin if the allies did not agree to Soviet plans.

Thus Khrushchev, in his blustery manner, impressed upon Humphrey his supposed sincerity about his ultimatum. His resolute voice rising, Khrushchev reiterated to the Minnesota Senator his desire to eliminate Western forces from Berlin. He protested to Humphrey that "some of your military men have made stupid statements lately, statements to the effect that the United States will break through [to West Berlin] with tanks if the East German Republic tries to get in the way. The Soviets have tanks, lots of them, and I warn you that we will use them. We have rockets, too. . . ." Dramatically jabbing his forefinger at Humphrey, Khrushchev sternly remarked: "Don't you threaten me!"

Like the consummate actor he was, Khrushchev swiftly softened his approach, telling Humphrey he was actually fond of Eisenhower and did not mean any harm to come to him or Berlin. "You must assure the President of this," he stressed. "When Khrushchev made this kind of switch," noted Humphrey, "I thought of my late father-in-law in South Dakota and the way he treated chilblains. He put his feet first in cold water, then in hot water. I was getting the Communist chilblain treatment from Dr. Khrushchev."

The wiley Soviet dictator continued to pour Communist propaganda into Humphrey's ear. He let Humphrey believe that the Soviets were seriously interested in a formal nuclear test ban and would make concessions to obtain it. Assured that Humphrey would carry back the word, Khrushchev cleverly implanted the idea that he could get along with Eisenhower if only that "imperialist" and "warmonger" John Foster Dulles were eliminated as Secretary of State.[8]

Khrushchev promoted the theme of expanded East-West trade, carefully nurturing the idea that such trade would be in the West's best interest. Using a bit of reverse psychology, he told Humphrey that the Americans were "stupid fools" to have turned down a Soviet request for credits to finance purchases of consumer goods in the U.S. Khrushchev professed to be delighted with the rejection. "You helped me," he contended. "You showed my people that you did not really care about them. You walked right into that."[9]

Before the interview was over, diplomat Khrushchev had thoroughly flattered his visitor's ego. Aside from making Humphrey feel important by talking to him for over eight hours, the Soviet Premier complimented Humphrey by suggesting he played an important role in the Senate and was a key shaper of American policy. To swell Humphrey's head even further, Khrushchev "impulsively" made the Minnesotan a trusted emissary: he decided to share with him two "secrets"—information unknown to any American—that Humphrey must carry directly to Eisenhower himself.

Understandably, Humphrey was intoxicated at the lavish attention he was getting from America's foremost adversary. The secrets themselves were, if true, rather spectacular. They consisted of the supposed Soviet construction of a super-bomb that could be carried in a relatively small warhead, and the development of an 8,700-mile missile. The purpose of revealing these "secrets" at this time should have been obvious: to scare the West into submission. By engaging in verbal pyrotechnics and threatening to rattle rockets, Khrushchev hoped to drive the Western allies from Berlin, or at least to force from them significant concessions. But Humphrey, at least initially, seemed oblivious to the real purpose of Khrushchev's propaganda thrust. Indeed, as events turned out, Humphrey gave Khrushchev's timely boast maximum publicity.

Almost from the time he left Khrushchev's presence, he

played into the hands of the Soviet dictator by promoting his "scare" diplomacy. Emerging from the Kremlin, Humphrey ominously warned New York *Times* reporter Max Frankel in Moscow that the Berlin controversy is "fraught with danger." There is no doubt, Humphrey told Frankel, that Moscow intends to get the Western powers out of Berlin. Hinting that he would even favor a compromise on the situation, Humphrey urged that whatever the West believed to be its legal position in Berlin,* the "legal questions will have to be tempered with prudent judgment."[10]

Humphrey later amended his remarks somewhat, but that initial statement was an open invitation for Khrushchev to put the pressure on. Arriving in London shortly afterward, Humphrey continued to stress the ominous aspects of his marathon talk. Wrapping his conversation with reporters in an air of mystery, he pridefully related that Khrushchev had entrusted him with a message to Eisenhower. "And it is significant," he added portentously. He revealed that Khrushchev had said to him: "I'm going to tell you a secret." And after telling it, Khrushchev added: "And now I'm going to tell you another." Asked as to what they were, Humphrey, assuming the posture of James Bond in the hands of Thrush, replied: "You couldn't pry them out of me with a crowbar."[11]

Returning home to a blaze of friendly headlines, Humphrey briefed the State Department and the Atomic Energy Commission about his talkathon with the Soviet Premier. He then went to the White House with his "secrets," spending more than an hour with President Eisenhower. When he left the President's office it was to savor the taste of more publicity as White House correspondents began crowding around him five deep. By this time Humphrey's "secrets" had been leaked to reporters through Humphrey aides.

Humphrey gloried in the attention he was receiving, and much of the American press avidly fed the Minnesotan's ego. *Time* and *Newsweek* gave rave reviews to the Humphrey sojourn,

*In actuality, Khrushchev, after the West refused to back down an inch, retreated on his ultimatum. The West, of course, is still in Berlin.

while liberal columnist Doris Fleeson came close to gushing. Even David Lawrence responded favorably to Humphrey's talkathon. Irrepressible himself, Humphrey enthusiastically spoke about his trip whenever he got a chance. "The Minnesota Senator was obviously exhilarated by the attention he has received since his mission to Moscow," noted columnist Willard Edwards at one point. "He called a press conference to which more than 100 reporters responded and talked steadily for 35 minutes."

While Humphrey continued to stress the "non-political" nature of his excursion, most of the commentary dwelt on how it had lifted his Presidential stock. Fleeson related that "It's a very Merry Christmas for the Hubert Humphreys. Circumstances have suddenly meshed to give the senior Senator from Minnesota the kind of attention which fixes his Presidential capabilities firmly in the mind of the public. His European journey took him to major points of danger where decisions of peace and war are being made. His handling of himself and his creative expression of his views won him serious consideration by the international press. . . ." Over a column headlined "Humphrey Stock on Rise," New York *Times* columnist James Reston claimed Humphrey was beginning to "get the political breaks, and he is now just old and experienced enough to know how to exploit them." In another column, Reston, noting Washington had been skeptical of Humphrey, remarked: "He has been suffering for years from the original impression he created here as a gabby, to-hell-with-the-consequences liberal. . . . Humphrey is still a pretty glib and cocky fellow, who looks like a cross between Bugs Bunny and James Cagney, but the Senate has amended its opinion of him upwards in the last six years." The elder stateswoman of the Democratic Party, Eleanor Roosevelt, said what Humphrey had most wanted to hear. He had, she said, that "spark of greatness" the next President would need.

Minnesota's Presidential hopeful, nonetheless, was not without his detractors. The Chicago *Tribune* acidly commented: "If Mr. Humphrey respected the dignity of his own government, he would refuse to serve as a Russian courier. This impertinent messenger boy has even forfeited any claim to good intentions.

"If he really thinks he is properly conveying something important and confidential between Moscow and Washington, surely even he must realize that it is indiscreet for him to talk about it in London. He is acting like a small child, taunting his playmates with 'I've got a secret' and butting into adult conversations with the demand, 'Look at me!' "

Columnist Arthur Krock of the New York *Times* related that Humphrey "squeezed the maximum amount of personal publicity out of his long interview with Premier Khrushchev in the Kremlin. He did this by means of an itinerant news conference, beginning in Moscow and ending at the White House. In its course, he successively shed information about what Khrushchev had said to him—a sort of publicity strip-tease. Thereby Humphrey got his name repeatedly on the front pages of the world press, and this prominence may have aided him in his aspiration to be evaluated as a much more important contender for the next Democratic Presidential nomination than hitherto he had been rated. But Soviet Russia's world propaganda in the cold war was also served by the Senator's personal publicity campaign. And in the division of benefits, the Russian interest made the greater profit."

Krock ventured the opinion that the biggest "secret" imparted to Humphrey by Khrushchev—that the Russians supposedly had operable an 8,700-mile missile—became the "secret" of everyone who read the Washington press dispatches on the same day the Senator confided it to the President.

"And," noted Krock, "this had been preceded by such a buildup by Humphrey—a hint here, a nod there, an ominous implication elsewhere, and all to news reporters—that it had an impact on the consciousness of the world public it never would have had if the Senator had not fed it out like a serialized commercial. Had not invested it with the 'scare' element by announcing 'you couldn't pry it out of me with a crowbar.' Had waited until he reported to the State Department and the President and then issued a dignified account of his Kremlin interview. . . ."

"Instead, Humphrey chose to make use of his eight hours with Khrushchev as a launching-pad on the steps of the Kremlin for his campaign to become President in 1961."

Krock noted that *Tagesspiegel*, a newspaper in West Berlin, was moved to remark:

"Senator Humphrey talked with Khrushchev, returned to Washington and told the public that he had a secret message from the Soviet Premier to President Eisenhower in his suitcase. All this can only create the impression that the world was facing an American statesman of the first importance. But the truth is that Humphrey needs bannerlines for a successful start of his campaign to become a candidate in the 1960 elections. . . . It takes an extraordinarily large amount of guilelessness to become a mouthpiece of Khrushchev's boasting. Humphrey appears to be the best propagandist the rulers of the Kremlin could wish to have at this critical time."

Krock supported the thesis with the thought: "The soundness of the comment by *Tagesspiegel* derives from Humphrey's use of the interview primarily as a personal publicity medium, and in a way bound to assist the 'scare technique' of the Kremlin."[12]

Human Events' late editor Frank Hanighen analyzed the Humphrey episode this way: "Soviet dictator Khrushchev played his card in the American political game when he lifted Sen. Hubert Humphrey from obscurity and gave him political 'visibility' as a contender for the Democratic crown in 1960. Only the myopic members of the Capitol press corps—who treated the whole fantastic story as merely that of an American legislator who happened to be in Moscow and by chance got an eight-hour private interview with the Kremlin head—think otherwise.

"Khrushchev, according to Diplomatic Row, surveyed the American political scene after the election, assessed the Democrats as the best bet, rejected their front-running Senator Kennedy because he is a Catholic and chose the far-Left Senator from Minnesota for exceptional favors. Mrs. Eleanor Roosevelt (whose husband awarded Soviet Russia its present potent status in the world power situation) cooperated well by tossing out

Humphrey's name as her candidate for the Democratic nomination.

"Why did Khrushchev pick this Senator, who is only in his second term, who enjoys no seniority position in the Senate and who rates only No. 4 among Democrats on the Foreign Relations Committee?

"The answer is not exactly enveloped in mystery. . . . For Humphrey has demonstrated his usefulness to the Kremlin on previous occasions. At the time of the Iraq-Lebanon crisis this summer, the Soviets used Humphrey as a transmission belt for conveying their sentiments to our government. Moreover, in the fall of 1957, when the Soviets had suffered one of their worst defeats at the hands of Secretary Dulles, the Minnesotan hurried to the rescue. In October of last year, the Kremlin sought to bulldoze Turkey; Dulles, after securing the okay of the Joint Chiefs of Staff, openly threatened to retaliate by bombing Soviet Russia if its government moved aggressively against our ally.

"Result No. 1: disappearance of anti-Turkish bluster by Russia. Result No. 2: a world-wide radio propaganda drive by Moscow against Dulles, calling for his resignation. Senator Humphrey was one of the first Americans who echoed this Soviet line, remarking that the President should ask Dulles to resign.

"Humphrey's far-Left position in the American political spectrum has long been noted; he is one of the founding fathers of Americans for Democratic Action (ADA), started by left-wingers who sought to avoid public odium by separating themselves officially from the obvious Communist stooges that were rampant during and just after World War II; he has been an advocate of surrendering the offshore islands of Quemoy and the Matsus to Peiping; he has taken a position on the cessation of nuclear testing highly palatable to the director of Kremlin policy.

"Washington's verdict: the 'liberal' Democrats, triumphant in the recent election, have their Kremlin-blessed candidate."[13]

A harsh judgment? Perhaps so. But in a pamphlet distributed to Communist Party members prior to the Democratic convention in 1960, the CP's national boss Gus Hall wrote that Humphrey's "public stand on the question of peace has taken a sharp turn for the better. Of all the candidates, Humphrey has the most advanced stand on the civil rights issue. Because he reflects the upturn of this movement he cannot be read out as a possible Democratic candidate [for President]."[14]

Whatever the final assessment of Humphrey's mission to Moscow, it had clearly thrust him into Presidential orbit. The Minnesotan himself had recognized the fact, and his only worry was how long his trip into the rarefied atmosphere of Presidential politics would last.

19

The Prince and the Pauper

When Hubert Humphrey officially tossed his hat into the Presidential ring on December 30, 1959, there was a curiously jarring note to his rhetoric. It was the age of the atom and the sputniks, but somehow Humphrey was oblivious to the new world. Here was no jet age candidate gearing his words to a youthful and prosperous America, but a politician dredging up memories of the depression over 20 years before and conjuring up the fading image of Franklin Delano Roosevelt.

Humphrey had been bred on depression politics and had made a success in Minnesota by hitching his wagon to Roosevelt's star—and he was determined to make these themes work in the 1960's.

The Minnesota Senator identified himself with the "plain people of this country" and said he would be the spokesman for the "victims of depression, distress and natural disaster." "My support," Humphrey stressed, "does not come principally from persons of position, rank or wealth"—an obvious dig at some of his Democratic opponents, especially Sen. John F. Kennedy of Massachusetts. "Rather," he continued, "it comes largely from people who, like myself, are of modest origin and limited financial means.

"I also know," he said, "that it is precisely these Americans—who lack the means, the power or the influence to fully control their own destiny—who most need and yet lack a voice in the conduct of their government. They need a spokesman, and I intend to the best of my ability to be that spokesman.

"Of one thing I am sure; if victory is to come to the Democratic Party, the plain people of this country must find in the Democratic standard bearer a man they sense to be their true friend, their spokesman."[1]

"Old Bob LaFollette and William Jennings Bryan would have loved it," noted "Scotty" Reston in the New York *Times*. "This was . . . the country boy with his chin out and his dukes up vowing to rescue the disinherited.

"Do the American people still like underdogs and 'hate the interests'? Are they against slums, disease, hunger and poverty? If so, suggested the honorable gentleman, let them rally to the banner of the Senator from Minnesota (and if they can spare a dime, that will be okay too).

"Washington hasn't heard anything like this since the last time. It was a perfect illustration of the classic log-cabin appeal, and the charming thing about it was that the Senator was obviously in dead earnest. . . .

"He is . . . an authentic son of the old agrarian reformers, and there is nothing wrong with his pitch that would not be cured by a plain, old-fashioned national depression."[2]

Arthur Krock thought he noticed something else about Humphrey's speech. In seeking his goals, suggested Krock, Humphrey had been willing to hand the Republicans some free ammunition. Asked whether he thought any Democratic rival "would make a good President," Humphrey responded: "If I thought so I wouldn't be declaring my intentions." In cold type, said Krock, "this remark conveyed the sole implication that Humphrey does not believe Senators Symington, Kennedy, Johnson . . . or any other Democrats for whom convention delegates are now being sought would 'make a good President. . . .' " All this may have been in jest, Krock contended, but it would still be played up by Republicans as serious.

"But the second issue which Senator Humphrey handed to the Republicans for development," said Krock, "could not have been raised unwittingly, having been furnished in his official announcement. He proclaimed not only that one of his 'main' reasons for aspiring was to become the 'spokesman' of the victims of depression. He singled himself out as uniquely qualified to become this spokesman because 'I know from personal experience what it means to be one of those victims.' "

It is as old as politics, said Krock, to be the poor man's candidate, adding wryly that this is "one wealth which people of small means have in overflowing abundance. But it just so happens that the 'means' of Humphrey's chief potential rivals—Symington, Johnson, Stevenson and particularly Kennedy—would not be measured as 'limited' on the personal yardstick he was using. It also so happens that Nixon's means would fit well inside that mark. Thus, if Humphrey is not nominated and Nixon is, Humphrey has left it open for the Republicans to avail themselves of the class issue he has invoked and claim that, unlike their convention, it takes a rich man to get a majority of Democratic delegates."[3]

Not all of Humphrey's fire was reserved for fellow Democrats, however, and if he had conceivably handed Nixon an issue, it was not because he had any love for the Vice President. Nixon, who undoubtedly would be the GOP nominee, was one of Humphrey's favorite whipping boys. At the press conference following his formal announcement for the Presidency, he called Nixon "one candidate with several points of view" on each issue and "a Republican with a capital R, and no amount of political pancake can cover up those Republican warts."

"When the people," Humphrey declared, "are called upon to vote on a Republican—an identified, clear-cut, unwashed Republican—I have a feeling they will vote for the Democratic Party and the Democratic candidate."

Discounting the alleged extent of Southern hostility toward his candidacy because of his civil rights stance, Humphrey claimed, "My friends in the South respect a man for his sincerity and convictions and not for tightrope walking. I am not engaged in a circus act."

While Humphrey may not have been performing in a circus,

he was, nevertheless, turning a neat somersault on the issue of national security. "This subject," he proclaimed, is "by far the greatest issue of all." Though Humphrey, himself, had been one of Ike's sharpest critics for not having done enough in the field of disarmament, he was now saying: "The Administration has permitted America to come in second-best in a two-nation race in the missile effort.* We have frittered away—the Administration has frittered away—our national strength so that when we go to the bargaining table, we go with less than complete superiority."[4]

The core of Humphrey's support included the Minnesota contingent, old FDR enthusiasts, and Eastern liberals of the Americans for Democratic Action variety. Minnesota Gov. Orville Freeman and Sen. Eugene McCarthy were in the Humphrey camp, along with the controversial Max Kampelman, who began his political career as a member of the Humphrey staff when Humphrey was mayor of Minneapolis. Oscar Ewing, a former high official in the New Deal and Fair Deal who had helped Humphrey form the Democratic-Farmer-Labor Party in Minnesota; James Lanigan of New York, an aide to Adlai Stevenson; W. Averell Harriman; and James Rowe, whose Washington experience dated back to FDR (and who also happened to be a friend of Senate Majority Leader Lyndon B. Johnson), were advising Minnesota's senior Senator. Also coaching him were Joseph L. Rauh, a vice chairman of the ADA and counsel for the United Auto Workers; Mrs. Eugenie Anderson, Ambassador to Denmark during the Truman Administration and also an ADA member; and Leon Keyserling, a high-ranking ADA member who had been a top economist in the Truman Administration.

Energetic and enthusiastic for the Minnesotan, they figured the biggest hope for a Humphrey nomination lay in the possibility of a convention deadlock. The pre-convention strategy

*The so-called missile gap was used by the Democrats repeatedly throughout the campaign and had largely become an issue because of statements vented by Lt. Gen. James Gavin, who later became an Ambassador to France under President Kennedy. When the Kennedy Administration took office in 1961, Defense Secretary Robert S. McNamara, in an unusual fit of candor, admitted that no missile gap had existed.

was to win the delegates from Minnesota, Wisconsin and South Dakota as a nucleus of a Midwestern block that would give Humphrey at least 150 votes on the first ballot. To achieve even this, however, Humphrey would have to prove to the party chieftains and delegates that he had what it took to win. And he could do this only by entering the primaries. Though a zealous champion of the "common man," the pros realized that Humphrey had never really been a popular figure outside of Minnesota.

"The ironical thing about him," Reston once noted, "is that, while he has many qualities normally regarded as popular in this country—the common touch, confidence, intelligence, experience, industry and eloquence—he is not really a popular political figure. Part of the reason for this is that he has never overcome the reputation he acquired in his early days . . . as a gabby extremist of the Left."[5]

Humphrey was out to prove Reston wrong. And the first time he would really have a chance to do so was in the upcoming April 5 Wisconsin primary, where he was scheduled to tangle with the young Lochinvar of the East, John F. Kennedy. "Everything is building in the direction of Wisconsin," a Humphrey spokesman said shortly after his man had tossed his hat into the ring. "And everything hinges on Wisconsin. Either this campaign will be way off the ground on April 6, or it will be all finished."

There were good reasons for believing that Wisconsin was crucial for Humphrey, if not for Kennedy. The Badger State was considered Humphrey's back yard—a stone's toss from Minnesota—and Humphrey was in a position to collect on political favors he had bestowed on some of the state's Democrats over the years. Moreover, the political landscape seemed suited to the flavor of a Humphrey campaign. Inheriting the progressive legacy left it by Bob LaFollette, Wisconsin possessed a Democratic Party whose structure in large part resembled the radical elements that comprised the Democrats in Minnesota. Wisconsin, furthermore, was a farm state, and Humphrey had a much better reputation for lavishing subsidies on the farmer than did the candidate from Boston. Humphrey, too, had the chieftains of organized labor in his camp, with one, a United Auto Workers (UAW) official, heading his Wisconsin campaign.

And he was not without some helpful manipulators who managed to fix the outcome to his advantage. Wisconsin backers of Humphrey won a key fight in late January over delegate apportionment, a move interpreted as a blow to supporters of Senator Kennedy. On the motion of Sam Rizzo of Racine, the United Auto Workers official who was state chairman of the Humphrey organization, members of Wisconsin's Democratic Administrative Committee voted 14-to-12 in favor of a new formula that would cut from ten to five the number of state delegates awarded to the candidate who won the majority of votes. It would also raise from two to two-and-one-half the number of delegates elected in each Congressional District. This alteration was clearly designed to aid Humphrey, for, despite the fact that Humphrey should have found it easier to take Wisconsin than Kennedy, the polls revealed that Kennedy would probably win the popular vote.

Kennedy accused Humphrey's backers of "manipulation" and "changing the deck." "Americans," he contended, "have always considered it unfair to change the rules of a game after the game has started. I am astonished at the effort of the Humphrey forces to change the delegate allotments after both Humphrey and I entered the Wisconsin primary." Furthermore, the Kennedy forces asserted with heated indignation that to weight a primary against the expressed statewide preference as a device to get convention delegates disproportionate to a candidate's statewide support corrupted the purpose for which the primaries were established. Humphrey, himself a champion of the one-man, one-vote concept, blithely ignored the whole rigging process, leaving it to his aides to justify.

When Kennedy formally announced his own entrance into the Wisconsin primary in January, he assumed the attitude of an underdog. Preparing alibis for a possible loss, he "acknowledged" there were "risks and difficulties" in running against a contender who lives in a next-door state that has personal and ideological ties to Wisconsin. Only partially tongue-in-cheek, he called for Humphrey to reverse the process by invading the "Massachusetts backyard," the New Hampshire primary on March 8. (Humphrey refused the contest. He frankly admitted he was staying out of the Granite State primary because "I happen to think Senator Kennedy is much stronger there.")

For all of Kennedy's hedging and pretending that he was really No. 2 in the race, however, he had not plunged into the Wisconsin popularity contest for the purpose of committing suicide. In actual fact, the polls revealed he could beat Humphrey by a three-to-two margin. Kennedy, furthermore, had plenty of money to throw around and was using high octane fuel for his machine. Whereas Humphrey could staff only a few offices with superior people—indeed, some of Humphrey's offices were left in charge of persons too young to vote—Kennedy was staffing a large percentage with high caliber personnel. Nor was this done solely with money. "It was the long established connection of Kennedy's friendships and social background that provided him with talent," noted Theodore White. "His sisters and brothers criss-crossed the state, and four of Wisconsin's 10 districts were staffed by Ivy League college classmates." As voting day approached, the good-looking Kennedy clan was pitching in to help, including three Kennedy sisters—Mrs. Sargent Shriver, Mrs. Peter Lawford and Mrs. Stephen Smith—brothers Bobby and Teddy, other assorted in-laws and Jack's mother, Mrs. Rose Kennedy.

While Humphrey also used members of his family, they were much less glamorous and a good deal more amateurish. Humphrey, for example, put his 12-year-old son on television with him one night.

"What do you do?" the announcer asked the boy.

"I pass out pamphlets."

"And what happens?" asked the announcer.

"Oh, I find a lot of people who won't take Dad's stuff."

"Nothing like this ever happens on the Kennedy shows," remarked Reston. "They are more professional than anything in politics." One case in point was a show designed to catch the women's audience. Beginning at 10:30 in the morning, it opened with a film clip of Kennedy, his wife and daughter at home in Washington. While this movie continued in the background, Mrs. Kennedy appeared on the screen and introduced her sister and a sister-in-law, both handsome and beautifully but simply dressed. Mrs. Kennedy explained that the viewers could call any one of the three women at three different telephone numbers and pass questions from them to the Senator, who appeared on the screen.

The professional Kennedy touch didn't end there. Voters in small towns received what seemed to be engraved invitations from Kennedy "to meet at such and such a place." "There they find the cover-boy in person," reported Reston, "not only glamorous but intelligent, well-informed, earnest and literate. Maybe it's all a show, like Eddie Fisher and Liz Taylor coming to town, but the politicians don't think so, and the new polls show Kennedy gaining on Nixon."

Author Victor Lasky remarked there were also receptions for other Kennedys. "Invitations sent well in advance gave the occasion a special touch. 'The pleasure of your company is requested at such and such an hour on such and such a day to meet Mrs. Peter Lawford. . . .' This had the glamor of Bel Air and the chic fashion magazines. Its appeal can well be imagined. The resulting publicity was enormous."[6]

On top of all this, Kennedy had his private, twin-engine Convair which enabled him to hopscotch across the Badger State (Humphrey had a private bus), and his very own private pollster, Lou Harris. (Humphrey was so incensed that Kennedy could afford to hire a private pollster that when asked once by a reporter who would win in Wisconsin, he lashed out: "Ask Senator Kennedy. He seems to have all the facts. We haven't the money to take polls like a mother taking her baby's temperature every hour.")

Another factor favoring Kennedy, of course, was the high proportion of Catholics—some 30 per cent—comprising the Wisconsin electorate. Whether the facts actually bore out the premise, it was considered history that Al Smith lost to Herbert

Hoover in 1928 because he was a Catholic. And few Catholics, who thought that one of their boys had as much right to first-class citizenship as the next fellow, were likely to forget that as they marched into the voting booths on election day.

Defeating the glamor boy from Massachusetts would be difficult, and Humphrey would rely on the one tactic he always liked to rely on: his querulous, combative, high-pitched voice. While Kennedy actually carried out a comparatively elevated campaign, Humphrey entered the fray attempting to level his opponent with a massive verbal assault. JFK was "soft on Nixon." Papa Joe Kennedy, Humphrey claimed, had kicked into Nixon's campaign when Nixon was running for the Senate in 1950. Jack had voted with Nixon on many occasions. (To prove he was definitely not for Nixon, Humphrey imported from California Mrs. Helen Gahagan Douglas, a liberal "martyr" who many Democrats believed had been vilified in her losing 1950 senatorial campaign against Nixon.)

Kennedy was "naive." He was "Pop's pet." "Jack had all the jack." When Kennedy graciously offered to sit down with Humphrey and work out a mutual limit on spending, Humphrey, before he had heard the details, responded that the offer was as "phony as a three-dollar bill." Aware that Kennedy was hauling in support because of his charismatic qualities, Humphrey could not refrain from uttering a desperate, almost childish, denunciation of his opponent. "I don't believe in razzle-dazzle, frizzle-frazzle synthetic phony politics," he declared. "We're not in American politics to select a lead star for Hollywood drama, but a Presidential candidate." Asked if that "razzle-dazzle" tag was aimed at Senator Kennedy, Humphrey said he would not confine it to the Massachusetts contender, but would "apply it generously."

Welcoming the tag of "labor senator," Humphrey drubbed Kennedy for having been involved in the passage of the union-despised Landrum-Griffin labor reform act of 1959. (This was another Humphrey somersault, for while denouncing Kennedy for setting the stage for passage of Landrum-Griffin, Humphrey had, albeit reluctantly and in the face of popular support of union restrictions, voted for it himself.)

Nowhere did Humphrey attempt to cut up Kennedy more than on his early endorsement of the flexible price support policies of Ike's Secretary of Agriculture, Ezra Taft Benson. In a speech to the radical Wisconsin Farmers Union in February, Humphrey, making available a list of times JFK voted with Benson, asserted: "I have never flirted with Ezra Taft Benson or his farm programs." Anyone who ever has supported the policies of Benson, he stated, has done a "great disservice" to the farmers, as well as to workers and businessmen. "Quite frankly," Humphrey threatened, "a setback for me would be a setback for you and would have a serious impact on farmers all over the nation."[7]

In March, Humphrey's forces issued a nine-page pamphlet called the "Kennedy Record," charging that Kennedy's voting "makes him at best a fair weather friend of American agriculture." According to this analysis, Kennedy had supported the Republican Secretary of Agriculture on 27 major farm legislation votes between 1953 and 1958. Kennedy "affects the stance of a statesman," the pamphlet went on, but one can coldly regard his public pronouncements "as a smoke screen set up to obscure his anti-farm voting record." Since 1956, the pamphlet related, there had been a "great Kennedy awakening" when the Massachusetts Senator began to shift away from the flexible support stand advocated by Benson and toward the high price support stand proposed by the radical National Farmers Union. "That was the year," the analysis caustically commented, "in which Kennedy lost the Presidential and Vice Presidential nominations partly because convention delegates from rural America found his legislative record on agricultural issues far from prepossessing."

While the Kennedy forces waged the campaign on less of a personal basis, they did not take these onslaughts lying down. Both Bobby Kennedy and Franklin D. Roosevelt, Jr., acting as JFK's "hatchet men" in the contest, began spreading stories that Humphrey's campaign was being fueled with tainted Teamster union money and claimed that Humphrey had condoned "vote stealing" when the number of at-large delegates was reduced from ten to five. They also struck at Humphrey by selling for $1 each a label insignia of PT 109, the boat Kennedy had captained in World War II. This was not only a reminder that Kennedy had been something of a war hero, but it also raised the issue of Humphrey's lack of a war record and brought up renewed suspicions that Humphrey had been less than eager to wear the uniform in World War II. But Jack Kennedy himself left most of the rough stuff to his supporters and campaign strategists. The closest he ever came to really striking back at Humphrey, aside from producing a letter in 1958 in which Humphrey extolled Kennedy's liberalism, was the remark that he was just as liberal as Humphrey but that he couldn't bring himself to "bleed all over the floor the way Humphrey does." Playing the statesman rather than the politician, he was following the advice given him by his own pollster, Lou Harris. Harris had warned: "At all costs, Kennedy must avoid being looked upon as a politician. Anything approximating name-calling can only hurt Kennedy. He must make every effort to resist the taunts and barbs thrown by Hubert Humphrey. Temptations inevitably will arise to slug it out with H. And slug it out Kennedy must, but on his own terms and in keeping with his own positive profile."

The Harris analysis was obviously quite correct, as the voters were clearly attracted to Kennedy's more dignified campaign style. "There is a world of difference between their personalities," noted Austin C. Wehrwein for the New York *Times*. Kennedy had flair, sophistication and good looks and would thread scintillating quotes from Jefferson, Hamilton and Lincoln into his pitches. Tossing in bread and butter issues sparingly, he liked to dwell on the philosophy of the Presidency and what sort of qualities a President should possess. Though he might advocate the same platform as Humphrey, he would "still appear the more conservative of the two," noted a Green Bay editor.

Humphrey was always coming out punching, but at times he resembled some small mongrel yapping at the heels of a thoroughbred. Typical of many reactions was that of Miss Mary Healey, a Beaver Dam lawyer. "I'd rather have him in the Senate than in the Presidency. He has great ability, but not the maturity or dignity. People are afraid he might move too fast." Sen. Humphrey commanded the support of most of the full-time organization Democrats, but Senator Kennedy's portrait as a young moderate was attractive to middle-class Democrats and Republicans. For both, noted Wehrwein, Humphrey is a "too much man." They think he is "too much for labor," "too much for the farmer," "too jumpy," "too cocky," "too sarcastic" and "too much of a blowhard." Even his labor image did not always go over with the blue collar crowd. The center of the Humphrey support, remarked Wehrwein, "is the leadership of the organized labor movement. But the biggest labor unit, Local 72 of the United Auto Workers, is split, with many of the 44,000 members in the Kennedy camp."

Part of the disdainful attitude toward Humphrey stemmed from a certain cornball quality to his campaign. Stumping the state for Humphrey, for example, was Philleo Nash, Wisconsin's Lieutenant Governor, who was also a guitar-playing minstrel. With something less than a minimum of coaxing, he would sing his latest Humphrey ballad to the tune of "Davey Crockett." The verse ran like this:

He is a Senator, neighbor and friend
We're gonna stick with him all the way to the end.
He used to come over just to help us out
And now it's our turn to help him without a doubt.
Farmers all around are taking a shellacking.
Money in the till is the thing that is lacking.
Get rid of Benson and your troubles will cease.
Put Humphrey in the White House, use our food (surplus) for peace.

While Philleo fiddled for the farmers, Joe Glazer, education director of the United Rubber Workers and head of the National Labor Committee for Humphrey, was Humphrey's labor troubadour. In Racine, Wisconsin, Humphrey stopped his campaign bus to greet the pickets from Local 180 of the United Auto Workers who were picketing the main gate of the J. I. Case Company plant. Introduced by Humphrey as his "Elvis Presley," Glazer unpacked his guitar and began plunking out "Solidarity Forever"—a militant labor song that Presidential candidate Humphrey lustily belted out along with the pickets. Some sample verses:

When the union's inspiration through the worker's blood shall run
There can be no power greater anywhere beneath the sun;
Yet what force on earth is weaker than the feeble strength of one,
For the union makes us strong.
Refrain:
Solidarity forever, solidarity forever, solidarity forever
For the union makes us strong.

They have taken untold millions that they never toiled to earn
But without our brain and muscle not a single wheel can turn;
We can break their haughty power, gain our freedom when we learn
That the union makes us strong.
Refrain

Is there aught we hold in common with the greedy parasite
Who would lash us into serfdom and would crush us with his might?
Is there anything left for us but to organize and fight?
For the union makes us strong.
Refrain

All the world that's owned by idle drones, is ours and ours alone.
We have laid the wide foundations; built it skyward stone by stone.
It is ours, not to slave in, but to master and to own,
While the union makes us strong.
Refrain

Visiting Local 180's strike headquarters, Glazer exhausted his bag of labor songs and Humphrey, caught up in the spirit of things, predicted the union would "bring the company to its knees in a week."[8]

Apparently, the spectacle of a Presidential candidate so obviously biased in favor of labor didn't bother Humphrey. As Glazer and Humphrey left, there were cries of "good-by, brother," the traditional union term for a member.

Inevitably, the religious issue was to rise in Wisconsin—as it was to rise wherever Kennedy appeared on the scene. And while both Humphrey and Kennedy made dutiful noises that one's religion should not play any part in the campaign, each candidate attempted to exploit the issue in a subtle manner. Kennedy used it by suggesting a vote against him was a vote for bigotry.

Humphrey was counting on the bigot vote to carry him into the Democratic convention with a solid bloc of delegates.

This Humphrey strategy, however, was not so apparent during the Wisconsin primary as it became evident afterward. Yet even during the Wisconsin contest there were questions raised concerning possible efforts by Humphrey forces to "cultivate" the Protestant vote.

By mid-March it was discovered that anti-Catholic literature was being mailed to Humphrey supporters, though such mailings were violently denounced by both Humphrey and Eugene Foley, the executive director of Humphrey's state organization in Wisconsin. Toward the end of March, Kennedy's Roman Catholic religion was made an issue in an advertisement that strongly hinted that Protestants should support Humphrey for President. Distributed to some 350 weekly newspapers by the Wisconsin Press Association, it had been authorized by the Square Deal for Humphrey Committee, an "unofficial" Humphrey group headed by Charles M. Schultz, vice president and political director of the Wisconsin State AFL-CIO.

The advertisement in question read: "Let's give Humphrey a square deal. The Democratic Party rose to its greatest heights with the New Deal and the Square Deal. How about a square deal for one of its greatest liberals? Is Humphrey getting a square deal?

"A leading political pollster reports: 'The solidarity of Catholic voters behind Kennedy shows up as far greater than that of Protestants behind Humphrey. Five out of six Catholics who were interviewed favor Kennedy over Humphrey. Included are many normally Republican voters who say they would back Nixon against any Democrat except Kennedy.' Should the Republican voters quoted above determine who the Democratic nominee for President shall be?"

Schultz, whose name was listed above the ad, repudiated it. He explained that he had been asked to head the committee formed by Charles F. Greene, but had not seen the copy of the ad before publication. Foley acknowledged that Greene had worked briefly as a volunteer in Humphrey's headquarters, but said he had become suspicious that Greene was a Kennedy supporter and had asked him to get out. Greene, himself, said he had "intended to help Humphrey but maybe I made a mistake and hurt him."[9] Whatever the truth of the matter, the religious issue proved a boon to Humphrey in Wisconsin.

As the votes rolled in on election day, April 5, it was clear that John F. Kennedy was the winner. The final tabulation revealed that Kennedy had won six of the state's 10 congressional districts, Humphrey four. In total number of delegates, Kennedy had 20½ to Humphrey's 10½. Under the primary rules before Humphrey's forces had slickly changed them, Humphrey would have fared even worse, with Kennedy picking up 22½ delegates and Humphrey only 8½.

Yet this seemingly solid loss for Humphrey had a silver thread that permitted the Minnesotan to hang on for at least another round. Indeed, Humphrey, ever optimistic, contemplated his loss as something of a triumph. What had bolstered his spirits was the plain fact that he had won all four predominantly Protestant districts, with Kennedy's popular margin having come from the heavily Catholic areas. In addition, there was evidence that Republican Catholics had crossed over into the Democratic primary to vote for Kennedy.

To the political pros—and to Humphrey—this meant that the primary could very well have split along the religious issue. It had not necessarily proved that JFK could win against Humphrey in a Democratic primary—it had only revealed that JFK could win with a high percentage of Catholic voters in his corner.

Humphrey had definitely hurt Kennedy's confidence, and there was the strong belief—now worrying Jack and encouraging Humphrey—that a predominantly Protestant America might still not vote for a Catholic for President. And while Humphrey continued to disavow any use of the religious issue, he had made up his mind that he would now contest Kennedy once again—this time in overwhelmingly Protestant West Virginia. It was Humphrey's belief that, although he had demonstrated he could not win in his own back yard, he could win in the peculiar bagpipe-shaped state of less than two million voters where rampant bigotry against Catholics was supposedly a fact.

Humphrey had been warned about getting into the West Virginia battle. Walter Reuther, James Rowe, Mrs. Eleanor Roosevelt and others close to Humphrey had advised that the contest might tear the two candidates apart. If he would not stay out of West Virginia, at least keep the campaign on a high level, Humphrey was told. The reasoning: both Senators Humphrey and Kennedy have more in common than in conflict. The major concern: If Senator Kennedy lost the primary and Senator Humphrey won, Humphrey, the liberal ideologist, might emerge with an anti-Catholic label, the candidate of the bigots. But Humphrey had no intention of following either of these requests. His combat spirit stirred by Wisconsin, Humphrey entered the West Virginia contest thirsting for Kennedy's blood.

As in Wisconsin, Humphrey ran on some familiar depression themes—a tactic that he thought would go over better in West Virginia, supposedly the poorest state in the nation. Over and over again he pounded home the "poor boy" theme, hoping that the voters would discriminate against the rich Jack Kennedy if not the Catholic Jack Kennedy. "I don't think elections should be bought," he told a courthouse square crowd. "Let that sink in deeply." He identified himself as the only Democratic candidate who was not a millionaire and the only one who had experienced poverty. He recalled that he had watched his mother "crying when our family home had to be sold." At Kingwood, a Republican stronghold, Humphrey protested that he was "running against tremendous odds." "I'm being ganged up on by wealth," he insisted. "I can't afford to run around this state with a little black bag and a checkbook."

"The suggestion," noted Arthur Krock, "was that Kennedy can and does. . . ." And noted Krock, the "little black bag" reference was to suggest crookedness on Kennedy's part.

As the campaign heated up, noted one commentary, the Humphrey-Kennedy political struggle became a name-calling contest. The Senators' respective camps, said another, were exchanging insults with a fervor not displayed in the West Virginia hills since the Hatfields and the McCoys stopped shouting and started shooting.

Robert Kennedy charged that Humphrey had distorted the record, attacked Kennedy's integrity and "played fast and loose with smears and innuendos." Humphrey retorted: "Jack will have plenty of chances to speak for himself without handouts through brother Bobby. Politics is a serious business, not a boy's game where you can pick up your ball and run home if things don't go according to your idea of who should win."

"It has always seemed rather amusing to me," Humphrey stressed, to see Jack publicly challenge other candidates to enter the primaries, and then when someone does enter he complains there is a conspiracy to stop him and deny him the nomination. . . ."

At one point the Kennedy forces published large advertisements purporting to show that votes for Senator Humphrey would land in a garbage can beside a road heading back to Minnesota, while votes for Kennedy would drop through the roof of the White House. Humphrey forces retaliated with a press release in the name of Lt. Gov. Karl Rolvaag challenging "the divine right of the Kennedys" to determine who should be the nominee.

There was also a sharp exchange of handouts between the two headquarters over the endorsement by the West Virginia Teamsters council of Senator Humphrey, the first open endorsement of any candidate by a large union.

While the Kennedy crowd saw the sinister Jimmy Hoffa behind the move, Humphrey forces maintained that the state Teamsters' choice was strictly a local decision by local people as to whom they favor in the local primary "and has nothing to do with Hoffa, regardless of how the Kennedy forces try to distort it."

The Kennedy attack, said the co-chairman of Humphrey's campaign, "looks more like another Bobby Kennedy desperation move and I am afraid Bobby is reverting to some of the 'guilt by association' tactics he learned while working for former Senator Joe McCarthy's committee during its heyday."

John Kennedy found himself ignoring the Harris advice in Wisconsin and slugging it out with Humphrey on a personal basis. He accused Humphrey of running a "gutter campaign." A blistering statement issued in his name charged that Humphrey could not win the nomination. "He cannot win the election," it continued. "He cannot be President of the United States. So why, you might ask, is he conducting a gutter campaign against me here in West Virginia? Why is he letting himself be used as a tool by the strangest collection of political bedfellows that has ever joined to gang up on one candidate? And why should he ask West Virginians to waste their votes on him?"

The biggest clout of the campaign, however, was engineered by Bobby Kennedy, condoned by Jack and executed by Franklin D. Roosevelt, Jr., a former Humphrey friend. "New bitterness was injected . . . into the Democratic Presidential primary," reported David Broder in an April 27 dispatch for the Washington *Evening Star*. ". . . Franklin D. Roosevelt, Jr., campaigning for Senator Kennedy of Massachusetts in this state's May 10 primary, said last night Senator Humphrey 'is a good Democrat but I don't know where he was in World War II.' "

Hotly denying the implication, Humphrey responded: "Roosevelt's inferences (*sic*) are the lowest kind of campaigning. He has been a friend of mine for the last 15 years and he knows my public and private record.

"He knows I was denied the opportunity of active military service and he knows I never sought at any time any special consideration. To the contrary, I tried repeatedly to volunteer." Humphrey claimed he was deferred from military service three times during World War II for physical disability (a claim that will be examined more closely in a following chapter).

Kennedy personally refused to disown Roosevelt's comments, stating only, "I have not discussed the matter of war records and I'm not going to. Mr. Roosevelt is down here making his speeches. I'm making mine."[10]

The junior Roosevelt was to be more specific just four days prior to the primary election. On May 6, Roosevelt unloosed another blast, charging that Humphrey had on three different occasions asked for deferments: first, to continue teaching school;

secondly, to manage a political campaign; and finally, to manage labor relations for a Minnesota company. In a statement that drew only cynical guffaws from politicos, Kennedy this time claimed, "Any discussion of the war record of Senator Hubert Humphrey was done without my knowledge and consent. I strongly disapprove the injection of this issue into this campaign."

Nothing made Humphrey more bitter than this slap at his having stayed out of World War II. The issue had been revived in every one of his campaigns since 1945, but now he was being done in by an old ADA friend.* Humphrey was positively raging. "All this material," he angrily responded, "has been completely discredited and recently exhumed by *Human Events*, a McCarthy magazine. If Franklin D. Roosevelt, Jr., and Jack Kennedy want to be the McCarthy spokesmen of 1960 they can be."

Did Senator Humphrey know that Kennedy had repudiated Roosevelt's statement in a press release? "That's a lot of baloney," Humphrey replied to a reporter. "These boys play both the high road and the low road, and they both get splashed. They cannot keep out of each others' ditch."

Charges concerning his war record had hurt Humphrey, but the major factor in the campaign remained the religious issue. Following Wisconsin, a poll by Harris had revealed that Humphrey was ahead and that much of his edge resulted from an anti-Catholic sentiment. Realizing he somehow had to break through a built-in bias against him, Kennedy dealt with the subject with ever increasing frequency. With an edge of anger in his voice, he told his audiences that the "real issue" in West Virginia was economic distress, "not where I go to church on Sunday." In Fairmont, he rasped that "one of the issues of this campaign is my religion. I don't think it's anyone's business but my business. . . . Is anyone going to tell me that I lost this primary 42 years ago on the day I was baptized?"

Addressing the American Society of Newspaper Editors in

*Roosevelt later told intimates that Bobby had put him up to raising the war issue, and rather than incur the crown prince's displeasure, he let his old pal Humphrey have it right in the groin.

Washington in the midst of the primary campaign, he stated: "There is only one legitimate question underlying all the rest: 'Would you, as President, be responsive in any way to ecclesiastical pressures or obligations of any kind that might in any fashion influence or interfere with your conduct of that office in the national interest?' I have answered that question many times. My answer was—and is—no." He assured his audience he was "not the Catholic candidate for President. Do not expect me to explain or defend every act or statement of every Pope or priest. . . . If there is bigotry in this country, then so be it—there is bigotry. If that bigotry is too great to permit the fair consideration of a Catholic who has made clear his complete independence and his complete dedication to separation of church and state, then we ought to know it. But I do not believe that this is the case." Kennedy pounded home the theme, with always the subtle suggestion that if he lost it would be because of bigotry. On the face of it, of course, there was only one way the people of West Virginia could erase their reputation, however unjust, of being narrow-minded—and that was to vote for JFK.

The Humphrey forces were also not above using the religious issue. Humphrey backers, related *Time* at the beginning of the West Virginia primary, "have already made a less-than-subtle move with a campaign song, 'I'm Gonna Vote for Hubert Humphrey,' which the instruction sheet notes is sung to the tune of the spiritual, 'Give Me That Old Time Religion.' "[11]

Reporter Joseph Alsop was more explicit. After sampling voter sentiment, the liberal columnist reported that "Sen. Humphrey owes to prejudice well over half his support in the four places polled . . . if Sen. Humphrey wins the West Virginia primary, as he well may do, he will owe his victory to Ku Klux Klan-minded voters.

"He will also win with powerful help from an admitted ex-Kluxer, Sen. Robert C. Byrd. . . ."

"The mystery of this West Virginia primary," Alsop wrote later, "is the role of Sen. Hubert H. Humphrey of Minnesota. Here is a hot, crucial Democratic contest, in which naked religious prejudice is the demonstrated source of at least half the voter support for Sen. Humphrey, the liberal enemy of prejudice in all forms."

In an intensive statewide survey, Alsop reported, the *Wall Street Journal's* Alan L. Otten found that "at least seven out of ten" prospective Humphrey voters were animated by prejudice. The New York *Times*'s William H. Lawrence wrote: "There are few voters intending to vote for him who identify themselves as 'for' Humphrey. Most simply say they are 'anti-Kennedy,' primarily on religious grounds."

In similar circumstances, said Alsop, if Kennedy's opponent were Sen. Lyndon B. Johnson of Texas, "the acknowledged voices of American liberalism would be making the National Welkin ring with their roars of indignation. Actually the Liberals have held off, because Sen. Humphrey is one of their own."[12]

When the final returns were tabulated in the Mountain State, John F. Kennedy had buried the religious issue—and Hubert Humphrey. He had captured 220,000 votes to Humphrey's 142,000. Kennedy had carried 48 of the state's 55 counties. Summed up the Baltimore *Sun's* Howard Norton: "It just proves you can't trust bigots."

Humphrey withdrew from the Presidential contest to concentrate on his campaign to be re-elected to the Senate, but he must have bowed out with a heavy heart. He must have realized that his chances for ever again being considered as a Presidential contender were remote. In 1956, he had not been able to persuade Democratic delegates to give him a shot at the Vice Presidency. Indeed, his own delegation was less than eager to see Humphrey on the national ticket. In 1960—after considerable publicity in the press, most of it favorable—he could not capture one primary against John F. Kennedy, either in his own back yard or in West Virginia, a state that would seemingly welcome a Protestant candidate who had mastered depression politics.

But in politics, as in gambling, nothing is ever certain. After he had easily won his 1960 Senate race, he became Majority Whip in the Senate. And when an assassin's bullet cut down

John F. Kennedy and his old friend Lyndon Johnson stepped into the Presidency, Humphrey once again moved within range of the Democratic national ticket. In August, 1964, not because he was genuinely popular, but because he was a friend of Lyndon Johnson, Humphrey was nominated by the Democrats for the Vice Presidency. As Johnson's running mate, he was swept into office on a landslide vote, a "heartbeat away" from the most powerful position on the globe.

20

Profile in Courage

When Franklin Delano Roosevelt, Jr., assailed Humphrey's World War II record in the West Virginia primary, Hubert Humphrey was unquestionably stunned and hurt. But it was not the first time his war record had ever been discussed—nor would it, probably, be the last. Though Humphrey's lack of military service has been bruited about in almost every campaign, many of his friends have pretended that it has never been an issue. Michael Amrine, for example, stated in a campaign biography published prior to FDR Jr.'s attack: "His lack of military record has never appeared as a campaign topic. When a 'hate sheet' once brought it up his friends—and even his political foes—answered the smear by pointing out that he had tried several times to get in the service and that none of his deferments had been sought by him."[1]

William Connell, Humphrey's administrative assistant, wrote in a letter to this author on June 17, 1966: "It is . . . noteworthy that no reputable person in Minnesota during the many campaigns the Vice President participated in ever raised this issue. It never became known as an issue, as such, being disposed of typically in a matter of a few hours by those who had known the young Humphrey in their official capacity as members of the Selective Service system or Naval recruiting system."*

*For the text of this letter and the "official" chronology of Humphrey's Selective Service record, see Appendix I.

But the plain truth of the matter is that Humphrey's record has become an important issue in virtually every one of his campaigns since 1944 and has not been disposed of as easily as Mr. Connell has suggested. Even Winthrop Griffith admits: "In almost every election campaign of his career he has been forced to defend himself against opponents' charges that he was a 'draft dodger' or that he 'didn't try very hard' to get into the armed forces during World War II. . . ."[2]

Answering the question whether Humphrey tried to avoid the draft is not especially easy, particularly since Humphrey's aides appear less than eager to respond to inquiries regarding the Vice President's war record. This author, for instance, wrote a letter to Mr. Connell on May 16, 1966, asking for specific information pertaining to Humphrey's military record. When no answer was received at the end of three weeks, another letter was dispatched on June 9. Mr. Connell replied this time, but his letter was not terribly enlightening. Not one of the major queries put to him was answered in a direct fashion. Some of the questions the author asked:

"When did Mr. Humphrey first attempt to get into the armed services?" No answer.

"According to Winthrop Griffith's book and a number of other articles on Mr. Humphrey, the Army induction center at Fort Snelling turned him down because he had a 'non scrotal hernia.' Is it also true that this was repaired after his election to the Senate in 1948?" No answer.

"Would it be possible for me to see the documents and affidavits Mr. Humphrey has to refute charges against him?" No answer.

Mr. Connell also discouraged me from seeing Humphrey, himself, and in fact any member of the Vice President's staff.

Mr. Connell did furnish one direct reply. I had asked him when Humphrey first gave a detailed refutation of the charges made against him. Mr. Connell responded in this fashion: "In handling the attacks which have been made . . . the then Senator preferred and made the judgment, and I think it was a wise judgment, to have the officials who had to do with the Selective

Service and Naval recruiting at the time set forth the facts for themselves. He preferred to let the record stand for itself rather than to dignify the attacks by any kind of personal reply."

For my own edification, Mr. Connell sent me a partial—but only partial—chronology of Humphrey's Selective Service record put out after Roosevelt's attack in West Virginia. Yet the chronology did not answer my major inquiries and, indeed, raised fresh questions. With Humphrey's personal assistants so reluctant to straighten out the record, it is not exactly a surprise that Humphrey's lack of military service keeps cropping up in his campaigns.

The beginning of the "war record" issue can be traced back to 1944. And, ironically, it was Humphrey himself who projected it into the political arena. In April of that year, the Democratic and Farmer-Labor parties were merged into the DFL largely as a result of Humphrey's drive and initiative. Because of his role in the DFL's formation and because he had nearly won the mayorship a year earlier, the delegates at the merger convention in Minneapolis' Radisson Hotel were intent on drafting Humphrey as the fusion candidate for governor. Humphrey, the newspapers and the political pros, however, figured that whoever was tapped for the job would probably be beaten. Chances for victory were slim for a variety of reasons, including the fact that the DFL was a newly formed party and that the Democratic Party nationally had taken a dip in popularity. But Humphrey was believed to have had the best possible chance, and, besides, he was the popular favorite of the delegates. The pressures to draft him relentlessly increased. Though word was let out that he had plans to enter the Navy, the nominating committee picked Humphrey as the DFL's gubernatorial candidate. A proposal to draft him was made from the convention floor on April 15 with a boisterous roar of approval from the delegates. After considering the draft clamor for several minutes, Humphrey strode to the platform to tell the delegates that he must decline their nomination because he had a higher cause to serve.

"I want to go into the armed forces if I am acceptable," he declared in his most eloquent manner. "I want to be with those other young men and women in the armed forces, and you can't deny me that privilege.

"I cannot be your candidate for governor."

Humphrey humbly admitted that he was only one individual, "But the individual is important in the armed forces, for it is of individuals that divisions and armies are made." Humphrey also said that after the war there would be many problems of readjustment and he wanted to be in a position to understand them.[3]

Humphrey's moving, impassioned speech was a heavy blow to those who had been counting on him to run, but it drew him a standing ovation and favorable coverage in the local press.

It is a virtual certainty that Humphrey saved himself from the nomination with this speech. And with the DFL gubernatorial candidate losing in a landslide that year, Humphrey probably saved his political hide in the process. Moreover, while Humphrey did get around to doing a lot of things during 1944 and 1945, he never did get around to going to war. Thus was raised a political issue that has plagued Humphrey in every subsequent campaign.

While Humphrey never donned a uniform, his supporters get angry when it is suggested he might have been less than enthusiastic about joining the armed forces. They picture Humphrey as desperately trying to beat a path to the door of the military, only to be frustrated because of his physical frailties, but the facts suggest that Humphrey was not so all-fired determined to be in uniform as he has led the public to believe.

Humphrey, in fact, managed to receive non-medical deferments right up until the war was over, and he obtained these deferments while running for mayor, campaigning for Roosevelt and Truman, and working in other political capacities for the DFL. Not only did he permit letters to be written asking for his deferment, but, even after his "I-want-to-be-with-the-boys" speech, Humphrey himself wrote letters to the draft board purporting to show how essential he was to the war effort as a civilian.

Humphrey apparently did try to enlist in the Navy in late

1943 and early 1944 and was rejected for medical reasons, but this strange interlude, which shall be explored in more detail, was a rather atypical period for Humphrey during the war. His actions are exceptionally curious, for there is no evidence that he ever volunteered to get into any branch of service either before or after this period of time. Furthermore, the facts strongly suggest he would not have been turned down for medical reasons had he undergone a minor hernia operation—an operation that he reportedly had after the war was well out of the way.

A more thorough look at Humphrey's activities during the World War II period is also revealing. War, it must be recalled, was declared on December 7, 1941. Humphrey was 30 years old at the time and had only one child. Yet not until the "winter of 1943"—according to the Connell chronology—did Humphrey feel an inner compulsion to serve in the military. Why this patriotic impulse had not overwhelmed him earlier remains an unanswered question. The Connell chronology suggests that Humphrey was classified 3A through August of 1943 because he was a father. Other fathers, however, were serving overseas. Barry Goldwater, suffering from an astigmatism and badly battered knees, was older than Humphrey and had three small children under six years of age when the war broke out. But by 1942 Goldwater was flying P-47 single engine fighter planes across the North Atlantic—a hazardous journey even under peaceful conditions. Later, he flew cargo from India across the Hump to China. Paul Douglas, father of two children, was 50 when the war broke out and promptly joined the Marines. No one suggests that Humphrey had to join the Marines or fly fighter planes to prove his heroism, but when Humphrey and his supporters suggest that regulations prevented him from joining the armed services, listeners have a right to be skeptical.

In August, 1943, the official chronology continues, Humphrey was employed at Macalester College as an instructor for the Air Force ROTC program. "This meant he was given automatic classification of 2A as a civilian in an essential job."

Yet that explanation is somewhat misleading. There was nothing "automatic" about Humphrey's job classification at all.

The college, itself, had to request deferment and draft board hearings had to be held. Both of these were done in Humphrey's case. John B. LaDue, the former draft board secretary in Ramsey, Minnesota, recalls that Dr. Charles J. Turck, the then president of Macalester, formally requested Humphrey's deferment, and he also recalls a board hearing regarding such deferment.[4]

The crucial importance of Humphrey's job to the war effort, furthermore, is bound to escape many persons. In a letter to this author dated January 11, 1966, G. Theodore Mitau, Chairman of the Political Science Department at Macalester College, wrote that Humphrey taught four courses in the fall of 1943 and three in the spring of 1944. Yet Mr. Mitau noted only one course, the "Survey of Social Sciences," taught each semester, which fell "within the framework of the Air Force College Training Detachment program" (see Mitau letter in Appendix).

Why Humphrey would have been deferred because he taught this general survey course to ROTC students is highly perplexing, and it is difficult to believe, assuming that it was vital, that it could not have been taught just as well in uniform. Besides, if Humphrey really did have an all-consuming passion to go to war, he would not have permitted Macalester College to write letters to his draft board asking for a deferment.

There are other credibility gaps in the Humphrey "war record." While Humphrey made an eloquent plea about wanting to go to war before the DFL convention in April of 1944, that speech has been viewed with a jaundiced eye by his critics. Scott Schoen, editor of the Redwood Falls (Minnesota) *Gazette*, noted in *Human Events* in December, 1959, that Humphrey's impassioned presentation didn't prevent him from "accepting the position of state campaign manager for Roosevelt and Truman. . . ." Schoen added, moreover, that Humphrey was "reclassified in September to continue in that capacity, at the request of Elmer F. Kelm, then state DFL chairman and later collector of internal revenue. Some critics have called this putting 'politics ahead of country,' and subsequent events have frequently reminded them of it."

In declining the gubernatorial candidacy in 1944, Schoen continued harshly, "Humphrey was being entirely practical, with the patriotic gesture as window dressing. The newly amalgamated Democratic-Farmer-Labor Party was in no position, with or without Humphrey, to win a state election. Its candidate Byron G. Allen . . . lost to Edward J. Thye (later Senator) that year, 701,185 to 430,132, and Humphrey was a lesser known figure than Allen."[5] Schoen went on to point out another significant fact. Humphrey, he noted, had no qualms about running for mayor in 1943; nor did he mind running for mayor in 1945 when his chances for winning were excellent. It was only when he was faced "with an impossible political race" that he chose to decline a nomination on the grounds that he must be with the military.

Schoen's charges are harsh, yet they have never been adequately answered. Nor does Schoen's damaging article exhaust the evidence revealing Humphrey's reluctance to serve in the Army. On July 11, 1944—again according to Humphrey's supporters—he was classified 1A. The Connell chronology, however, again insists that Humphrey was deferred because of a new draft regulation which exempted men who were 30 years of age or over and who had children. How this deferment differed from the one Humphrey received in 1941 is not clear. Again there is no hint that Humphrey tried to get his exemption waived, and indeed there is much evidence that he actually desired an exemption. Several published accounts show that on September 15, 1944, DFL state chairman Elmer Kelm wrote to Local Board No. 2, Hennepin County, 800 Washington Avenue, Southeast, Minneapolis, to request that Humphrey be deferred. The letter read:

Gentlemen:

It is my understanding that men over 26 years of age, engaged in responsibly necessary employment, are now deferred: therefore this letter is written to request deferment of Hubert H. Humphrey, Jr., of 622 Fifth Street, S.E., Minneapolis 14, Minnesota, who is acting as campaign manager for the Democratic-Farmer-Labor Party in Minnesota. He is now devoting, and has been devoting, his full time to such employment since June 15, 1944.

This request is made in the belief that men of his age are entitled to consideration for deferment under present regulations.

Yours very truly,

EFK:rk (signed) Elmer F. Kelm[6]

Twelve days later—on September 27, 1944—Humphrey was reclassified from 1A to 2A by this board, according to still other published—and undenied—reports. The 2A classification was for a civilian in an essential job. Thus, on the face of it, Humphrey was deferred because he was the campaign manager for the DFL in Minnesota!

The Kelm letter has never been satisfactorily refuted by the Humphrey forces. And one can hardly believe that Kelm, on his own, would have written it without Humphrey's permission. Humphrey was not only the founder of the DFL, but he had expressly made his wishes known that he wanted to serve with the armed forces. That Kelm would not have consulted Humphrey before sending it is difficult to imagine.

There is still further evidence that Humphrey's zeal for being in mufti was less than ardent.

The *Northwest Industrial News,* a publication put out by Claude Efnor of Minneapolis, has reproduced copious amounts of material dealing with Humphrey's draft status during World War II. He also published copies of letters between Humphrey and his draft board that certainly suggest that Humphrey was seeking a way to avoid induction into the Army during 1944 and 1945. Efnor's *News,* for example, published a copy of a letter from C. M. Norton, a clerk at the draft board. Dated January 26, 1944, the letter (addressed to Humphrey) says: "Before we can consider a further deferment for you, we must have a request from Macalester College. Will you please have them submit the usual letter?"[7] The *News* does not show any letter, though it says that one was signed by Macalester's president. And it has been substantiated elsewhere that Macalester College did write letters to get Humphrey deferred.

The *Northwest Industrial News* also shows that Humphrey sent a letter to his draft board on December 9, 1944—eight months after his famous speech about going off to war. Humphrey explained in his letter that he was now engaged in public relations, employer-employee counselling, and industrial and government research. A good deal of his business activity, he insisted, included representing either labor or employee associations "before any one of the war agencies created by state and federal government . . . I wish to also report for purposes of your records that I have another son born on March 26, 1944, at University Hospital, University of Minnesota. My family now consists of my wife, Muriel F.; daughter Nancy F., five years nine months; son Hubert H., two years eight months and a son Robert A., eight months."[8]

In a letter dated January 10, 1945, Humphrey sent still another letter to his draft board to amplify information in the December 9 letter. In this letter, he says he has been retained by two industrial concerns in the Twin Cities, both of "which are engaged in the manufacture of war materials. . . . Over 90 per cent of all productions in both concerns is devoted to filling war contracts as let by the War Department."[9]

Humphrey does not use the word "deferment" in these letters, but there seems no mistaking their purpose: to prove he should not be drafted because he felt he was "essential" to the war effort as a civilian.

Efnor says he was able to obtain copies of these letters that "someone in the draft board supplied from the files," but they could, of course, be forgeries. Still, they have not been tagged as such. The author, in fact, asked Mr. Connell to explain them away. Writing to him in May of 1966, this author asked Mr. Connell the following question: "Enclosed is a copy of the *Northwest Industrial News* for September, 1964. The back page prints what purports to be copies of correspondence between Mr. Humphrey and others with Mr. Humphrey's draft board. Are these copies authentic and do you have any comments about them?" In response to this particular inquiry, Mr. Connell said: "The character of the *Northwest Industrial News* is well known to any informed citizen in Minneapolis, and I think you can determine that character by making a random sampling of any group of newspaper, radio or television people in the Twin

Cities, for example." In actuality, there are pros and cons about Mr. Efnor, but that, of course, was not the issue. These letters are either forgeries or the real thing. Mr. Connell's avoidance of a direct answer suggests they are all too authentic.

There is other information indicating Humphrey's reluctance to join the Army. Emil E. Holmes, who had been a past national commander of the World War Veterans and past Minnesota State Commander of the Disabled American Veterans, prepared an ad that took after Humphrey's war record in the 1948 campaign. This ad, so far as the author is aware, has also not been refuted. The ad noted that Humphrey was a registered pharmacist and licensed to fill out medical prescriptions. "There was a crying demand for men of that training during World War II," said Holmes, but Humphrey did not volunteer to serve in this capacity. In January of 1945, said Holmes, Humphrey went to Washington for the Presidential inauguration, but before he left he filled out a filing affidavit for mayor of Minneapolis. This time, at any rate, Humphrey was making no claims about how he had to serve with the boys in the military. "After talking to officials in the East on housing," Holmes continued, "he telephoned his wife to file him for mayor, and she did. Then he returned to Minneapolis and went to Fort Snelling for his induction physical examination." (Holmes does not mention it, but apparently Humphrey's attempts at obtaining a deferment had not come through.) On February 13, 1945, noted Holmes, the Minneapolis *Times* (now defunct) carried a front page story on Humphrey of much interest. The *Times* report said that Col. John A. Buxton, Fort Snelling executive officer, had noted that Humphrey had passed his physical examination "when he first appeared at the Fort and was passed for general service." Holmes said, however, that Humphrey did not "volunteer to go at the time he was physically cleared. Whether or not he should have offered his services as a pharmacist was for his own conscience." The *Times* story goes on to say that on subsequent examination Humphrey was accepted for "limited service" when a right—not "double"—hernia was discovered. Major H. Shapiro, Chief Medical Officer of the induction station, said, "The cause for physical rejection was definitely not present at the time Humphrey was previously examined. It would not keep him from being accepted for limited service."[10]

"The official record of state Selective Service," said Holmes, "has this final ruling on Humphrey:

" '2-14-45: Qualified for limited service administratively. Rejected because of right non-scrotal hernia. . . . (Signed) H. Shapiro, Maj. Med. Corps., Ft. Snelling, Minn.' " Even though Humphrey was qualified for limited service, however, he never was inducted—nor did the possibility that he might be called up prevent his running for mayor.

The available evidence strongly suggests that Humphrey definitely tried to avoid military service in the Army. But one period in Humphrey's life still needs to be explained: the late '43-early '44 period when he supposedly made repeated attempts to get into the Navy. The Connell chronology states:

"During the Winter of 1943 and 1944 Humphrey sought repeatedly to enlist in the Navy. According to Rollo Mudge of Minneapolis, who was a chief specialist recruiter for the Navy in Minneapolis in 1942 through 1944, Humphrey made at least 20 attempts to enlist in the Navy and 'he was so persistent as to be almost embarrassing to us. We had to turn him down both for color vision defect and for double hernia.' Mudge said that a person with a simple hernia would be acceptable to the Navy if the applicant agreed to surgery which Humphrey agreed to, but double hernia* was a cause for rejection."

For verification, the author placed a long-distance telephone call to Mr. Mudge in Minneapolis on March 24, 1967. There is no question that Mudge, who toiled in the DFL vineyard with Humphrey, is the strongest witness on Humphrey's behalf in regard to his military record. Though Mudge knows nothing about Humphrey's attempts—or lack of attempts—to get into the Army, he insists he diligently tried to get into the Navy but that the "double hernia" barred him from entrance. He also says the "double hernia" (lay term for bilateral hernia) was discovered in late 1943 or very early in 1944.

*Why the Navy discovered a "double hernia" and the Army found only a single hernia has never been clarified.

Humphrey, however, never underwent an operation to have his hernia repaired until after the war was over.[11] Mr. Connell says Humphrey agreed to be operated on for a single hernia, but why he did not agree to have his "double hernia" repaired is difficult to fathom. Contrary to the impression left by Connell, Humphrey—at least according to Mudge—would have been accepted by the Navy if he had had his hernia fixed. An interview with several doctors reveals that Humphrey's bilateral hernia—which was non-scrotal—would have been easy to repair. A Pomona, California physician who served as an Army doctor told the author, for example, that if Humphrey had agreed to be operated on, he would have been on his feet in one day, ready for active duty in three months—"six months at the maximum." Mudge himself admits this. Acknowledging that Humphrey could have undergone an operation and had his "double hernia" repaired, Mudge, though not a doctor, tried to make it seem that such an operation would be difficult. Even so, when he said that after such an operation it would have been "Six months before he would have been any good," Mudge was indirectly admitting that Humphrey could have been accepted into the Navy had he undergone surgery.

Humphrey's hypocrisy about desperately trying to get into military service is revealed by the fact that he never had his hernia repaired during the war. Since the hernia is given as the central reason for his rejection by both the Navy and the Army, there seems little question that he would have been accepted once it had been fixed. There were others with physical defects who had served in the war. Gov. Harold Stassen served in the Navy with a tubercular lung and former Minnesota State Treasurer Val Bjornson, who opposed Humphrey for Senator in 1954, was turned down for military service because of a hernia. But he had it repaired at his own expense and served in the Navy four years, most of that time overseas.[12]

There are still other thoughts raised by Humphrey's physical ailment. Assuming Mudge is correct in saying that Humphrey's hernia was discovered in late 1943—early 1944 at the latest—then Humphrey's repeated attempts to get the Navy to accept him after the hernia was discovered were purely for show, as he must have realized he would *not* be accepted until it was repaired. His performance before the DFL delegates at the 1944 convention would also be doubly suspect. Humphrey told the clamoring delegates that he could not run for governor because he wanted "to go into the armed forces if I am acceptable." Yet Humphrey must have known there was little likelihood that he would be accepted because he had refused to have his "double hernia" repaired.

Humphrey's failure to serve in the military has somehow haunted him all his life. As the years have gone by, declares Amrine, Humphrey "feels steadily worse" about missing military service, and his friends think this helps to explain his staunch support of veterans' legislation. By itself, Humphrey's non-service was not necessarily a badge of dishonor. Many patriotic persons did not go to war. But unlike most of those who remained civilians during World War II, Humphrey and his supporters have portrayed Humphrey as a man who zealously sought to defend the United States in uniform. Humphrey's failure to serve would probably have been thrown up at him no matter what he or his supporters had ever said, but it is highly unlikely that he would have been as repeatedly and as savagely whiplashed with this issue had he not dramatically forsaken a gubernatorial nomination on the grounds that he wanted to "be with those other young men and women in the armed forces." Precisely because he was so publicly determined to "go to war" does the question keep popping up: why didn't he?

21

The ADA's Obedient Servant

Hardly had Hubert Horatio Humphrey been nominated as the Democratic candidate for Vice President than he managed to put his foot in it. During a weekend campaign-strategy-planning trip to the LBJ Ranch in Texas, Hubert was summoned by the President for a walk in a cow pasture. He promptly slipped on some cow dung, but recovering his balance, cried out: "Mr. President! I just stepped on the Republican platform!"

Since the whole scene took place in front of newsmen, some Johnson and Humphrey aides winced at the bad taste of it all, but the Boss himself thought it was about the funniest thing he had ever heard[1]—*Time* Magazine, September 11, 1964.

Humphrey, however, probably surpassed this display of tastelessness at Euclid Beach Park in Cleveland, Ohio, where some 6,000 Democrats had gathered to assail a steer roast and to hear words of wisdom from their Vice Presidential candidate. In an aside from his prepared speech, Humphrey asserted:

John Kennedy drew the largest crowds of the campaign in 1960 in Ohio. . . .

John Kennedy loved Ohio more than any other state except his beloved Massachusetts. Yet he lost this state in 1960.

You owe something to his memory. You have the opportunity to redeem your state. I want you to undo what you did in 1960. I want you, in honor of our late President, to go to work between now and

November 3. Vote—and send the message so that John Kennedy in heaven will know we won.[2]

Attacking the GOP platform and appealing to JFK's ghostly spirit, however, were only minor themes in Humphrey's campaign. Mostly, Humphrey, along with the rest of the Democratic Party, desperately waged a demagogic campaign against Barry Goldwater, picturing him as a bizarre "radical" and "extremist" who had used ignoble methods to capture the Republican Party and who rather fancied the idea of plunging the nation into nuclear war.

There was no question about it, according to Humphrey: Goldwater was just plain evil. In Athens, Georgia, Humphrey insinuated that Goldwater represented a "reactionary" and "money grubbing" force. In Ardmore, Arizona, Goldwater was a "radical and an extremist." Elsewhere, Humphrey predicted a "nuclear reign of terror" if Goldwater were elected. In Los Angeles, Humphrey stressed that Goldwater "seeks to destroy the social and economic achievements of the past generation." Because Goldwater believed that state and local governments, combined with private enterprise, should do many of the jobs now being done by the federal government, Humphrey complained that Goldwater was opposed to the young, the old, the businessman, the laborer, the farmer, the white and the Negro. Hardly a speech went by when Humphrey wasn't wickedly wielding his verbal hatchet.

Goldwater's progressive attitude on civil rights was known to almost anyone in politics. He had voted for numerous civil rights bills; he had contributed to such Negro organizations as the NAACP and the Urban League; he had voted for public accommodation laws in Arizona; and he had helped to desegregate the National Guard there. A vocal opponent of enforced segregation, he had condemned that practice many times over and he had even assailed it in the South during the 1964 campaign. Theodore White, America's unofficial historian for the Presidential campaigns, has categorically stated that Goldwater refused to cater to racism in the 1964 contest.

Half Jewish himself, Goldwater has always felt at home with "minority" groups and has actively championed the cause of the Mexican and Indian Americans in Arizona. This genuine compassion for all peoples—no matter what their color or religion, or heritage—did not prevent Humphrey from suggesting that Goldwater was in league with the bigots.

Goldwater was opposed to civil rights, Humphrey liked to suggest, because he did not believe that the 1964 civil rights bill was the best way to achieve racial equality. He and his followers were appealing to "our ancient curse of race prejudice" because they had suggested that race riots and street violence be curbed—a battle cry subsequently sounded by LBJ. Humphrey didn't want Goldwater in the Presidency because "I don't want a man in the White House who has no respect for ethnic groups."[3]

At the August 12, 1964, Hershey, Pennsylvania unity meeting of big-wig Republicans, Goldwater proclaimed publicly:

> I seek the support of no extremist, of the Left or of the Right. I have far too much faith in the good sense and stability of my fellow Republicans to be impressed by talk of a so-called extremist take-over of the party.
>
> Such a thing cannot happen under Bill Miller and me. We repudiate the character assassins, vigilantes, Communists and such groups as the Ku Klux Klan which seeks to impose its views through terror or threat or violence.

Blithely ignoring such statements, Humphrey, like a famous cold drink, decided to "pour it on." Goldwater, he proclaimed, represented "the radicals and the extremists." In Humphrey's fevered imagination, Goldwater was encouraging support from the anti-Semites and the gun-toting Minutemen, whose leaders suggest they have assassination plans for America's leaders. Though Humphrey was a long-time opponent of "McCarthyism" and "guilt by association," he was not above pointing out that "Gerald L. K. Smith, leader of the extreme right-wing Christian Nationalist Crusade" had announced support for Goldwater. He also charged—in spite of the Hershey statement —"there has been no indication from the Goldwater leadership that such support is not welcome. . . ."[4] (Humphrey did not, however, point out that Nazi leader George Lincoln Rockwell vigorously opposed Goldwater.)

True enough, Goldwater didn't go crusading against every single right-wing kook that might have happened aboard his bandwagon, but then neither did Johnson or Humphrey repudiate every pacifist, black nationalist and pro-Communist that happened across their path. And one wonders whether Humphrey will ever repudiate the Stokely Carmichaels of this world.

Goldwater simply was not permitting an "extremist" take-over of the GOP—and Humphrey knew it. While Humphrey was shouting from the roof tops that Goldwater was an extremist run by extremists—and that extremism equalled the Minutemen and Gerald L. K. Smith—the facts were that none of the persons attached to Goldwater's personal staff or who ran the GOP National Committee belonged to any organization that Humphrey tagged as "extremist." Moreover, his policy advisers —far from bordering the outskirts of lunacy or extremism— were comprised of an attractive array of noted scholars and intellectuals such as Dr. Milton Friedman, the University of Chicago economist who writes a column for *Newsweek*, and Professor Robert Strausz-Hupe, the cold war academician who heads the scholarly Foreign Policy Research Institute at the University of Pennsylvania.

The "extremism" issue was only part of a larger theme that Humphrey liked to play: that Goldwater would plunge the country into nuclear war. Relentlessly, Humphrey portrayed the Arizonan as a man with an itchy finger on the nuclear trigger. In Madison, Wisconsin, Humphrey declared the election of Goldwater would make the United States "a garrison state in a nightmare world, isolated from everything except a nuclear reign of terror." "If we were to do as he bids us," Humphrey declared, "we would find ourselves eventually at war all over the globe—war fought with nuclear weapons in Eastern Europe, escalated war in Southeast Asia, war against Cuba, war in Berlin."[5]

The catchy theme of nuclear irresponsibility never left Humphrey's lips. *Time* magazine would note: "Democratic Vice Presidential nominee Hubert Humphrey is going around asking audiences: 'The question before the electorate is simple, prophetic, profound—which of these men, Lyndon Johnson or Barry Goldwater, do you want to have his hand on the nuclear trigger?' "[6]

The U.S. President, Humphrey would tell an audience in Carbondale, Illinois, "holds in his hand the power to maintain the peace of the world or annihilate virtually all life on this planet." And Goldwater, Humphrey added, "has made millions of Americans uneasy and apprehensive about placing his nervous finger on the nuclear trigger."[7]

In a wind-up speech in Los Angeles on October 31, Humphrey declared: "On July 12, 1964, a leading American told Senator Goldwater: 'You have too often casually prescribed nuclear war as a solution to a troubled world.'

"He continued: 'Goldwaterism has come to stand for nuclear irresponsibility . . . Goldwaterism has come to stand for being afraid to forthrightly condemn right-wing extremism. . . . In short, Goldwaterism has come to stand for a whole crazy-quilt collection of absurd and dangerous positions. . . .'

"This was on July 12, 1964. And the author of those statements was Gov. William Scranton of Pennsylvania. The governor has since chosen to rise above his principles—but the condemnation he issued that July day has been confirmed a *thousandfold* in recent weeks."[8]

Goldwater, of course, never "casually prescribed" nuclear warfare anywhere. True, he had received an outpouring of sharp criticism from liberal Republicans, LBJ and Humphrey because he had suggested that authority for the use of nuclear weapons should be given to the supreme commander of NATO. While Goldwater was being roasted for such advice, however, a number of periodicals discovered that such authority already existed. *Time* magazine, for example, pointed out: "Johnson gets across the notion, for instance, that Goldwater is irresponsible and reckless because he has suggested that NATO's supreme commander ought to be given some sort of contingency authority for using tactical nuclear weapons—at a time when Gen. Lemnitzer, under a delegation of power from Johnson, already has just such authority."

U.S. News and World Report put it this way: "Even now the understanding is widespread among NATO allies that U.S. commanders in Europe—not just the supreme commander—have orders, issued in advance, to use nuclear weapons in certain emergencies with no further instruction from Washington."

Pursuing the story, the New York *Times* reported that ". . . it is widely assumed in the capital that certain field commanders now have authority to employ nuclear weapons under certain circumstances."

The public, unfortunately, was not about to catch up to the truth and Humphrey wasn't about to make it available. On the September 20, 1964, *Meet the Press* television program, he again conveniently misrepresented Goldwater's position regarding the use of nuclear weapons in Southeast Asia. Program moderator Lawrence Spivak asked Humphrey: "On the nuclear power issue, Senator Goldwater has said over and over again that he is not in favor of using nuclear bombs in Southeast Asia. Why, in view of that, do the Democrats keep insinuating that he is?"

Humphrey replied: "It is a little difficult for me to keep up with this shifting target of Mr. Goldwater. He did once say that he thought it would be well to use nuclear weapons to 'defoliate,' I believe it was, the jungles in Viet Nam. There isn't any doubt but that he said that. I think that was a very reckless statement, and I have said so. . . ."

Humphrey's no-doubts to the contrary, Goldwater positively had not made such a statement. That canard resulted from the ABC-TV show *Issues and Answers* in June of 1964, when Goldwater was interviewed by Howard K. Smith. Asked by Smith if there were any methods that might be employed to defoliate the jungles in South Viet Nam, Goldwater responded by saying there were several methods under Pentagon consideration and that "defoliation of the forests by low-yield atomic weapons could well be done." But he had also carefully prefaced that remark with: "I don't think we would use any of them." In no sense did he advocate such action, nor did he in any way imply that he "thought it would be well" to use such devices.

Indeed, he denied such an interpretation and it was plain from his remarks that such an interpretation was false.

Campaigns, to be sure, are always rough and tumble exercises and Humphrey was not exactly new to the role of political hatchet man. In 1960 he had turned on Richard Nixon, tagging the Vice President a "juvenile delinquent." Thus, his gut-cutting of Goldwater was not a surprise. Nor was it a surprise when he didn't stick to the facts. What counted, so far as he was concerned, was reinforcing the image of Goldwater as a mad man surrounded by mad men, someone who just might "annihilate" life on this planet. The campaign was tailored neatly to the theme of those little "ads" the Democratic National Committee put on television, depicting innocent children being vaporized by nuclear bombs if Barry Goldwater were elected President.

Politicians with a wry sense of humor must have smiled, inwardly at least, as they watched Hubert Humphrey mount his podium to hurl down such thunderous accusations at his opponent as "radical" and "extremist." For the truth, of course, was that few persons in the Senate had ever been more radical than Hubert Horatio Humphrey. Indeed, Humphrey had fancied himself as a radical throughout the years. "Insofar as I am sorry for anything," Humphrey had once remarked, "it is not because I am a liberal, but it is because I am not more liberal than I am."[9]

While the press did its energetic best to put Humphrey in the "mainstream" of political life in 1964, the pitch was difficult to sell. A close look at the Humphrey record does not indicate any particular "mellowing" on his part. Bill Miller, Goldwater's Vice Presidential candidate, had highlighted Humphrey's own radical outlook in Lockport, New York, on September 5, 1964. The blast tore off the cover of "moderation" in which the anti-Goldwater press had conveniently cloaked the Democratic Vice Presidential nominee.

"From 1949 to 1950," Miller claimed, "Hubert Humphrey

served as chairman of the ADA. And every year since 1950 he has continued his service as vice chairman in the ADA, a fact which Senator Humphrey himself was proud to include in his own biography listed in *Who's Who*. [Typically, Humphrey conveniently dropped any mention of his ADA membership in the 1964 edition of *Who's Who*—feeling he had a better chance at the nomination by not stressing his radical ties.]

"His program is clear from his record . . . and his record is clearly one of the most radical in Congress. During his fifteen years in the Senate, he has voted the official ADA line on 191 occasions and has voted no on only three occasions."

Miller continued: "Today our nation confronts many grave and dangerous crises in every area of the world. Perhaps the greatest threat to peace and freedom comes from Red China. American soldiers have already fought this threat in Korea and are fighting it today in Laos and South Viet Nam. Do we want a Vice President from the Americans for Democratic Action, which advocates diplomatic recognition of Red China . . . which advocates the admission of Red China to the United Nations . . . which advocates removal of the travel ban so that Chinese Communists can come travel through this country . . .?

"The American people have learned through bitter experience that a coalition government with the Communists today means a Communist satellite government tomorrow. Nowhere is this more clear than in Laos, communism's latest acquisition. Do we want a Vice President from the Americans for Democratic Action, which advocates that we now extend this same disastrous coalition program to Cambodia, to Viet Nam, and indeed to all of Southeast Asia. . . ?

"Communism in Cuba stands today as the greatest single threat to peace and freedom in our own hemisphere. Only recently, the O.A.S. condemned Castro for his attempts to export communism to other Latin and South American countries. Even today, the presence of Soviet troops just 90 miles from our own shores—together with reports that offensive missiles still remain there—makes our own national security questionable. Do we want as a Vice President the vice chairman of the Americans for

Democratic Action, which advocates that both the United States and the O.A.S. adopt a completely "hands-off" policy toward Castro . . . not even economic sanctions . . . which, as a matter of fact, urges that we re-admit Cuba to the O.A.S. and welcome Castro into the Alliance for Progress, to pour upon him gifts of our own American economic aid. . . ?"

The Miller speech had struck a sensitive nerve among top Democrats, who didn't exactly relish the fact that Humphrey's record was being unveiled in this fashion. Senate Majority Leader Mike Mansfield protested that Humphrey had opposed some of ADA's stands and Senate Foreign Relations Committee Chairman William Fulbright—who normally agrees with the ADA—fulminated that Miller was guilty of "foul-mouthed vituperation." (Fulbright, however, didn't mind comparing Goldwater with Mao Tse-tung.)

Humphrey, it was true, had not gone along with every jot and tittle of every ADA resolution ever passed, but he could not escape responsibility for its leftist hue. He was founder, past chairman and vice chairman of the ADA. He had been intimately involved with it since its birth. Even now as he was running for the Vice Presidency he was still a member (though he had resigned as ADA vice chairman when he was nominated).

And there could be no mistaking the positions of the ADA: they were far, far to the Left. Since its inception in 1947, the ADA, while non-Communist, has tilted to the port side of the political spectrum. Within the United States, it was bent on spreading the gospel of the welfare state and scattering the seeds of socialism. The first foreign lecturer to tour the United States under ADA auspices was Jennie Lee, a leading British socialist and wife of left-wing socialist Aneurin Bevan. Elucidating economic doctrine, the ADA's house organ, the *ADA World*, revealed its sympathy toward socialism in the March 29, 1947, issue, claiming that "there must be drastic regulation, dispersal, and, in some cases, public acquisition of (American business) monopolies. . . ."[10]

The organization regularly sent its members to England to study socialism, and the January 27, 1950 *ADA World* supported the socialists for re-election in England. As ADA's national chairman, Humphrey himself enthusiastically welcomed a Labor victory.[11] Steeped in socialist thought, the ADA group feverishly fought for rampant federal control over the economy. Centralization of power in the federal government pervades every economic issue to which the ADA addresses itself. A research paper on the ADA put out by the Republican National Committee reveals the broad outlines of its philosophy. Some typical quotes culled by the committee from successive ADA platforms: "The government must undertake to build firm foundations for enduring prosperity by bold, long-range programs for the development of our resources, the rebuilding of our cities, the elimination of our slums, and the provision of full and equal opportunities for health, education and security for all our people."

"Government subsidies and financing and, if necessary, government plants must be used to provide more power, more steel and other vitally necessary raw materials."

"Housing goals must be set by the federal government."

A year never goes by when the ADA isn't calling for massive increases in federal spending over the previous year on housing, health, education, slums, public power, mass transit, recreational centers and other assorted welfare programs.

Yet domestic socialism—or one of its variations—isn't ADA's only goal. While ADA was founded as an anti-Communist organization within the framework of the democratic Left in the United States, it has, more often than not, advanced a program of wholesale appeasement of the Communists in foreign affairs. Even back in 1947—according to friendly biographer Clifton Brock—the ADA, after considerable internal struggle, just barely backed the Truman Doctrine of giving military aid to Greece and Turkey to prevent a Communist takeover. On the other hand, as Brock revealingly points out, the ADA enthusiastically embraced the Marshall Plan because it "omitted the military aid features which had turned many of them against the Doctrine, it pledged U.S. aid not to two small and reactionary regimes, but to all of Europe, *including Russia. . . .*"[12] (emphasis added).

The ADA's Obedient Servant

The ADA has continued to take a "soft-on-communism" approach. It has called for total disarmament under United Nations control, aid to Communist countries (including, as noted, the Soviet Union), a hands-off attitude toward Cuba, military withdrawal of American forces from Western Europe, recognition of East Germany, U.N. control over Panama, and U.N. control of major portions of Southeast Asia.

As an active "Red China lobby," it has drawn up an enormous rehabilitation program for mainland China, including recognition, admission to the United Nations, inclusion in international nuclear talks and removal of U.S. trade and passport barriers applying to it.

As James Burnham documented in his study, "Does ADA Run the New Frontier?," the organization has equally tried to rehabilitate Castro's Cuba. ADA welcomed Castro's assumption to power, and fifteen months after his takeover Prof. Robert J. Alexander could write in the April, 1960 issue of *ADA World* that Castro's condemnation of the United States was deserved because of "the recent history of our relations with the Latin American countries."

"The Cuban crisis," an ADA editorial stated in October, 1960, " will be solved . . . as the Cubans realize that the rest of Latin America is moving forward with our help. . . . Castro's hold in Cuba comes from what he has done for the people, not what he has done for the Russians."

In February, 1962, the ADA remained unbothered by the fact that Cuba was rapidly being transformed into a Soviet military base. Noted the *ADA World:* "Action by the U.S. to intervene militarily or to support military invasion by Cuban exiles . . . would be not only wrong but self-defeating. . . . (This is) no time to take unilateral economic sanctions against Cuba."[13]

Regarding the war in Viet Nam, it has continued to oppose military escalation, the northern bombing, and in fact has insisted that the United States recognize the Viet Cong and bring them into a coalition government.

It is no wonder that Gus Hall, Moscow-trained head of the U.S. Communist Party, had praise for the ADA in the June 23,

1963 *Worker*, because of its role in turning America leftward. The "serious Left," said Hall, must work within the Democratic Party to shape left-wing movements and issues and "on many of these issues the ADA has fulfilled a limited role."[14]

Perhaps Humphrey could not be blamed for every one of the utterances of the ADA, but he had fostered it, spoken for it, and lent it his prestige over the years. And over those years its members—particularly under the Kennedy Administration—had managed to gain influential jobs in government. ADA members like Arthur Schlesinger, Jr., Arthur Goldberg, Orville Freeman, Ted Sorensen, John Kenneth Galbraith and others became major powers in the American governmental system.

If Humphrey was not directly responsible for all of its programs, pronouncements and influence, he was certainly indirectly responsible. And if he had vigorously opposed its stands, then why hadn't he resigned? Other liberals—notably David McDonald, former head of the Steelworkers union and Sal Hoffman, head of the Upholsterer's union—dropped out of ADA because of its left-wing extremism, but not Hubert Humphrey. Along with the socialist-minded Walter Reuther and Arthur Schlesinger, Jr., he remained with ADA for the purpose of enhancing its prestige.

The point, of course, is that Humphrey didn't oppose its positions on major issues of the day. Miller had accurately stated that on 194 votes tabulated by ADA, Humphrey had voted with the organization 191 times. That, alone, would suggest a striking similarity in philosophy. And when he has disagreed with the ADA he has abjectly apologized. On June 20, 1957, Humphrey rose on the Senate floor to state:

"So far as the ADA is concerned, I, too, am one of its officers. I think it no secret that on occasion this great organization has seen fit to chastise me, and perhaps properly so. Perhaps I did not understand why at the moment but their judgment was undoubtedly better than mine."[15]

The ADA had not changed by 1964—and neither had Humphrey. Indeed, Humphrey's name is attached to the radical program ADA presented in that year to the platform committee of the Democratic National Committee at Atlantic City, N.J. Insisting that the trouble with the United States is that it doesn't like "big" government, the ADA requested the Democrats to adopt in their platform plank an "accelerated public works program," a "large-scale public housing program," and the establishment of more TVAs. It also suggested that the Democrats promise to "increase public employment by developing comprehensive programs to meet the unmet needs of the American people."

In the field of internal security, the ADA demanded the elimination of laws and congressional committees that maintain it. "First and foremost," said ADA, "we pledge the abolition of the House Un-American Activities Committee and the Senate Committee [*sic*] on Internal Security. . . . We pledge to those who have been dismissed in the past as loyalty or security risks the opportunity to have their cases re-examined on their merits. . . . We pledge the repeal of statutory provisions limiting such freedoms, such as those contained in the Smith Act, the Internal Security Act of 1950, and the Communist Control Act of 1954. We pledge the abolition of the Attorney General's list of subversive organizations." The House Committee on Un-American Activities has conducted literally scores of investigations which have notably improved America's internal security. As a result of its probes, the HCUA has helped to clean the Communists out of the movie industry and security risks out of the super-secret National Security Agency. The Committee, of course, was also responsible for the exposure of Alger Hiss. Under the Smith Act, high-ranking American Communists have been convicted and sent to jail. The Senate Internal Security Subcommittee has proved an invaluable source for scholars on the subject of communism. But the elimination or castration of such legal anti-Communist instruments does not bother the ADA; indeed, it welcomes their destruction.

Nor has ADA's foreign policy grown more resistant to the blandishments of communism. The 1964 platform called for "unilateral" disarmament initiatives on the part of the United States; the extension of "neutralism" to Southeast Asia (to be guaranteed, in part, by "mainland China"); recognition of Red China; and "the lifting of barriers to trade in nonstrategic goods with mainland China."[16]

Not only did Humphrey permit his name to be attached to this radical platform, but during the campaign he sought out and used as speech writers ADA chairman John P. Roche and ADA vice chairman Arthur Schlesinger, Jr. At that time both Roche and Schlesinger were taking dovish positions on the war in Viet Nam. Roche, too, had long been in favor of pro-socialist, "soft-on-communism" doctrine. And so, too, had Schlesinger. In 1964, Schlesinger told columnist Henry Taylor that he would "neither withdraw nor apologize" for a 1947 article in which he had claimed, "There seems no inherent obstacle to the gradual advance of socialism in the United States through a series of New Deals. . . ." Thus, despite Senator Fulbright, it was not exactly "foul-mouthed vituperation" to throw the ADA issue up at the "mellowing" Hubert Humphrey in 1964.

22

The "New" Humphrey I

Humphrey's ties to the ADA are only one test of his essential radicalism. Another test involves specific votes and pronouncements made on specific issues. And despite the persistent argument that he had mellowed by 1964, it was difficult to see how his own philosophy differed from the ADA's own socialist and "soft-on-communism" precepts.

In the field of domestic legislation, it is clear that he fully accepted the ADA's belief in galloping federal intervention into the economy. A compilation of Humphrey's voting record on key issues from 1949 through 1964 was put out by the nonpartisan *Congressional Quarterly*. Of the 156 votes recorded, one cannot find any—not one—in which Humphrey voted to cut spending in domestic affairs. There is the overwhelming feeling that Humphrey would ante up the federal pot no matter what the price or the purpose. Nor is there any measure on which he voted that he would reduce the awesome power of the federal government. Like the ADA, he has been for peacetime price and rent controls, seizure of private industry through executive powers, a rapid proliferation of public power projects, for more rather than less federal aid to education, more aid to foreign countries—preferably channelled through the United Nations—and against cuts in appropriations for the executive departments or public works appropriations—even when proposed by such stalwart liberals as Sen. Paul Douglas.

Humphrey had been a sponsor of medicare-type legislation as early as 1949, and he was instrumental in pushing "Food for Peace" and the Peace Corps programs through the Congress. Mass transportation, federal aid to housing, extended unemployment benefits, aid to depressed areas, increased Social Security benefits, aid to veterans, aid to veterinarians, etc., Humphrey had a voracious appetite for spending, and to list the federal projects Humphrey favored and favors is long and probably endless.

In 1953, he peremptorily decided that the cattle raisers of the country should start getting a subsidy because of a decline in cattle prices—even though the prices were higher at that time than during the midst of the Korean War, when there was a worldwide boom on for cattle. Commenting on Humphrey's proposal, the Chicago *Tribune* remarked: "There have been no cooperative moans from the prospective beneficiaries of this generosity. The American cattle industry is the one major segment of agriculture which has never received government subsidies, except for some minor payments under OPA, hasn't asked for them, and doesn't want them."[1] Nevertheless, for Humphrey, a government subsidy was the right nostrum for almost any economic ailment.

Humphrey came to the Senate in 1948 broke, but by 1964, according to his own statement, his net worth was $180,000; thus he had managed to put aside the tidy sum of $11,000 or so per year. But Humphrey obviously didn't apply the same "penny earned, penny saved" philosophy to the federal government. A "balanced budget," he proclaimed in 1953, is a "futile dream." In typical Humphreyana, he declared that income would never meet outgo until the "world is in balance. . . ." Whatever those words actually meant, it was a cinch that Humphrey was not calling for government economy.

"There is one factor—one condition—in the executive branch which does cause concern," Humphrey complained in 1959, the year in which the Republican administration had, up to that time, scored the biggest budget and biggest peacetime budget deficit in history. "It is what I call 'budget-itis,'" Humphrey opined, "a condition which spreads like contagion from the accountant of the Bureau of the Budget." Just seven days after the record $12.5-billion deficit was history, Humphrey could not refrain from saying: "This is an administration with a bookkeeper's mentality, which is more interested in dollar signs and ledger books than in the real problems, needs and desires of the American people."[2]

Humphrey once paid a curious tribute to the late President Roosevelt—considered a wild spendthrift in his day—for his "wisdom in curtailing expenditures." Humphrey could get positively irate when spending cuts were proposed by some of his colleagues. "If some member of Congress offers a little two-bit amendment in the name of economy to cut off $25 million from the school lunch program," he once snapped waspishly, "or $100 million from the soil conservation program, that makes him a hero for economy!"[3] Not everyone thinks of a $100 million proposed spending cut as a "two-bit amendment" for economy, but Humphrey was not everyone.

Humphrey was positively succinct about his spending philosophy on still another occasion: "I have always said that between the platforms of Santa Claus and Scrooge, I will stick with jolly Santa. Any time anyone wants to run on that platform, they can count me in. . . ."[4]

No issue ever really seemed too insignificant for Humphrey's wide-ranging interests. Thus, with equal fervor he could be found fostering a federal crusade to wipe out "noxious weeds," promoting a federal "home-gardening program to assist needy persons," or trying to get the Congress to erect a monument in Washington, D.C. for the wildly radical Floyd B. Olson, the late Minnesota governor.

In 1963 he demanded the establishment of a "Conservation Hall of Fame" that "will honor the men who have worked to protect and conserve the natural resources and beauty of our land." With visions of our government cranking out super athletes that could defeat any opponent, Humphrey thoughtfully called for the creation of a federal sports agency in 1964. "Never again," Humphrey solemnly intoned with atypical chauvinism, "should our country run a mere eighth, as we unfortunately did in the Winter Olympics in Austria."

Contemplating Humphrey's penchant for spending the taxpayers' dollars, columnist Raymond Moley, once a key adviser to the late FDR, remarked in the Los Angeles *Times:* "The infinite variety of Sen. Hubert Humphrey's contrivances to spend taxpayers' money and to thrust the federal proboscis into private affairs is a source of amazement, wonder and occasionally, a source of innocent merriment.

"No cranny of our civilization escapes his roving eye and no subject flags his energetic tongue. Recently, he unfolded in the Senate a scheme to federalize what he calls the 'living arts.' "

Moley sarcastically suggested that Humphrey had added deeply to our knowledge about this subject by revealing there were now 10 arts rather than the proverbial seven. The Minnesota Senator explained that he wanted to "expand our counter-offensive" in this area and to implement this activity through a federal advisory commission that would plan handouts to would-be artists and the establishment of a national gallery. "We already have a national gallery in Washington," noted Moley, "but since it was contributed by Andrew Mellon, the Senator probably believes that it smells too much of capitalism and harbors too much bourgeois art."[5] Humphrey, of course, has had the last laugh, for the Great Society, beginning in 1964, had already begun federal subsidization of the arts in a grand manner, including the funnelling of funds to the "hate-whitey" plays of black racist LeRoi Jones.

A global giveaway artist, Humphrey has always been seeking new ways to pour the taxpayers' funds overseas as well as at home. "We should increase substantially our foreign aid program in all its aspects," he said in June of 1959, just after Ike had submitted his multi-billion dollar foreign aid budget. Indicative of his attitude about shovelling money abroad was the statement: "Some of our colleagues sometimes say that a country occasionally defaults on a loan. So what?"[6]

And for Humphrey, as for the ADA, there is always a spanking new scheme lurking just around the corner. "The Council of Economic Advisers," he wrote in *The War on Poverty* in 1964, when he had reportedly metamorphosed into a moderate, "states that every family's income could be brought above the $3,000 cut-off point by a direct subsidy of $11 billion a year to the lowest income groups. . . . Certainly this nation could pay such a price, if need be, to provide a reasonable standard of living for all citizens." Humphrey did not suggest scrapping other welfare programs by replacing it with this new plan; he implied that he wanted it added to the existing welfare programs on the books.

Humphrey has repeatedly denied he is a socialist, but he has consistently held a hostile view of business and has favored a socialistic approach to the economy. Part of this may stem from the influence of his father or his teachers at the University of Minnesota, or from Max Kampelman, who was Humphrey's legislative counsel from 1949 through 1955 and is still very close to Humphrey today. When Humphrey was running for office in 1948, Kampelman belonged to a group that openly supported Socialist candidate Norman Thomas for President. Along with ADA members like Benjamin McLaurin, Kampelman signed a statement endorsing Thomas that said: "We believe that the United States needs a President who stands for peace and against the get-tough policies of the Democratic and Republican parties and the war-breeding appeasement of the Communist-dominated Wallace movement.

"America needs a President who opposes the 'free enterprise' slogans of Truman, Taft and Wallace—slogans which have led us repeatedly into the jaws of cruel unemployment and misery. America needs a President who will bring us democratic social ownership of America's major industries. . . .

"And America needs a mass political party of all workers of hand and brain dedicated to a program like that of the British Labor Party."[7]

Whether it was through Kampelman's persuasion or not, Humphrey championed such socialistic measures as peacetime price and rent controls and demanded the seizure of American industry. As Mayor of Minneapolis, he called for seizure of company plants when they violated union concepts of economic justice. Rather than have the government use the union-hated Taft-Hartley law to solve the 1952 steel crisis, Humphrey vigorously supported the President's unconstitutional seizure of the steel mills.

Actually, Humphrey had championed the federal government's seizure of private industry a few months after he had come to Washington as a Senator. In May of 1949, for example, he had publicly called for the Congress to pass a law that would permit the government in a national emergency to take over a plant or industry lock, stock and barrel, including the profits and loss.[8]

Humphrey favored the government's using the mailed-fist approach toward the steel industry in 1962 as well as in 1952. In the spring of 1962, President Kennedy received word from major steel companies that they were going to implement their first hike in prices since 1958. Though neither the President nor his economic advisers had ever met a business payroll, Kennedy asserted in cold anger at his press conference the next day that "there is no justification for an increase in steel prices." Moreover, he aimed a series of hammer blows at the companies for the purpose of getting them to rescind the price increase. Barely had the steel firms announced their decision when they began to feel the entire weight of the federal government on their backs. Federal Trade Commission Chairman Paul Rand Dixon announced April 11 that the FTC had begun an informal inquiry into the possible violation of a 1951 consent order barring the steel industry from collusive price fixing. The Justice Department threatened anti-trust action; the Treasury suggested a tax penalty would be imposed; and Administration-controlled Congressional committees promised probes of the industry. In addition, the Defense Department, by-passing the competitive bidding process, began automatically awarding defense contracts to companies which had not raised their prices. Under such pressure, the companies rolled back their price hikes, but the brass-knuckling of the industry caused consternation in the business community and JFK's popularity among businessmen fell to a low ebb. Nevertheless, Humphrey upheld as perfectly proper the President's brazen interference in the steel companies' right to raise their prices.[9]

So enthralled has Humphrey been with socialistic concepts for American business that in 1959 he called for the United States to begin "a seven-year plan of our own."[10]

Pointing out that the seven-year plan was a Soviet concept, the *Wall Street Journal* editorialized that "Everything possible is wrong with this idea. First, it is asking the U.S. to imitate the Soviet Union, which could only mean abandoning the free-market economy and replacing it with a centrally and politically directed economy. Indeed, Mr. Humphrey said as much: 'It is time we took planning out of the dog house and put it in the White House.' " Quite apart from the dubious political implications of the scheme, said the *Journal*, the system of the planned economy doesn't work. "The Soviets have been trying to make it work for some 40 years and they have repeatedly had to resort to imitations of capitalistic practice. . . ."

At any rate, declared the *Journal*, not central planning but "the complex interaction of millions of individual economic judgments and adjustments is the powerhouse that has generated our present living standards and the push to future economic growth. . . . Yet it is this free economy, truly the marvel of the ages, that Senator Humphrey apparently wants to junk. . . ."[11]

Humphrey's love affair for socialism hasn't seemed to lessen much over the years. To bone up on the latest socialist doctrine, he, along with one other American, UAW president Walter Reuther, sojourned to the Socialist Conference held in Harpsund, Sweden on July 13-14, 1963. While Humphrey's trip was obscured from the American public, the *Socialist International Information*, a weekly newsletter published in London for socialists throughout the world, reported on August 3, 1963, that the meeting took place at the invitation of the Socialist Prime Minister of Sweden, Tage Erlander. In addition to Humphrey and Reuther, those present included such European socialists as

Herbert Wehner and Willy Brandt (the Chairman and Vice Chairman of the German Social Democratic Party) and Harold Wilson (the British Labor Party leader).

Nowhere has Humphrey been more outrageous—or more radical—than in his demands for socialistic programs for the American farmer. As Senator from the largely agricultural state of Minnesota, he relentlessly pushed for huge agricultural subsidies. High price supports, government loans, paying the farmers not to farm, farm trade with Communist countries, tax-exemptions for co-ops, sale of surplus food abroad at subsidized rates, school lunch programs, food stamps, guaranteed income—Humphrey beat the drums for these farmer "welfare" measures and many more. Humphrey's motives were as much political as ideological, for there was no doubt he liked to curry the farmers' vote with the taxpayers' money. In the 1960 campaign, in fact, Humphrey would unabashedly seek votes from the farmer by proclaiming: "I have never swerved or hesitated in my support of the REA [Rural Electrification Administration] programs, or the soil conservation or public power programs that are so vital to the American farmer. Not every political candidate can make that claim."[12]

On September 7, 1950, Sen. Styles Bridges (R.-N.H.) launched a full-scale attack on the National Farmers Union, claiming it had been infiltrated by Communists. Bridges' speech documented the fact that Communists, Communist-fronters and Soviet apologists had penetrated the leadership of the NFU. He revealed that the president of the North Dakota Farmers Union, who was also chairman of the Farmers Union national executive committee, boasted that he welcomed Communists into the organization. Bridges claimed that "Archie Wright, president of the Northeastern Farmers Union," had been identified under oath as a Communist by two former Communists. He also demonstrated that such well-known liberals as Gardner Jackson, former legislative representative of the Farmers Union in Washington, had been drummed out of the organization because of their opposition to communism. Jackson, himself, had related in a letter that he was booted out because of his "insistent, uncagey, and unsilenceable opposition to Communist infiltration to official positions of power of NFU." Jackson's letter also charged that James G. Patton, head of the Farmers Union, had a great tolerance for Communists and pro-Communists and appointed them to various important positions.[13]

Not unexpectedly, Humphrey immediately sprang to the NFU's defense. Though unable to deny Bridges' accusations—indeed, they were obviously true—Humphrey denounced the charges as nothing more than "warmed-over dried biscuits—the same old accusations coming out again and again in an effort to frighten the American people."[14] There was, of course, every reason Humphrey might want to defend the Farmers Union, since it had a large following in Minnesota and since it favored Humphrey's own policies of greater federal aid to almost everyone, particularly the farmer.

Humphrey has always been inclined to statist agriculture. For many years he was a champion of the Brannan farm plan. Under this proposed program, which even Democratic Congresses repeatedly turned down, the farmer could sell his products on the open market for whatever he could get and the government would directly pay him the difference between an average market price and a high price the government believed the farmer should receive. Along with this munificence went stringent government controls, but the farmer would be virtually guaranteed a profit at the expense of the American public.

In discussing a proposed farm program once, Sen. Spessard Holland asked Humphrey: "Does the Senator from Minnesota agree with me that a price support program calling for 100 per cent government price supports on all farm products, both perishable and storable, on a family-unit basis, with the announced purpose to force thereby a redistribution of land and a division of the profits of the land is socialism, pure and simple?" Humphrey replied: "No, I do not agree with the Senator."[15]

Humphrey constantly cried for the scalp of Ezra Taft Benson, Ike's Secretary of Agriculture, because Benson thought the American farmers should not necessarily have a guaranteed high income, that parity—or the support price—on commodities should be lowered, and that the government might reduce its control over how much the farmer could produce or sell. Yet not only was he a critic of Benson, who rejoiced in the free enterprise concept for the American farmer, but he rather marveled at the *Soviet* system of agriculture.

In May of 1959, Humphrey issued the astonishing prediction that within five years Russia would "start pushing the United States out of world markets" with its own agricultural surpluses.[16] He claimed that the Russians would develop surpluses in cereal grains, fats and oils and dairy products.

Communist countries, of course, are notorious for their inability to produce surplus agricultural commodities, and why Humphrey was so admiring of Soviet farming methods is still a darkly kept secret.

One wonders what he thought when, in 1963, the Soviets came to the Western countries, hat in hand, for enormous quantities of wheat because of poor harvests in their great agricultural paradise. By 1968, the Soviets still have not caught up to America's farmers. While the U.S. was literally giving away billions of dollars worth of food to the outside world, the Soviets were unable to supply food to their own satellites. "In order not to default entirely on her trade agreements," wrote Fred Smith, a retired Naval Intelligence officer and a long-time observer of Soviet bloc operations, "the U.S.S.R. often imports food from the West to sell to her satellites. As an example, many times Soviet ships have loaded wheat in Canada and sailed directly to Havana, Cuba, to unload. . . ."

In 1966, according to Smith, Czechoslovakia was compelled to import 800,000 tons of grain from the West because the U.S.S.R. could not supply it. Even France delivered a million tons of wheat to the U.S.S.R. in 1966. "One of Moscow's top planners," Smith continued, "recently admitted that American farm labor is four times as productive as Russian farm labor. . . . Therefore, in spite of an occasional good harvest or reports of various farm improvements, it is doubtful that the Soviets can feed themselves or their satellites, without importing from the West for years to come, if ever."[17]

As an admirer of Soviet agriculture, Humphrey did not find it difficult to embrace a farm plan outlined by John F. Kennedy in 1960 and introduced to the Congress in 1961. In fact, Humphrey had worked closely with Orville Freeman—his protégé and Kennedy's Secretary of Agriculture—in its formation. Under this plan, the Secretary of Agriculture would be invested with increased coercive power over the individual farmer and would have an enormous say over what and how much he could produce for the free market. The American Farm Bureau Federation, the biggest of the nation's farm organizations, blasted the program—whose main features were eventually scrapped—as a "bid to concentrate unprecedented power over the destiny of American agriculture in the executive branch of government." With a strong bent toward free enterprise, the farm bureau's outburst was not unexpected. But criticism was also levied by a surprise source: the late Henry Wallace, a former Secretary of Agriculture and Humphrey's radical adversary during the late 1940's. Wallace, who had many times expressed socialistic views regarding agriculture, said he had "grave concern" over the Kennedy program. "I think," he continued, "it would require stricter controls than they have in most Communist countries."

"A similar plan was proposed in the depression days," he said, "but when I became Secretary of Agriculture I found there was no way to put it across unless we tied up everything tight as a drum and raised tariffs to match."[18]

Norman Thomas, six times the Socialist candidate for President, was not without his reasons when he said in 1964 that Humphrey was his choice for President and that he "is the type of Democrat I like and one who would be a Socialist if he got to England."[19]

23

The "New" Humphrey II

How was it that the idea spread that Humphrey had mellowed? Part of the explanation, no doubt, is that the entire country had turned to the Left under Kennedy and Johnson, and Humphrey's proposals no longer appeared as outlandish as they had when such men as Taft, Knowland and Lyndon Johnson (who appeared far more conservative as a Senator) had ruled the Senate. On occasion, moreover, Humphrey enjoyed shedding his Santa suit and posturing before the electorate as a man with a tight grip on the public purse who championed the free enterprise system. Though Humphrey actually voted constantly to tax and spend—and even hailed the philosophy behind it—he was not averse to switching images for the purpose of tossing a few bones to some of his more conservative supporters.

Thus, even at the very time he was helping to support and write a farm program that Henry Wallace could say was similar to Communist farm programs, he could blithely contend—as he did on March 10, 1961—that he had "become skeptical of what we call the rigid control program. I make this statement frankly because in my earlier days in the Senate I argued vigorously for the most rigid type of controls."[1]

Humphrey relished making economy noises when it suited his purposes, such as the time he lambasted Sen. Harry Byrd's committee on nonessential federal expenditures as "extravagant" precisely because it was doing what Humphrey really didn't want: saving the government money. While voting to hock future taxpayers up to their ears in welfare measures, he could be quoted as saying, "Either we learn how to properly utilize the vast sums of public revenues and how to appropriately control and manage their use, or we will bleed our economy into an impoverished condition."[2] Discussing President Eisenhower's request to raise the debt limit in 1958, Humphrey asserted: "I don't think we should rush into this pell mell." With thoroughgoing piety, Humphrey said he felt such big decisions ought to be carefully and thoughtfully pondered.

For years, also, Humphrey capitalized on a conservative approach to financing education by pushing legislation which permitted parents to deduct student educational expenses from their taxes. This sort of legislation, of course, avoided federal controls and Humphrey's support for it lent the impression that he was gradually turning away from the concept of a coercive central government. In actuality, however, Humphrey continued to press for both this measure *and* direct federal school subsidies to the states. For Humphrey, the tax-deductible approach was never an alternative to the direct subsidy; and, indeed, when the two came in conflict he opted for the subsidy. On Feb. 4, 1964, for example, Sen. Abraham Ribicoff, a liberal Democrat from Connecticut, introduced an amendment—similar to legislation previously sponsored by Humphrey—that would have allowed students or parents a tax credit for college expenses for tuition, books, fees and similar costs on a sliding scale up to a maximum credit of $325. Sen. Barry Goldwater, who had also been introducing such legislation for years, voted in its favor, but not Humphrey. In turning down the amendment, Humphrey felt impelled to rely upon conservative argumentation. "I have sponsored similar legislation for many years," he related, "and I have been deeply concerned with the plight of parents seeking to provide their children with the advantages of a college education. I still express this concern and will continue to seek federal assistance in their behalf. . . ." But, said Humphrey, "The adoption of this [Ribicoff] amendment, however meritorious . . . would wreak havoc with the federal budget."[3]

Humphrey's solicitous plea for the federal budget was interesting but hardly believable, and political observers think Humphrey actually betrayed his pledge to college students because the Ribicoff measure would have weakened the chances for passage of the Administration's federal aid to education bill, a proposal preferable to Humphrey since it involved federal taxes and federal controls, and because Sen. Russell Long, the Administration's floor manager, had made it clear the "amendment is not recommended by the Executive Department"—words which always carried considerable weight with Humphrey when a Democratic Administration was in power.

Whatever the reason, it revealed Humphrey's resourcefulness in attempting to create—from time to time—the impression that he was inspired with conservative instincts. Such gimmicks shouldn't have fooled anybody, but apparently Humphrey found such stunts sly enough to outsmart many of his fellow Minnesotans and those reporters who were touting Humphrey as a "moderate" in 1964.

Humphrey's vote in 1959 for the Landrum-Griffin labor reform law—an act despised by union leaders—has also led some people into believing that Humphrey has the stamina to rebuff the wishes of organized labor. Yet, as shall be shown, Humphrey voted precisely the way the union leaders wanted him to on this law. Far from resisting organized labor's demands, Humphrey has slavishly pursued them. Invariably he has done its bidding, whether on voting for minimum wage increases, endorsing federal welfare schemes, or campaigning for the repeal of labor laws that dissatisfy union bosses.

Humphrey's labor union loyalty has been long-standing. In forming the Democratic-Farmer-Labor Party, Humphrey relied heavily on union support; in fact, the unions controlled the party. As mayor of Minneapolis, he bowed to almost every whim of the unions and he rode into the Senate on a wave of union support. Figures on file with the Clerk of the Senate disclose that Humphrey's major contributions in three Senate campaigns came from unions like the United Auto Workers and the United Steelworkers. And the labor unions have received more than their money's worth. Since coming to the Senate in 1949, Humphrey has never deviated from a pro-union position—including his vote on Landrum-Griffin. The AFL-CIO's political arm, COPE, has scored Humphrey on 60 major votes throughout his Senate career. On every single vote, Humphrey sided with big labor. Through 1964, he had consistently urged passage of legislation which would scrap two major sections of Taft-Hartley, the injunction provision which permits the federal government to prevent for 80 days a strike that threatens serious harm to the nation, and the right-to-work provision. Contrary to popular conception, the right-to-work clause does not automatically allow a worker to hold a job without belonging to a union; all it does is permit the states to pass laws along these lines. But Humphrey never even endorsed this small measure of states' rights and voluntarism because of organized labor's opposition.

Humphrey's willingness to toady to the union bosses—not the average working man—is notorious. During his years in the Senate, for example, he boycotted the Senate recording studio because the unions call it a "non-union, low-wage shop." During the 1959 steel strike, Humphrey's picture was flashed in *Solidarity,* the United Auto Workers' house organ, dropping money into the steel striker's fund.[4] In 1960, as noted in a previous chapter, he lined up with pickets outside the J. I. Case Company to sing the militant labor song, "Solidarity Forever," and root for the union to "bring the company to its knees." A more brazen bias by a legislator in favor of unions would be difficult to discover.

Accused in 1964 of wearing non-union underwear, Humphrey fired off an indignant denial to the Amalgamated Clothing Workers, "but whether he stepped into a booth and provided visual evidence of the label is not reported," the Chicago *Tribune* remarked sarcastically. It added: "We should have thought that Hubert's abject loyalty to the union bosses was by now so thoroughly documented that no question of his fealty would ever arise. But union party discipline apparently is so rigid that a political slave must be regimented right down to his lingerie. 'Love us,' the labor bosses growl, 'and wear our products next to your epidermis.' "[5]

Humphrey was not above condoning labor union violence either. He condoned it as mayor of Minneapolis, and he winked at it as Senator. In June of 1950, armed pickets ambushed workmen attempting to enter the rayon plant of the American Enka Company at Morristown, Tennessee, riddled an automobile with rifle fire and wounded three men, one so severely he was expected to die. The gunmen were identified and a grand jury returned indictments within 24 hours. The Morristown strike, conducted by the CIO United Textile Workers, had been marked with frequent disorders and, finally, Gov. Gordon Browning of Tennessee sent national guardsmen to reinforce local officers and state police, who found themselves badly outnumbered by union mobs. Instead of condemning the union goons, Humphrey decided to go down to Morristown to see whether Gov. Browning was "justified" in calling out the guard.[6]

Nine years later, Humphrey was still appeasing union militants. In Albert Lea, Minnesota, after mobs of strikers had clashed with non-union workers in the Wilson & Company meat packing plant, Minnesota's Democratic Gov. Orville Freeman, Humphrey's protégé, sent state militia into Albert Lea after the local police (members of a union affiliated with the AFL-CIO) had failed to maintain order. Instead of protecting workers who wished to enter the plant, the commander of the militia announced, "the plant is closed . . . there is martial law. There will be no production. Go on home." The glee of the strikers was not concealed. One of them said, "It makes a beautiful picket line, doesn't it?" pointing to the guardsmen as they stopped workmen at the plant gates. In short, by resorting to violence the union strikers won their major objective of getting the plant closed and thereby preventing operation by non-strikers. While editorials scored Freeman and a three-man federal court castigated him for bowing "to the demands of a law-violating mob," Humphrey supported Freeman's action and accused Wilson—an enlightened company—of "living in the dark ages."[7]

Humphrey's lack of concern for union violations of law and order was further demonstrated in 1962 when he used his political influence with the Justice Department to have a long-time political crony and former Minnesota DFL National Committeeman Ray Hemenway appointed as a United States Marshal. News stories datelined Albert Lea in February, 1935, tell of grand jury indictments and jail sentences involving Hemenway and others on a charge of using force and violence in a labor dispute at a local foundry. Hemenway and the others pleaded guilty to "gross misdemeanor, unlawfully entering a building with intent to commit a felony or any malicious mischief," and were sentenced to 60 days in jail at hard labor. Two years later, in 1937, newspapers reported a second incident. The headline in one paper read: "Ray Hemenway and 50 Others Barricade Themselves in Union Hall. Missiles Thrown at Deputies by Union Men."[8] Nevertheless, Humphrey felt no qualms about making him a marshal.

The belief that Humphrey "bucked" union labor with his vote for the Landrum-Griffin labor reform act of 1959 is not true, though the myth has taken hold even in some Republican quarters in Minnesota. Humphrey did vote for this act, which labor opposed, but what is forgotten is that organized labor itself refused to condemn any Senator for his vote on final passage. Recognizing the intense pressures upon Congress to enact some labor reform law because of the union scandals bared by Sen. John McClellan's rackets committee, the AFL-CIO realized that even its friends would feel compelled to endorse the final version of Landrum-Griffin.

Therefore, the AFL-CIO decided to gauge whether a lawmaker voted pro-labor on Landrum-Griffin by analyzing his stand on key amendments.[9] A look at the record reveals there is no vote Humphrey cast in which he crossed his union friends. In actual fact, the Congress began debating labor reform legislation back in 1958, and both in that year and 1959 Humphrey voted to weaken proposed restrictions on labor unions every time. Among the amendments he opposed were those permitting states and territories to regulate or prohibit strikes in public utilities; allowing states and territories to assert jurisdiction over labor disputes the NLRB declined to handle; and barring access to the NLRB of any union that had not filed with the Secretary of Labor and made available to members certain organizational and financial documents and reports. He also opposed McClellan's famous "Bill of Rights" amendment, which guaranteed union members the right to vote in union elections, nominate candidates, speak at union meetings, participate in union business and be free of arbitrary fines and punishment.

Also forgotten is the fact that Humphrey immediately issued a clarifying statement after his vote for Landrum-Griffin in which he blasted the measure as "punitive." Organized labor, he warned, "should never forget that it was the Republican-Dixiecrat coalition which passed Landrum-Griffin for the purpose of tying labor's hands and making it more difficult to organize—especially in the South." Humphrey explained that when the bill came to the Senate from the House, he and his fellow pro-union legislators did much to rewrite the House version. Though he voted for the softened Senate version and the Senate-House compromise, Humphrey proclaimed that he certainly did not approve of all the features of the final bill. But he insisted he was "firmly convinced that this was the best bill we could get under the circumstances which prevailed."[10]

If Humphrey really thought Landrum-Griffin was as bad as he said, of course, he should have voted against it anyway. His vote, however, made no difference so far as passage was concerned—only two Senators opposed it—and by having it on the record that he voted for Landrum-Griffin Humphrey was able to have his cake and eat it. For though big labor knew full well that Humphrey was in its hip pocket, some citizens in Minnesota were beguiled into believing that their senior Senator was willing to stand up to the unions.

Humphrey's fervent support of union militancy and his fetish for ham-fisted regulation of private industry may spring from a deep-seated antagonism that he has toward business and the free-enterprise system—a bitterness that can be found in most socialists.

During his days as mayor he was calling the National Association of Manufacturers "evil." Back in 1952, he was quoted as saying: ". . . the Association of American Railroads, the private utilities, the investment bankers, they represent special privilege. They have been lobbying the American Congress for years seeking to check progress at every turn. It is about time they were put in their place."[11]

True, that was many years ago. But Humphrey had also revealed his antagonism toward business in later years, as we have seen. Yet Humphrey may have poured out his most vitriolic opinion regarding the American free-enterprise system in 1963—less than a year before he was tapped for the Vice Presidential nomination.

On September 17, 1963, Hubert Humphrey led a group of colleagues in asking the President to proclaim a day of national mourning for four young Negro girls killed in the vicious church bombing in Birmingham, Alabama. That bombing had shocked the nation and had brought outpourings of protest from civilized leaders everywhere—including Gov. George Wallace of Alabama. While most people concluded this malignant bombing had been perpetrated by the Ku Klux Klan or some other fanatical element, Humphrey chose to lay a major share of the blame on the capitalist system and businesses in both the North and South. Here was no "moderate" speaking, but a flaming Populist with Marxist interpretations coursing through his speech.

In passionate, rambling rhetoric, Humphrey stated that the "combined forces of the business and professional leadership in the South—those men who own and control the banks and the factories, the newspapers, the radios, the televisions, who own the land, who are the big contributors to the politicians" were responsible, for they had not created a "rational and humane pattern of equality for the Southern Negro."

Humphrey declared: "I know the power of these men. And I also know that much of their power is linked with, and subservient to, the economic power of the Northern and Eastern banks, insurance companies and other corporations. The responsibility of the Southern establishment for the state of affairs in the South during these past decades must be shared with their associates in the North who have at the very least acquiesced in the policies of racial degradation and humiliation.

"Many large institutions—corporations, manufacturing establishments, and banks—are owned by people in the North. They profess to have policies of equal opportunity in the Northern areas or in the Western areas, but they do not advocate the same policies in the South. . . .

"What is so sickening about the whole matter is that these policies have been to a large degree followed because of money—to save money that might otherwise have been used to educate, to save money that might otherwise have been used to raise workers' salaries and to improve their working conditions.

"It is no accident that those who most loudly espouse the meanest and most reactionary of racist policies also oppose every effort to improve working conditions, to improve education, to provide more social security—not just for Negroes but for all Americans. . . .

"And so—for profit, for money—the whirlwind of racial hatred and violence has been encouraged—not permitted, but encouraged and invited, by the stubborn and determined hard core of segregationists who are reactionary, politically and economically.

"I repeat, they are a limited, small number, but they have maintained control and power, frequently with the help of powerful and political influences in other areas of the country. . . .

". . . When we talk of evil and atheism in Russia and the closing of churches in the Soviet Union, we should think of citizens becoming so deeply moved by hate and passion that they bomb synagogues and bomb churches and kill people who worship. . . ."[12]

From almost every point of view, Humphrey's incredible outburst made little sense. Contrary to Humphrey's description, there is no such thing as one, monolithic South; there are, in fact, many Souths, and the treatment of the Negro varies from state to state and from county to county within the states. Furthermore, the Southern states, both individually and collectively, had made enormous progress in improving job and educational opportunities for the Negroes over the years—and vast proportions of that improvement stemmed from those very industrial and business leaders Humphrey was railing against. These men, particularly in the post World War II years, had moved their businesses into the South's urban areas, expanded opportunities for Negro and white alike, and poured funds into the state treasuries which, in turn, were used to construct hospitals and schools for the benefit of all races. None other than Ralph McGill, the liberal editor of the Atlanta *Constitution,* remarked in his *The South and the Southerner* (1963 version): "Changes came fast at the war's end. Even in 1945 Southerners in cities had ceased to be startled by Negroes appearing on juries. Voting rights, still crudely, often viciously, denied in rural areas, were increasingly granted in the cities. Politicians were seeking those votes and there began to be a more equitable justice in the courts." In short, improvement, when it came, came to the South's industrial areas. "By 1960," stressed McGill, "there was at least a beginning of school desegregation in twelve of sixteen Southern states, including Delaware and Maryland. In 1961, two Negro students were accepted at the University of Georgia, the first break in the heatedly and repeatedly pledged defiance of 'never' by the tier of Deep South cotton states. To one who had been part of it for a lifetime the changes were dramatic."[13]

Finally, it is palpably untrue "that those who most loudly espouse the most reactionary of racist policies also oppose every effort to improve working conditions, to improve education, to provide more social security—not just for Negroes but for all Americans. . . ."

Historically, the well-known racists in this country have been pro-welfarist, and have employed the rhetoric of Populists like Hubert Humphrey. Ben "Pitchfork" Tillman became a master of South Carolina politics by directing hatred toward the Negro and the wealthy merchants and planters alike. Mississippi's James Kimble Vardaman and Georgia's Tom Watson hurled their invectives at the same targets—and drew the support of the Populists.

Alabama's former Gov. George Wallace, who is a modern-day symbol for segregation in the South, learned his political trade at the hands of "Kissin'" Jim Folsom, who was a champion of welfare for the poor. Wallace, himself, has hailed federal handouts and created a miniature welfare state.

Humphrey's outburst revealed less about the traditions of the South than it did about Humphrey's intense feelings concerning business and free enterprise. Whatever else it did, it hardly revealed his supposed "moderation."

The Birmingham speech—as his 1948 speech at the Democratic convention—also laid bare his radical feelings in regard to civil rights. Throughout the years Humphrey, more often than not, has been considered a firebrand on the subject of Negro equality. But, as on other issues, he had tried to bank the fires of zealous righteousness burning within him. Thus, the man who drove much of the South out of the party in 1948 was cooing to segregationists in 1951. At the 1952 convention, he was for a watered-down platform on civil rights. In 1955, the New York *Post's* liberal correspondent William Shannon wondered whether Humphrey was turning conservative because he had refused to join Sen. Herbert Lehman in a fight to dilute the Southerner's mightiest weapon against civil rights legislation: Senate Rule 22, which protects the filibuster.

Humphrey's response was filled with moderating overtones. "I could have made a whiz-bang speech on civil rights on opening day," he asserted. "I like to make speeches and I would have loved to do it." But he added that "an opening day fight on the Rules would have cemented the old Republican-Southern alliance," which, he maintained, would damage the liberals' attempts to reach an accord with the Democratic Southerners on objectives other than civil rights. So "soft" on civil rights had Humphrey become in 1956 that he was arguing that he was not so sure that it was "vitally necessary" to mention specifically in the Democratic platform the Supreme Court decision against racial segregation in the schools.[14]

Some of this "softness" undoubtedly sprung from his desire to soothe Southerners, so he could win at least a Vice Presidential nomination on the Democratic ticket in both 1952 and 1956, but part of it also stemmed from Humphrey's belief that softer tactics not only turneth away wrath but might accomplish more in the final result.

When President Lyndon Johnson tapped Humphrey to steer the 1964 civil rights bill through the Senate, for instance, Humphrey again used the subtle rather than the saber-rattling approach. Anxious that the debate not become bitter, Humphrey resisted suggestions to be tough on the filibusterers and keep the Senate in longer sessions. He went out of his way to be courteous to the Southerners and to accommodate Senate Minority Leader Everett Dirksen, without whose help no civil rights bill would pass. Again, of course, Humphrey was bucking for a Vice Presidential nomination—a goal that partially explained his excessive kindness to Democratic Southerners.

But Humphrey's "moderation" was more in style than in substance. For in failing to light up the sky with oratorical fireworks, Humphrey managed to help pass one of the most far-reaching civil rights bills in history. Reporters, moreover, might have been less convinced of Humphrey's "moderation" had they recalled his bitter anti-South, anti-free enterprise speech following the Birmingham bombing, or if they had come across a curious letter by Humphrey published in the National Lawyers Guild *Newsletter* on June 30, 1964, from its Detroit headquarters.

The Humphrey letter, dated June 2, 1964, read:

> The National Lawyers Guild is surely to be congratulated for its program of providing legal assistance and counsel to persons involved in civil rights cases in Mississippi.
>
> From my discussions with members of the Department of Justice I had been aware of the difficult situations which exist in that state for those persons involved in civil rights demonstrations. Your efforts to redress this balance are certainly courageous and commendable.
>
> Many thanks for your kind words about my attempts to bring about passage of an effective and meaningful civil rights bill.
>
> Best wishes,
>
> Hubert H. Humphrey

Praising the Guild was not exactly the most moderate of actions.

The most recent issue of the House Committee on Un-

American Activities *Guide to Subversive Organizations and Publications* says on page 121 that the Guild "is the foremost legal bulwark of the Communist Party, its front organizations, and controlled unions and which since its inception has never failed to rally to the legal defense of the Communist Party and individual members thereof, including known espionage agents."

24

The "New" Humphrey III

As Lyndon Johnson's Vice President, Hubert Humphrey has turned into something of a hawk when he speaks of the Communist menace. Retorting to Bobby Kennedy's remarks suggesting the Viet Cong be brought into a South Vietnamese coalition government, Humphrey shot off that this was like bringing the "fox into the chicken coop." Unlike so many of his liberal brethren, he has backed the bombing of North Viet Nam and has been signally honored with an attack—both verbal and physical—from the peaceniks. In the year 1967, Administration supporters were feverishly circulating material on Viet Nam to rally dissident Democratic doves to the LBJ banner. The speech considered most persuasive on the matter: Hubert Humphrey's.

Yet how much can one rely on Humphrey's current rhetoric, knowing that he solemnly agreed to support publicly the President's policies as the price for the Vice Presidency? Humphrey, of course, may vigorously back the current war effort, but it is not unfair to wonder whether his views are colored by his commitments to LBJ and the hard fact that he could easily be bumped from the 1968 ticket if he refused.

Whatever Humphrey actually believes for the moment, his instincts prior to the Vice Presidency were clearly tinged with dovish qualities. He was not only "soft on the Soviets" in many cases, and he not only favored coalition governments, but he extolled or apologized for pro-Communist or Communist revolutionaries, including Fidel Castro. Humphrey led the appeasement-minded forces in the Senate on more than a score of different occasions and he lined up with those who somehow thought it best for the United States to surrender its sovereignty to that impotent gaggle of non-countries which comprise the majority of the United Nations.

Humphrey tough on communism? His demonstrative opposition to the policies of John Foster Dulles hardly reflected such an attitude. Almost from the time Dulles entered the Republican Administration in 1953, Humphrey was squaring off against Ike's Secretary of State. Humphrey rapped Dulles for "yielding" to such hard-liners in foreign policy as Senators William Knowland and Joe McCarthy, and he was in the forefront of those suggesting or demanding that Dulles resign. Humphrey led the fight to prevent Dulles from protecting the off-shore islands of Nationalist China and he battled Dulles' request for executive authority to repel Communist aggression in the Mideast.[1]

No action revealed Humphrey's lack of understanding of how to deal with the Communists more than his bitter denunciation of a Dulles interview published in a 1956 issue of *Life* magazine.[2] Dulles claimed the threat of "massive retaliation" had prevented Communist China from walking out of the Korean truce talks, intervening openly in Indo-China and capturing the Nationalist Chinese islands of Quemoy and Matsu. Humphrey not only attacked Dulles' assertions, but took particular issue with the Dulles statement that "The ability to get to the verge without getting into war is the necessary art. If you cannot master it, you inevitably get into war. If you try to run away from it, if you are scared to go to the brink, you are lost. . . . We walked to the brink and we looked it in the face. We took strong action."

Whether the United States had acted as firmly as Dulles contended was open to question, but Humphrey's major assault was against the philosophy that lay behind the statement. To the joy of liberals and left-wingers, Humphrey exclaimed, "No other responsible American statesman in our lifetime has ever so described an American diplomatic objective. Yesterday Mr. Dulles refused to affirm or deny his responsibility for his statement. I called upon him to repudiate it."[3]

Taken literally, Humphrey said later, the *Life* article "in effect expounds a new basis for American foreign policy. Dulles' art of getting to the verge of war comes precariously close to rejecting the traditional American conviction that we must never strike the first blow."[4]

Humphrey's facts were not entirely correct. Secretary of War Henry Stimson had once written that the object of our diplomacy should be to maneuver the Japanese into firing the first shot. The Dulles doctrine was far less militant, and, in fact, had nothing whatsoever to do with initiating war but much to do with preventing it.

In order to escape war or surrender, a country must take strong action against an aggressor, even at the risk of the holocaust. That, in essence, was the Dulles thesis. Though boldly stated, it was hardly revolutionary and had been practiced by various American presidents throughout the years. Military aid to Greece and Turkey, the Berlin Airlift, Truman's demand that the Soviets vacate Iran—each of these policies was a form of "brinksmanship." Surely Humphrey must have been aware that if the Soviets or the Communist Chinese were willing to go to the "brink of war" for an objective and the West refused, the Communists would automatically win that objective. To shrink from the verge of war would be to let a determined foe win its goals in every crisis.

But part of Humphrey's trouble is that he has consistently been unable to recognize a determined foe. Take, for example, the case of Dominican poet-leftist Juan Bosch, who assumed the Presidency of the Dominican Republic in 1963. After Bosch was forced out following seven months of misrule, and after he tried to make a comeback in 1965 with full-fledged Communist support, Humphrey was still defending Bosch—at least in private conversations. Humphrey rose to Bosch's defense, according to a Humphrey aide, even though the Senate Internal Security Subcommittee had labeled him "an ideological Trotskyite" who had allowed the Communists free rein of power when in office.

An even more devastating account of Bosch's ties to radicalism has been told by Latin American specialist Peter Nehemkis, a Washington lawyer who had helped JFK form the Alliance for Progress program and had been appointed by the Organization of American States to monitor the Dominican voting that elected Bosch president in 1963.

In his *Latin America—Myth and Reality*, Nehemkis wrote that Bosch "sought to foment racial antagonism," put in power "political henchmen," "packed the judiciary with party followers, thus destroying its independence" and created a phony war with Haiti. On September 25, 1963, Manuel Tavarez Justo, "maximum leader" of the pro-Castro 14th of June Movement, addressed the Dominican Republic over government facilities. "His speech," Nehemkis wrote, "was a defense of Bosch's dismal record—a record of irresponsibility, international deception and betrayal of democracy. A shocked Dominican public asked: 'Why should the leader of the Castro Communist movement be given radio time on the government-owned station to defend the Bosch regime?' After this performance, even the die-hards wondered if Bosch—intentionally or unintentionally—was a puppet whose strings were pulled by a bearded showman on a neighboring island."[5]

While Humphrey recognized that Bosch had a weakness toward communism, he was still assuring Democratic friends of his in 1965 that the Dominican leftist could be an excellent leader of his country—even though history had proved otherwise. Soft on Bosch, Humphrey was equally soft on another Latin leftist: Fidel Castro. In January of 1960, nationally syndicated columnist Holmes Alexander wrote that Humphrey appeared extremely sympathetic toward the Castro government. "The Senator," said Alexander, "spoke with disparagement of the 'Batista dictatorship' and with forbearance of the 'Castro regime.' When I asked him if his choice of words could be considered significant, and if he did not think Castro also ran a 'dictatorship,' the Senator said he would let his statement stand.

"It was a clear case of Hubert Humphrey's refusing to turn his back on Fidel Castro. For a man aspiring to be President of the United States at this hour of history, the statement is less than reassuring."[6]

When Humphrey finally learned that Castro was not just an agrarian reformer, he still managed to advocate vigorously a policy that, in effect, protected Castro's position. In May of 1961, Humphrey expressed flat opposition to military intervention, declaring that a military crackdown on Cuba "could entangle the United States in a fruitless and dangerous policy."

A little over a month before the Cuban missile crisis, Humphrey denounced Republican advocates of a U.S. invasion of Cuba as "jingoists." Humphrey stated that the Senate must "get tough"—not with Castro—but with "swaggering irresponsibles in these very halls of Congress" who were for eliminating Castro through U.S. military might. On October 18, 1962, just three days before President Kennedy made his historic speech about Soviet long-range missiles in Cuba, Humphrey charged that those who termed Cuba a military threat were doing so "for narrow partisan purposes." Those Republicans who proposed an invasion of Cuba, he insisted, were "damn irresponsible" and those who urged a blockade—as JFK was to urge—were "over 65, have hardening of the arteries, and usually have congressional immunity."[7]

Humphrey was no less buffaloed by pro-Communist extremists in Africa. Indicative of Humphrey's policy in this area of the world was his support of the American Committee on Africa, one of the most militant organizations in the United States dealing with African affairs.

In a letter to Mr. Martin T. Camacho of the Portuguese-American Committee on Foreign Affairs, Humphrey gave a resounding vote of confidence to this radical group. Defending it against accusations of leftism, Humphrey said: "Without going into the substance of the charges, let me say that the American Committee on Africa used my name on its letterhead with my full knowledge and consent. I appreciate your concern, but I am confident that this is a reputable organization pursuing a worthwhile cause."[8]

Sponsored by such liberals as Arthur Schlesinger, Jr., Bishop James Pike and socialist Norman Thomas, the American Committee's "worthwhile cause" appears to be that of waging war against the pro-Western regimes in Southern Africa. (The committee's October, 1966 *Bulletin* on Southern Africa labels Angola, Mozambique, Rhodesia, South Africa and South West Africa as "captive nations.") Furthermore, it openly supports terrorists and Communists who oppose these governments.

Though ostensibly against unjust rule for black Africans, the committee's glaring racial bias can be seen from the fact that it refuses to criticize totalitarian African nations if they are black-controlled. Among the terrorists and Communists the committee has openly endorsed: Holden Roberto, whose anti-Portuguese insurgents butchered more than 1,500 men, women and children in northern Angola during the March 15, 1961 uprising; and Communist Braam Fischer. The committee, which admits that Fischer joined "the South African Communist Party in the 1930's," makes an elaborate defense of him in its March, 1966 South Africa *Bulletin*.

Humphrey's affinity for African extremists is no less great than the American Committee's. Not only has Humphrey been an apologist for Holden Roberto, but in a letter to a constituent dated May 23, 1962—shortly before Algeria had formally won her independence from France—Humphrey described the National Liberation Front as "basically friendly toward the West." Within two years, the "basically friendly" National Liberation Front, now ruling Algeria, had outlawed all political parties save one, suppressed freedom of public opinion by confiscating newspapers and other communications media, ordered withdrawn non-Communist newspapers from France while welcoming Communist publications from other countries, nationalized practically every business and farm, and turned Algeria into a base for pro-Communist and black nationalist revolutionaries bent on overthrowing moderate and pro-Western regimes in

Africa. Furthermore, Algeria's ruler Ben Bella openly propagandized against the United States and hailed Castro as a "brother."

The Congo crisis again revealed Humphrey in the corner of hot-blooded African nationalists. In September, 1961, Humphrey defended on the floor of the Senate the character of such pro-Communists as Antoine Gizenga, then vice-premier of the central Congolese government, and Christophe Gbenye, a Gizenga follower who became the government's Minister of Interior (i.e., chief of police).

Many in the U.S. State Department—though by no means all—recognized Gizenga as an untrustworthy radical, and the bearded Gbenye, no doubt to Humphrey's horror, emerged as the swashbuckling leader of the Peking-backed Congo People's Republic in Stanleyville—the same "Republic" which sparked the bloody 1964 massacre of native Congolese and white hostages, including the murder of the famous Dr. Paul Carlson. Moreover, Gbenye had personally spurred his rebel Simba soldiers on to the slaughter with the statement: "As fetishes we will wear the hearts of Belgians and Americans; we will dress in the skins of Americans and Belgians."[10]

Humphrey's judgment of character in the international arena obviously leaves something to be desired. Castro, Bosch, Ben Bella, Gizenga, Gbenye—each has violently turned against the United States and each has been infected with the virus of communism. Nor are Humphrey's foreign policy miscues confined to Latin America or the African continent, for he has equally misgauged the situation in Asia. Moreover, he has defended proposals to bring the "fox into the chicken coop" when applied to various Asian countries.

The Minnesota Senator, for instance, lashed out at Republicans in 1961 for opposing a coalition government in Laos. W. Averell Harriman, noted an AP dispatch, "made it clear in a television interview . . . he thinks the West is going to have to accept the presence of some Communists in any neutralist regime in Laos."

Incensed at Harriman's remarks, Sen. Thruston Morton excoriated such comments as fallacious and indiscreet, adding: "Everyone knows that forcing Laos to accept a coalition government would be the same as delivering it into the hands of the enemy." When Morton urged the President to repudiate the Harriman suggestion, Humphrey chastised Republicans for "their political guerrilla warfare" against efforts to solve the Laotian crisis. Humphrey said attempts to suggest a coalition government would be Communist-dominated amounts to "emotional misrepresentation."[11]

Pursuing his Communist accommodation policies, Humphrey led the opposition in the Senate in 1955 to ratification of a resolution empowering the President to defend the Nationalist Chinese offshore islands of Quemoy and Matsu, whose seizure by Red China would undoubtedly have dealt a terrific military and psychological blow to the Nationalists on Formosa.

Humphrey suggested that these islands were an irritant whose possession by the Nationalist Chinese worsened our relations with Communist China. He referred to the offshore islands—inhabited by 50,000 anti-Communist Chinese—as an internal matter, and contemptuously claimed their defense would only win the friendship of "Syngman Rhee and Chiang Kai-shek"—as if these anti-Red rulers, whose countries had shed blood against a common Communist foe, were somehow unworthy of support. Humphrey protested there was not "one iota of evidence to show that Quemoy and Matsu are essential to the defense of Formosa"[12]—thus airily dismissing such experts as Admirals Arleigh Burke, Ike's Chief of Naval Operations, and Charles M. Cooke, former commander of the Seventh Fleet, which patrols the waters near the China Coast.

One of 13 Senators to vote for the Lehman resolution opposing the defense of Quemoy and Matsu, Humphrey asserted just three years later: "To stake the prestige of the United States on the defense of these offshore islands I believe to be incredible folly, militarily precarious, and diplomatically indefensible.

"On this issue I would not want to risk or commit the lives of my three sons or yours."

Yet the hard fact remains that the United States has helped

the Chinese Nationalists successfully defend these islands since 1949; that the Chinese Communists have suffered a humiliating defeat because of their inability to seize them; and that the pro-Western government on Formosa has been immeasurably strengthened as a result of the islands' remaining out of Communist hands. Because the United States has resolutely refused to follow Humphrey's advice, some 50,000 anti-Communist Chinese have not had to relinquish their ancestral homes for a Taiwan refugee camp or capitulate to a Communist enemy.

Humphrey was not content to appease the Communist Chinese on the offshore islands alone, however. In 1957 Humphrey proposed a "fresh look at our policy" toward Red China and advised that we should consider modifying a number of our policies "such as the trade embargo, which force China into ever closer relations with the Soviet bloc."[13] The Minnesotan also pressed for a U.S. policy that would strip the Nationalist government of its seat on the Security Council at the United Nations and replace it with neutralist India.[14]

Such pleas for accommodation with Communist China have been brushed aside or covered up when Humphrey has found it wise temporarily to shift his political posture from dove to hawk for political reasons. After GOP Vice Presidential candidate William Miller had made a devastating exposé of the ADA and its China policy in 1964, Humphrey decided to show that he was significantly less radical than the organization which he had founded and supported ever since its inception. While Humphrey's radicalism enabled him to capture certain Democratic votes, he often found it the better part of valor to reveal himself as less of a radical to the public at large.

He received some help in his image making from Paul Niven on *Face the Nation.* Niven asked Humphrey: "Senator, I want to get back to ADA for a moment. You explained there were diversions of views in the organization. . . . I know that you don't agree with it on negotiations leading to U.N. admission of [Red] China because you belong also to the Committee of One Million, whose whole purpose is against that."

Humphrey replied: "You are surely right."[15]

Yet Niven was surely *not* right—and Humphrey was well aware that Niven was wrong. The Committee of One Million's September, 1964 declaration to keep Red China out of the United Nations was endorsed by 345 incumbent Republican and Democratic lawmakers. Among the missing names: Hubert Humphrey's.

While Humphrey had been a member of the Committee, the Committee does not show him to be a member as far back as 1962. In June of 1964, Humphrey had explained in writing to Committee member Walter Judd that while he had been on record in opposition to the seating of Communist China, "I do not wish to be considered a member of the Committee of One Million."[16]

Humphrey's failure to disabuse Mr. Niven or the viewers about his connections with the Committee conveyed the impression he was far more serious in his intent to bar Red China from the United Nations than was actually the case. And the plain, unvarnished truth of the matter is that over the years Senator Humphrey vigorously pressed for a U.S. policy of conciliating the Communist-controlled government on mainland China.

As announced over the years, Humphrey's foreign policy could only have weakened the United States and the Free World in relation to the Communist bloc. Indeed, he has worked to scrap American sovereignty over strategic areas, disarm the United States without the faintest sort of inspection system, and support Communist countries—including the Soviet Union—with both trade and aid.

In 1960 he spurred on the fight in the Senate to eliminate the famous Connally Amendment, which permits the United States to prevent the World Court from automatically deciding conflicts involving the United States and other nations. To give the World Court—upon which are seated jurists from Communist countries—automatic power to render judgments regarding vital American interests is sheer folly. For the United States, once agreeing to dispense with the Connally Amendment, would be honor-bound to live up to a World Court decision even if it went against American interests. Yet the Soviet bloc, as history has clearly revealed, would refuse to obey any judgment it believed would be damaging to Communist goals. Nevertheless, Humphrey has frantically pushed for the Connally repealer, whose sole effect would be to jeopardize American security. In 1959 he proposed internationalization of a strategic U.S. waterway—the Panama Canal—a move that could hardly help Amercan security.[17] And he has consistently called for the U.S. to surrender more and more of its power to the United Nations and to such agencies as the U.N. Special Fund (now the U.N. Development Fund)—an organization that has channelled many of its projects into Communist Poland and Cuba.

Perhaps persuaded less by the international implications and more by the fact that his Minnesota business and farm supporters could become enriched, Humphrey has zealously pushed for trade and aid to Communist countries.

In 1958, Humphrey called on President Eisenhower to stand up and fight for an Administration-backed plan to extend foreign economic and agricultural aid to Iron Curtain nations.[18] When Humphrey visited Warsaw in 1961, he argued that the United States should extend the length of credit terms to Communist Poland. "If other countries are selling to Poland," said Humphrey, "the United States should join the bandwagon."[19]

In September, 1963, Humphrey said he planned to take personal command of a drive to persuade the Kennedy Administration to reverse its supposedly restrictive policy on farm exports to Russia. His campaign was touched off by the announcement that Canada was to sell more than 200 million bushels of wheat to the Soviet Union. In a few months—after Kennedy had agreed to sell wheat to the Soviets—Humphrey asserted the United States should take the initiative "to create a constructive and conciliatory climate" with the Soviet Union at the United Nations, with the aim of expanding East-West trade.

Humphrey then called for a "bold review" of United States trade policy with the Soviet Union, claiming there should be a relaxation of restrictions on "non-strategic, pro-people" items. The proposed sale of wheat to the Soviet Union, he insisted, indicated "definite possibilities" for extending East-West trade.

In making his pitch for expanded trade with Communist

countries, Humphrey shamelessly pandered to the American businessman's desire to make money, apparently unconcerned by the fact that these same Communist countries were supplying the enemy in Viet Nam. Thus, in *The Cause is Mankind,* Humphrey declared: "The wheat sale was a beginning. . . . Until the American wheat sale to the Soviet Union, our trade policy remained based on the most rigid possible concept. . . . Obviously, a tremendous amount of American business is being lost through such a restrictive trade policy. . . ."

Humphrey argued that it was perfectly all right to expand private trade arrangements—guaranteed with government credits—because if we didn't supply the Communists our allies would anyway. Put another way, if our allies wrongfully gave the enemy vital goods that it needed, the United States should compound the sin.

Veteran diplomatic observers have scored Humphrey's remarks as fatuous. In the first place, as those with any knowledge of Soviet trade matters have stressed, the Communist countries cannot get everything they want from Free Europe. In the second place, the United States, if it really desired, could sucessfully pressure our allies into vastly reducing the amount of trading they do with Communist nations. Thirdly, it is pointed out, Humphrey obviously has no comprehension about what it takes to deal with the Soviets. An argument can be made for carrying on expanded trade with the Soviets, but those in the diplomatic business say trade should be used as a weapon to compel Communist concessions in the cold war.

Yet Humphrey, at precisely the time the Soviets desperately needed American food, was willing to offer it to them on a silver platter—with no strings attached.

Humphrey has been equally as ready to appease the Soviets in the area of disarmament. While vigorously claiming upon occasion that the United States should enter into mutually inspected disarmament agreements with the Soviets, he has actually championed disarmament measures that have contained no inspection provisions whatsoever.

As chairman of the Senate Foreign Relations Committee subcommittee on disarmament, Humphrey has led the United States into an atomic test-ban moratorium and test-ban treaty without inspections. When Nikita Khrushchev used the United Nations to make a plea for control-less disarmament in 1960, Humphrey responded, "Mr. Khrushchev's speech was the speech our President should have made."[20]

In the same year, Humphrey said: ". . . the United States finds that the Soviet position on controls is still inadequate . . . the U.S. position perhaps could be modified. . . ."[21]

Humphrey had been a fervent apostle of the uninspected moratorium on nuclear weapons tests reached with the Soviet Union in 1958. Though the test-ban was hailed in peace circles, some notable scientists, such as Dr. Edward Teller, often referred to as the "father of the H-bomb," cast a gimlet eye toward the moratorium. He believed it had produced just what the Soviets desired: the thwarting of the U.S. testing program while permitting the Soviets to conduct tests of their own on a clandestine basis. Teller's view was more than mere speculation.

On August 30, 1961, the Soviet Union announced it was unilaterally breaking the "moratorium," and the subsequent massive series of atmospheric tests revealed to virtually every nuclear scientist of stature that meticulous planning had gone into the Soviet program. Not only Dr. Teller, but a number of other American nuclear experts believed the Soviets could not have conducted such a thorough testing program unless they had consistently violated the moratorium as a means of preparation. Yet Humphrey had long championed this moratorium and had been given credit, because of his subcommittee hearings, for having brought the 1958 test ban to fruition.

Humphrey's reaction to the Soviet tests was bizarre. While he flayed the Soviets for having "dealt a cruel and vicious blow to the cause of peace," he refused to call for the immediate resumption of America's nuclear program. While the Soviets were initiating the most extensive series of atomic tests in history, the Minnesota Senator seemed positively unconcerned that America's avowed enemy might be leaping into the nuclear lead.

Bewilderingly, Humphrey's almost immediate response, registered in a speech at the Waldorf-Astoria Hotel, was that the Soviet action was a *plus* for the United States, albeit not a plus for American and Free World military security. Humphrey insisted that the Soviet ripping up of the unsigned, uninspected test ban pact was "a great psychological and moral victory" for the United States since it proved Soviet treachery—though on that basis the Soviet conquest of Eastern Europe was also a great psychological and moral victory. While the Soviets were improving their nuclear weapons, Humphrey took great comfort in the fact that, "We have refused to be stampeded into nuclear weapons testing. We have put the welfare of the world ahead of our immediate military needs."

Equally astounding, Humphrey preached in this same major address that the Soviet violation of the moratorium had not proved that we needed to strengthen our defense program, but that it is "important that Congress complete action on the President's proposal for a United States Disarmament Agency on World Peace and Security." Nor did it prove the need to re-arm our allies. Quite the contrary. "Now more than ever we should bolster the areas of freedom in the world. . . . Our attention cannot be restricted only to national defense and weaponry. Our concentration must be upon the needs of the people in Latin America, in Africa, in Asia, in the other parts of the world."[22]

President John F. Kennedy revealed the stark defeat of our nuclear diplomacy in a speech announcing the resumption of U.S. atmospheric tests in March of 1962. In what many believe to have been an understatement of the facts, Kennedy stressed: "Had the Soviet tests last fall merely reflected a new effort in intimidation and bluff, our security would not have been affected. But, in fact, they also reflected a highly sophisticated technology, the trial of novel designs and techniques, and some substantial gains in weaponry.

"Many of these tests were aimed at improving their defenses against missiles—others were proof tests, trying out existing weapons—particularly those of greater explosive power. . . .

"And I must report to you in all candor that further Soviet series, in the absence of further Western progress, could well provide the Soviet Union with a nuclear attack and defense so powerful as to encourage aggressive designs. . . .

". . . We now know enough about broken negotiations, secret preparations, and the advantages gained from a long test series never to offer again an uninspected moratorium."

Undeterred by the failure of moratorium diplomacy, Humphrey was searching for even more radical approaches to disarmament in late 1961. Barely a month after the Soviets had renewed their atmospheric nuclear tests, Humphrey dropped a bombshell on United States foreign policy when he told a Polish television audience on October 16 that the United States was giving "very thoughtful and very serious consideration" to the Rapacki plan for an atom-free zone in central Europe. The plan also called for a thinning out of armaments in a central European area that would include East and West Germany, Czechoslovakia and Poland.

When the television interviewer pointed out that the Rapacki plan—proposed by the Polish Foreign Affairs Minister and supported by the U.S.S.R.—had already been rejected by the West, Humphrey replied: "That was by a previous Administration. . . . There is a new President and a new policy and a new disarmament program. . . . The disarmament agency will be giving the Rapacki plan and other plans to stop the arms race very thoughtful and very serious consideration."[23]

Humphrey's announcement that the United States was considering a withdrawal of nuclear and conventional forces from Europe could not have been more ill-timed. It came within two months after the Soviets had erected the Berlin Wall, closing off East Berlin from the Free World, and within two months after the Soviets had deliberately violated the unofficial test-ban pact. Western Europe, already shaken by these violent Soviet actions, feared some new and even more dangerous Soviet move was in the offing. Nothing could have been more primed to instill panic in our Western allies than Humphrey's prattle about the Rapacki plan.

Following Humphrey's announcement, there was a flurry of Administration statements reassuring our allies that the Rapacki plan was absolutely unacceptable. Referring to the Polish proposal, State Department press officer Lincoln White stressed that the U.S. considers such schemes "transparent devices intended to weaken and ultimately destroy the Atlantic alliances."[24]

The following day Secretary of State Dean Rusk echoed similar sentiments. Rusk emphasized that military disengagement in Central Europe would be catastrophic and that a withdrawal or reduction of troops or other zonal arrangements to reduce nuclear armaments would imply an "abandonment of responsibility."[25]

President Kennedy, finally, personally had to calm the fears of the West German Ambassador that Humphrey's disengagement plan was not a serious proposal.[26]

25

Through a Glass Darkly

"I became Vice President because he made me Vice President," Stewart Alsop quoted Humphrey as saying in 1965. "I became Whip because he made me Whip. As a matter of fact, I've had a helping hand from Lyndon Johnson from the beginning. I remember him saying to me, 'Hubert, you should get better acquainted with more Senators,' and we'd have lunch with Walter George or Dick Russell, or someone like that, in the private dining room."[1]

Humphrey is always aware of the political umbilical cord linking his fortunes with those of Lyndon Johnson. A Humphrey assistant told Fletcher Knebel about one of Humphrey's first staff meetings as Vice President, when he walked to the window, pointed across to the White House and said: "That's how close we are to the President of the United States. Every word we utter, everything we do reflects directly on the President and on the White House. Each of us must conduct himself with that in mind. We must dress, act and speak with dignity, wisely and prudently, and when we act, we must be sure it's right. I'd rather have delays than to come up wrong."[2]

So faithful a lieutenant has Humphrey been that this story floats about Capitol Hill: LBJ and Humphrey were attending a swank dinner affair when the President suddenly whispered into Humphrey's ear, "Hubert, did I hear you belch?" To which Humphrey responded, "No, Mr. President, was I supposed to?"

As in all relationships between human beings, there have been some difficult moments of stress and strain. At a meeting with his legislative leaders, the President spoke testily about someone leaking information and then cast a withering glance at the No. 2 man. The President has complained about Humphrey's large staff and still feels he is a compulsive talker. But the Vice President has gone that extra mile to avoid such abrasive occurrences.

"Humphrey," reported *Newsweek* in 1965, "has curtailed his own taste for talk; he has suddenly become too busy to grant many interviews ('Johnson,' groused one reporter, 'is more available than Humphrey'); and he submits most of his speeches to review. . . . For so compulsive an ad libber as Humphrey, that screening doesn't always work: in one speech . . . he strayed from his text, caught himself, and said: 'I don't know whether I should have said that or not. That part wasn't cleared.' "[3]

At LBJ's request, he has helped coordinate and implement the federal government's responsibilities in the areas of civil rights and poverty, he has coaxed LBJ legislation through the Congress, and he has traveled both in the United States and abroad to plump for the President's foreign policy. And, unlike his earlier free-wheeling days in the Senate, his role as Vice President has given him an ideologically conflicting image.

Thus, out of loyalty to the President, he has established close ties with Georgia Gov. Lester Maddox, who ran Negroes out of his private restaurant with ax handles, and he has supported Negroes Carl Stokes and Richard Hatcher as mayoralty candidates.

He has steered Johnson's radical civil rights programs through the Congress, but he successfully organized opposition in the Senate to legislation to abolish poll taxes—legislation that Humphrey had consistently campaigned for during his Senate years.

He is for the President's policy in Viet Nam—indeed, no more vigorous a champion of the war exists. He has tangled with Bobby Kennedy over that war, he has been pelted by peaceniks for defending it, and he has been shelled in Saigon by the Viet Cong for verbally shoring up South Viet Nam's anti-Communist regime. From New Delhi to New York, the peripatetic Vice President has rehearsed America's aims and achievements with all the evangelical fervor he once brought to such causes as disarmament and America's appeasement of Communist China.

Yet his crusade for the American war effort in Viet Nam has not prevented his supporting "Nervous Nelly" Democrats at home—the very doves that LBJ and Humphrey have stressed are prolonging the war because of their constant criticism of our presence there. He is supporting Fulbright and Morse, Gruening and Church—the Senate's most conspicuous anti-war element—for re-election in 1968. In 1967, Humphrey even endorsed for the state senate in California none other than peacenik assemblyman John Burton, who wholeheartedly supported a San Francisco referendum demanding an "immediate" U.S. withdrawal from South Viet Nam.

Humphrey has received some sharp criticism for his loyalty to the Johnson Administration, particularly from his old left-wing friends who cannot understand why their long-time ally is supporting the war effort. Yet his friends ignore the practical realities of politics. Assuming Humphrey desperately wishes to succeed to the Presidency—which, of course, no one doubts—he must be at least as royal as the crown.

His extravagant eulogizing of the President may be entirely in earnest, yet it is also the surest road to the White House. If Johnson were unhappy with the Vice President's performance, one can be certain that Lyndon would be making plans to unload Humphrey in 1968. Furthermore, Humphrey is well aware that his popular appeal is less than overwhelming, and that his most likely chance of succeeding to the Presidency is either through Lyndon Johnson's death, or by becoming LBJ's hand-picked successor after the Texan has retired.

Whatever Humphrey actually believes, his future welfare rests with what voters think about the Johnson Administration.

Thus, it is clearly to his advantage to be the Saint Paul of the Great Society, the total defender of the faith.

His role as special pleader, however, may obscure his deepest feelings on matters of national importance. There is some reason to believe, for example, that without Lyndon Johnson hovering in the foreground, Humphrey might actually be opposed to the war. Washington lawyer Max Kampelman, a close Humphrey adviser who breakfasts with him frequently, has called the Vice President essentially a "pacifist." Kampelman should know, since Kampelman himself was a conscientious objector during World War II (though he has since repudiated the philosophical concepts of pacifism). Even with Lyndon's presence directly influencing his opinions, Humphrey's goals for Viet Nam are not exactly those one associates with "hawks." As he told *Newsweek* commentator Emmet John Hughes, himself a spokesman for the appeasement faction in the country: "How do we speed the day of peace? We must not only accept the results of free elections—including any winning Communist candidacies. We must also make crystal clear—perhaps clearer than we have done to date—our total acceptance of true independence and nonalignment. This does not apply merely to Viet Nam. It applies to all Southeast Asia. We want no permanent enclaves or bases. We seek not one Gibraltar, nor one Guantanamo."

If the United States truly seeks neither enclaves, nor Gibraltars nor alignment, it seems—to some observers at any rate—that we must then be fighting the entire war in Viet Nam in vain. What tough-minded diplomats hope we are seeking is not some "nonaligned" Southern Asia that cowers before the Red Chinese and the Soviet colossus the way "nonaligned" Cambodia trembles every time Mao Tse-tung sneezes, but a powerful network of stable Southeast Asian countries that are willing to be our allies and to resist the Red tyranny that threatens to engulf them.

There are other indications that Humphrey's heart is not exactly in "hawks' corner." When LBJ sent troops to the Dominican Republic in 1965 to impede a Communist takeover, reporters close to Humphrey on the New York *Times* were saying that the Vice President was not really pleased with Johnson's course of conduct. And as has been revealed earlier, Humphrey has always had a particularly soft spot in his heart for Juan Bosch, the radical Dominican poet whom the Communists were attempting to restore to power as their puppet.

But Humphrey's essential "softness" in the field of foreign policy is not all that has been glimpsed in his role as Vice President. Even more than during his latter days in the Senate, Humphrey has assiduously cultivated the image of moderation. But hard as he obviously tries to strike this pose, he seems incapable of extinguishing the radical passions that obviously well within his being. After the riots in 1967, Humphrey's instinctive reaction—which brought him a verbal cuffing from the President—was to call for a "Marshall plan" for the cities, a phrase suggesting giant infusions of additional federal funds into America's metropolitan areas. With prices and interest rates soaring and predictions that the federal government would go into debt $20 billion in fiscal '68, Humphrey's clarion call caused LBJ to go through the roof. Humphrey has not used the term since, but the outburst certainly suggested that his radical cast of mind had not necessarily matured while assuming the responsibilities of affairs of state.

Addressing the National Association of Counties conference in New Orleans in 1966, Humphrey again expressed some rather extreme views—this time in regard to preventing riots in the cities. He warned there would be "open violence" in every major city in America unless rent subsidy legislation was passed, a statement, many observed, that appeared to invite violence should Congress have refused to adopt such a law.*

While deploring violence as a means of solving the problems of the poor, Humphrey then went on to condone the very violence he had just deplored. He contended that he would

*Congress did pass a rent subsidy bill, and, in fact, had previously voted for a rent certificate and public housing program to aid the poor in attaining better living quarters. But the riots came in 1967 anyway, the worst America had ever suffered—a fact that suggests Humphrey was dead wrong in predicting that rent subsidy legislation would cure the riots.

hate to "be stuck on a fourth floor tenement with rats nibbling on the kid's toes—and they do—with garbage uncollected—and it is. . . ." And if he suddenly found himself in such a predicament, "I think you'd have more trouble than you have had already, because I've got enough spark left in me to lead a mighty good revolt under those conditions."[4]

This towering apology for mayhem was blasted in numerous editorials and columns all over the country, for clearly—despite the qualifying remarks made prior to it—the Vice President was telling potential rioters he could not only understand the reasons for their instigating riots, but that he too would find it possible, under certain circumstances, to lead such an outburst. Whatever Humphrey may have intended, his remarks could only have emboldened those bent on provoking massive chaos in urban America.

Much of the business community is also not convinced that Humphrey's Vice Presidential role has mellowed him substantially. Liberal in its outlook on business affairs, *Fortune* magazine has commented:

> Humphrey, himself, has encouraged the new-Humphrey notion by telling business audiences that he has "changed." He never specifies how he has changed, and he always adds a remark to the effect that everybody changes, but the message comes across. . . .
>
> Actually that message is a bit misleading. . . . In getting at the realities behind the new-Humphrey image, it is essential to distinguish between style and substance. The Humphrey of 1965 is a far smoother and more reflective man than the Humphrey who in 1949, at thirty seven, took his seat as a freshman Senator. . . .
>
> But Humphrey's maturing and his ascent in Senate status were not accompanied by a change in the pattern of his voting record. During his four years as Whip, 1961–64, his voting record rated 97 per cent right according to ADA, and 100 per cent right according to the AFL-CIO's Committee on Political Education. And for all the current talk of a new Humphrey, he would undoubtedly be scoring close to 100 per cent if he were still a Senator.[5]

Thus, there is every reason to believe that Humphrey, should he become President tomorrow, might be a good deal less anti-

Communist than LBJ and a good deal more radical in regard to domestic policy. Even should Humphrey desire to continue the course of the nation in the direction LBJ has put it, there are doubts as to whether he would have the fortitude to withstand the liberal pressures as much as LBJ himself. Unlike LBJ, Humphrey's friends and supporters and aides largely spring from the ADA or ADA-thinking crowd that has dominated DFL politics in Minnesota. The John Blatniks, the Eugene McCarthys and the Don Frasers, each an influential Democratic lawmaker from Minnesota and each dovish in regard to the Communist menace, have sprung from the loins of the DFL. Not only the socialist-leaning Kampelman, but even more left-leaning liberals like ADA vice chairman Joseph Rauh and UAW president Walter Reuther readily have Humphrey's ear. Furthermore, the AFL-CIO, whose policies have had an enormous influence over Humphrey, may no longer be in a position to anchor Humphrey's views to the Right in foreign policy, as the more "conservative" element, represented by the aging George Meany and Jay Lovestone, fade from the union scene. And could Humphrey, whose passion for being well liked is considerable, resist trying to please his liberal friends in the press without either a Meany-oriented AFL-CIO or a Lyndon Johnson controlling his instinctively radical nature? Judging from the record, it is highly doubtful that Humphrey would have the necessary will power.

Hubert Humphrey has travelled a long way from his drugstore days in South Dakota. Still exuberant at 57, still the compulsive talker, still eager to dream up new federal plans for conquering poverty, disease, war and old age, he would like to go one more step up the political ladder. But as the 1968 election campaign began brewing, his future seemed most uncertain.

His fortunes rest with the popularity of LBJ and the Democratic Party, but neither were faring well in early 1968. And problems for the country were mounting. The United States was still bogged down in a seemingly endless war in Viet Nam. At home, the country was being convulsed by a mounting crime wave, student protests, peace marchers and fiercesome, bloody turmoil in the nation's cities.* The finances of the government were going from bad to worse, with inflation and taxes eroding the income of every working individual.

Despite the LBJ-Humphrey theory that the Soviets could be appeased, they were stirring strife in the Mideast, Latin America, Africa and Asia. And there were strong indications that they were catching up to us in the field of nuclear weaponry, as they had developed a fractional orbital bomb in violation of the spirit, if not the letter, of the space treaty; more powerful nuclear weapons through deliberate violation of the test-ban treaty; and an anti-ballistic missile system that the U.S. had foresworn at one time on the grounds that the Soviets would escalate the arms race if we erected one ourselves.

The liberal philosophy with which Humphrey has so long been identified was not only failing in the eyes of conservatives but also in the eyes of many certified liberals. No matter how much money the federal government poured into America's urban areas year after year, for example, the cities were continually in chaos and disorder. Both Richard Goodwin and Daniel Moynihan, each harboring impeccable liberal credentials, were now suggesting that the key to the country's welfare perhaps did not rest with the central government in Washington after all. Moynihan, in fact, maintained that liberals "have paid too little heed to the limited capacities of government to bring about social change. These failings have been accompanied, moreover, by a formidable capacity to explain them away. . . ."

As if directing his comments at Humphrey himself, Moynihan said: "In the aftermath of the Newark riots one could already detect our self-defense system at work. Newark, we were beginning to say, was after all a backward city, doubtless run by the Mafia. . . . Unemployment was high. . . .

"But Detroit . . . what have we to say after Detroit.

*A former Humphrey staff member once told intimates that the Vice President was so disheartened by the world situation after the riots in 1967 that one day he suddenly folded his arms across his forehead, laid his head down on the desk and tearfully stated: "We're being torn apart in Viet Nam and in our cities, and we don't know what to do." Humphrey has since denied this statement, but the source for this information insists the event did occur.

"Detroit had everything the Great Society could wish for a municipality. A splendid mayor and a fine governor. A high paying and, thanks to the fiscal policies of the national government, a booming industry, civilized by and associated with the hands-down leading trade union in the world.

"Moreover, it was a city whose Negro residents had every reason to be proud of the position they held in the economy and government of the area. Two able and promising Negro congressmen are from Detroit. Relations between the Negro community and City Hall could hardly have been better. . . ."[6]

Yet, noted Moynihan, Detroit too burst into flames. Obviously, he implied, neither the Great Society nor Humphrey's "Marshall plan" was the proper response to the nation's ills.

There were other problems facing Humphrey in his goal of becoming President. Neither Humphrey nor his associates had ever been seriously implicated in major scandals in previous years. But in 1967 and 1968 his close advisers were finding themselves involved in indiscreet roles in questionable activities.

In October, 1967, it was revealed that Max Kampelman, Humphrey's close friend and unofficial adviser, was a central figure in a controversial Agency for International Development transaction in India. The United States is faced with a $4 million loss as a result, and the matter is now under investigation by the Justice Department. Partly as a result of Kampelman's role in this affair, he was turned down as chairman of Washington, D.C.'s new City Council. And in February, 1968, Herbert J. Waters hurriedly resigned a $26,000-a-year post as head of the Agency for International Development's "War on Hunger" program when it was discovered that certain of his subordinates had accepted improper kickbacks from a Belgian contractor accused of overcharging the United States. Waters, whose own role in the affair is not yet clear, managed Humphrey's 1954 and 1960 re-election campaigns and served as his administrative assistant before being appointed in 1961 to AID.

Two other close Humphrey associates were also under fire. Both Neal Peterson, a current member of Humphrey's staff, and Eugene Foley, a Humphrey employee on the Senate Small Business Committee staff in 1961 and later head of the Small Business Administration (SBA), have been under some stiff criticism for an SBA transaction involving Universal Fiberglass. As a result of efforts by Peterson and Foley, the SBA had approved a certificate of competency for Universal Fiberglass *despite* objections of financial experts in the General Services Administration (GSA) and the SBA itself.

The certificate was money in the bank for Fiberglass, for it meant that GSA was required to award a $13.3 million contract to the company for three-wheel mail trucks. Peterson pushed for approval of the controversial certificate of competency when he was a staff member of the Senate Small Business Committee and his brother, Roger Peterson, was the lawyer for Universal Fiberglass. An official of the Fiberglass corporation is George Bookbinder of New York, a friend of Humphrey's and a contributor to his campaigns.

Bad omens for Humphrey could also be read into the resurgence of the Republican Party. The 1967 elections saw the Republicans make important gains in major cities around the country, gains pointing the way toward further GOP victories in 1968. And the Democratic Party was suffering a traumatic split. In the South, Dixiecrats were lining up behind segregationist George Wallace, and in the North, liberals were rallying behind anyone who might reverse LBJ's policy of steadfastly confronting the Communists in Viet Nam. Even Humphrey's Democratic-Farmer-Labor Party in Minnesota, whose strength had been eroded considerably in the 1966 elections, was split on the war issue, with Humphrey protégé Sen. Eugene McCarthy spearheading a move against LBJ in the Democratic primaries. Ironically, McCarthy was spouting an appeasement philosophy similar to that of Humphrey's in days gone by, though McCarthy's stance was even more radical, since he stoutly defended Red China's aggressions as those that might have been committed by any nationalistic country bent on securing the integrity of its own borders. (The Minnesota Senator even went so far as to defend Red Chinese aggression in Korea in his book *The Limits of Power*. "What the United

Nations officially labeled Chinese aggression in Korea," McCarthy stated, "was, in fact, a move which the Chinese considered, with some justification, given the statement of U.S. military leaders at the time, a defense of their vital interests close to their own frontier."[7]

And, as always, there was the massive threat of Bobby Kennedy. Staking out positions invariably to the Left of LBJ, Bobby had carefully put himself into a position so he would at least have a chance of wresting the nomination from Johnson. He had, to put it bluntly, initially been afraid of taking on the President. But when Sen. Eugene McCarthy not only had the courage to take on LBJ but proved he could be "had" in the New Hampshire primary, Bobby suddenly discovered that his conscience would not rest unless he jumped into the race. Lusting after a crown he believed might elude him in subsequent years, Bobby plunged into the contest with a fervor that was rending even further a terribly-torn Democratic Party.

Even after the President announced his intention not to run for re-election, Humphrey's own future was extremely vulnerable. For even if Humphrey were nominated to succeed his former boss, the Democratic Party appeared to be facing certain defeat in November.

Though storm clouds were gathering on the political horizon, Hubert Humphrey, whose first name literally means "bright spirit," was still the optimist. For he could recall that on several other occasions, his Presidential ambitions had been dashed to the ground only to take wing again through a stroke of fortune. Why should he give up hope now when he had come so tantalizingly close to fulfilling his dreams?

Appendix

The following letters were written to the author regarding Hubert Humphrey's Selective Service record. For an analysis and rebuttal of the "official" history of the Vice President's wartime record, see Chapter 20, "Profile in Courage."

January 11, 1966

Dear Mr. Ryskind:

President Harvey Rice has asked me to reply to your request for information about Vice President Humphrey. According to our records, Mr. Humphrey taught the following courses here at Macalester:

Fall Semester, 1943:
- Pol. Sci. 201 Survey of Social Sciences
- Pol. Sci. 231 American Government (2 sections)
- Pol. Sci. 351 International Politics
- Pol. Sci. 491 International Philosophy

Spring Semester, 1944:
- Pol. Sci. 202 Survey of Social Sciences
- Pol. Sci. 232 American Government
- Pol. Sci. 451 Seminar in Government

The *Survey of Social Sciences* was taught within the framework of the Air Force College Training Detachment program.

I hope this information will be of value to you.

Sincerely yours,
G. Theodore Mitau
Chairman
Department of Political Science
Macalester College
St. Paul, Minnesota

June 17, 1966

Dear Mr. Ryskind:

My apologies for not having written earlier in reply to your letter of mid-May. The attached copy of a chronology of Senator Humphrey's Selective Service record was prepared in 1960 when some of the questions were raised. The facts are set forth in that chronology. There is nothing that is "involved and confused" about the matter at all. The character of the *Northwest Industrial News* is well known to any informed citizen in Minneapolis, and I think you can determine that character by making a random sampling of any group of newspaper, radio or television people in the Twin Cities, for example.

In handling the attacks which have been made by such people as the publisher of the *Northwest Industrial News,* the then Senator preferred and made the judgment, and I think it was a wise judgment, to have the officials who had to do with the Selective Service and Naval recruiting at the time set forth the facts for themselves. He preferred to let the record stand for itself rather than to dignify the attacks by any kind of personal reply.

It is also noteworthy that no reputable person in Minnesota during the many campaigns the Vice President participated in ever raised this issue. It never became known as an issue, as such, being disposed of typically in a matter of a few hours by those who had known the young Humphrey in their official capacity as members of the Selective Service system or Naval recruiting system.

As you have already interviewed Dr. Kampelman, and you have read the extensive materials on the Vice President, I am sure that you have at least as good a picture of the Vice President as you would receive from any member of the staff. Dr. Kampelman has known the Vice President longer than any of us and has remained a close observer of the Senator and the Vice President, in that succession.

Sincerely,
William Connell
Administrative Assistant
Office of the Vice President
Washington, D.C.

Chronology of Senator Humphrey's Selective Service Record (Attached to Connell Letter)

(1) Hubert Humphrey was classified 3A in 1940 as the father of a small child—Nancy was then 1 year old.

(2) In August of 1943 Hubert Humphrey was employed at Macalester College as an instructor for the Air Force ROTC program. This meant he was given automatic classification of 2A as a civilian in an essential job.

(3) During the Winter of 1943 and 1944 Humphrey sought repeatedly to enlist in the Navy. According to Rollo Mudge of Minneapolis, who was a chief specialist recruiter for the Navy in Minneapolis in 1942 through 1944, Humphrey made at least 20 attempts to enlist in the Navy and "he was so persistent as to be almost embarrassing to us. We had to turn him down both for color vision defect and for double hernia." Mudge said that a person with a simple hernia would be acceptable to the Navy if the applicant agreed to surgery, which Humphrey agreed to, but double hernia was a cause for rejection.

(4) On July 11, 1944, Humphrey was classified 1A. He was called up in August and reported on September 6. He was informed that he would be deferred because of a new draft regulation which exempted men who were 30 years of age or over and who had children. Also Humphrey's medical exam revealed the hernia. Humphrey at that time was 33 years old and was the father of 3 children. Induction quotas at that time had been reduced because the Army had decided that it was too expensive to draft and support men with dependents.

(5) However, after the Battle of the Bulge on December 12, 1944, heavy draft calls again were resumed and those who had been deferred were called back. Humphrey was among those who reported back on February 12. However, he was rejected again for physical reasons. At no time did Humphrey ever ask for a deferment.

Notes

CHAPTER 1

1. Chapter by Elie Abel in *The Kennedy Circle* (Robert B. Luce, Inc., New York, 1961), p. 180.
2. *Ibid.*, p. 168.
3. *Congressional Record*, September 17, 1963, p. 17205.
4. New York *Times*, p. 51, March 13, 1960.
5. *Congressional Record*, September 17, 1963, p. 17205.
6. Theodore H. White, *The Making of the President: 1964* (Atheneum, New York, 1965), p. 273.
7. *Ibid.*, p. 273.
8. *Ibid.*, pp. 288-289.

CHAPTER 2

1. Winthrop Griffith, *Humphrey: A Candid Biography* (William Morrow & Company, New York, 1965), p. 35.
2. *Ibid.*
3. *Ibid.*, pp. 36-37.
4. Michael Amrine, *This is Humphrey* (Popular Library, New York, 1964), p. 29.
5. *Ibid.*, p. 30.
6. *Ibid.*, p. 46.

CHAPTER 3

1. *On the Economic Theory of Socialism*, ed. by Benjamin E. Lippincott (University of Minnesota, 1938). Introduction to essay by Oskar Large of the University of Cracow, Poland.
2. Michael Amrine, *This is Humphrey* (Popular Library, New York, 1964), p. 66.
3. *The Socialist Call*, May 7, 1948.
4. Hubert H. Humphrey, Jr., *The Political Philosophy of the New Deal*, A Thesis submitted to the Graduate Faculty of the Louisiana State University and Agricultural and Mechanical College in

partial fulfillment of the requirements for the degree of Master of Arts in the Department of Government, 1942, p. 119.
5. *Ibid.*, p. 7.
6. *Ibid.*, p. 8.
7. *Ibid.*, p. 33.
8. *Ibid.*, p. v.
9. *Ibid.*, p. vii.
10. *Ibid.*, pp. 35-36.
11. *Ibid.*, p. 80.
12. *Ibid.*, p. 81.
13. *Ibid.*, p. 55.
14. *Ibid.*, p. vi.
15. *Ibid.*, the Abstract.

CHAPTER 4

1. Minneapolis *Morning Tribune*, June 3, 1943, p. 20.
2. Minneapolis *Morning Tribune*, June 12, 1943, p. 9.
3. David J. Saposs, *Communism in American Politics* (Public Affairs Press, Washington, D.C., 1960), pp. 58-59.
4. *Ibid.*, p. 59.
5. *Ibid.*, pp. 59-60.
6. *Ibid.*, p. 61.
7. Minneapolis *Sunday Tribune*, March 5, 1944, Minnesota Section, p. 6.
8. Minneapolis *Morning Tribune*, March 6, 1944, p. 1.
9. Minneapolis *Morning Tribune*, April 18, 1944, p. 4.
10. *Minnesota Labor*, August 10, 1945, p. 1.
11. *Investigation of Un-American Propaganda Activities in the United States*, Special Committee on Un-American Activities, Report 1311, 1944, p. 16.
12. *Communist Activities in the Minneapolis, Minn., Area*, Hearings before the Committee on Un-American Activities, U.S. House of Representatives, June 24, 25, 26, 1964, p. 1791.
13. Max Kampelman, *The Communist Party vs. The CIO* (Frederick A. Praeger, New York, 1957), p. 113, and *Minnesota Labor*, April 7, 1944, p. 1.
14. Minneapolis *Morning Tribune*, November 1, 1946, p. 15.
15. Winthrop Griffith, *Humphrey: A Candid Biography* (William Morrow & Company, New York, 1965), p. 146.
16. Minneapolis *Sunday Tribune*, April 16, 1944, Minnesota Section, p. 1.
17. Minneapolis *Morning Tribune*, July 23, 1944, p. 3.

CHAPTER 5

1. *East Minneapolis Argus* (Digest of Speech), January 12, 1945, p. 1.
2. Max Kampelman, *The Communist Party vs. The CIO* (Frederick A. Praeger, New York, 1957), p. 113.
3. *Ibid.*, p. 115.
4. *Minnesota Labor*, February 16, 1945, p. 1.
5. Kampelman, *op. cit.*, p. 117.
6. Minneapolis *Morning Tribune*, April 9, 1945, p. 9.
7. Minneapolis *Star-Journal*, May 28, 1945, p. 8.
8. Minneapolis *Morning Tribune*, May 19, 1945, p. 7.
9. Minneapolis *Morning Tribune*, May 22, 1945, p. 9.
10. *Minnesota Labor*, May 18, 1945, p. 1.
11. *Minnesota Labor*, April 27, 1945, p. 3.
12. Minneapolis *Sunday Tribune*, April 22, 1945, Minnesota Section, p. 4.
13. Minneapolis *Morning Tribune*, May 6, 1945, p. 4.
14. *Minnesota Labor*, April 27, 1945, p. 1.
15. Minneapolis *Star-Journal*, May 26, 1945, p. 3.
16. *Daily Worker*, June 13, 1945, p. 3.
17. *Minnesota Labor*, June 15, 1945, p. 2.
18. *Ibid.*
19. *Ibid.*
20. *Ibid.*

CHAPTER 6

1. Minneapolis *Morning Tribune*, March 31, 1947, p. 6.
2. Minneapolis *Star-Journal*, May 6, 1947, p. 18.
3. Minneapolis *Morning Tribune*, June 7, 1947, p. 4.
4. Minneapolis *Morning Tribune*, June 5, 1947, p. 6.
5. Minneapolis *Morning Tribune*, March 22, 1947, p. 11.
6. *Minnesota Labor*, April 18, 1947, p. 1.
7. Minneapolis *Morning Tribune*, May 16, 1947, p. 6.
8. Minneapolis *Star-Journal*, March 11, 1948, p. 20.
9. Minneapolis *Morning Tribune*, December 22, 1947, p. 6.
10. Minneapolis *Morning Tribune*, June 24, 1948, p. 15.
11. Minneapolis *Star-Journal*, July 29, 1948, p. 18.
12. Minneapolis *Morning Tribune*, January 12, 1948, p. 13.
13. Minneapolis *Morning Tribune*, February 26, 1948, p. 13.
14. Minneapolis *Morning Tribune*, June 4, 1947, p. 15.
15. Minneapolis *Morning Tribune*, May 10, 1947, p. 22.
16. *Ibid.*

17. Minneapolis *Sunday Tribune*, June 8, 1947, Section L, p. 10.
18. *Ibid.*
19. Minneapolis *Morning Tribune*, May 9, 1947, p. 17.
20. Minneapolis *Morning Tribune*, February 24, 1947, p. 13.
21. Minneapolis *Morning Tribune*, May 7, 1947, p. 1.
22. Minneapolis *Morning Tribune*, May 8, 1947, p. 6.

CHAPTER 7

1. Minneapolis *Morning Tribune*, April 30, 1946, p. 11.
2. Minneapolis *Morning Tribune*, August 28, 1946, p. 13.
3. Minneapolis *Morning Tribune*, January 13, 1947, p. 1.
4. Minneapolis *Morning Tribune*, January 17, 1947, p. 1.
5. Minneapolis *Morning Tribune*, January 14, 1947, p. 1.
6. Minneapolis *Morning Tribune*, January 15, 1947, p. 13.
7. Minneapolis *Morning Tribune*, January 17, 1947, p. 4.
8. *Minnesota Labor*, August 23, 1946, p. 2.
9. Minneapolis *Star-Journal*, August 22, 1946, p. 2.
10. *Minnesota Labor*, August 23, 1946, p. 2.
11. Minneapolis *Morning Tribune*, August 30, 1946, p. 13.
12. *Minnesota Labor*, October 19, 1945, p. 1.
13. Minneapolis *Star-Journal*, April 28, 1947, p. 16.
14. Minneapolis *Star-Journal*, April 21, 1947, p. 1.
15. Minneapolis *Morning Tribune*, May 7, 1947, p. 6.
16. Minneapolis *Star-Journal*, April 30, 1947, p. 1.
17. Minneapolis *Star-Journal*, April 28, 1947, p. 12.
18. Minneapolis *Morning Tribune*, April 27, 1947, p. 1.
19. Minneapolis *Star-Journal*, April 29, 1947, p. 16.
20. Minneapolis *Star-Journal*, April 30, 1947, p. 1.
21. Minneapolis *Morning Tribune*, May 7, 1947, p. 1.
22. *Ibid.*
23. Minneapolis *Sunday Tribune*, May 11, 1947, Section L, p. 5.

CHAPTER 8

1. *Minnesota Labor*, August 31, 1945, p. 2.
2. *Minnesota Labor*, November 16, 1945, p. 6.
3. *Ibid.*, p. 1 & ff.
4. *Ibid.*, p. 6.
5. Anthony Kubek, *How the Far East Was Lost* (Regnery, Chicago, 1963), p. 171.
6. *Minnesota Labor*, November 16, 1945, p. 1.
7. *Minnesota Labor*, December 7, 1945.
8. *Ibid.*

9. Minneapolis *Morning Tribune*, August 11, 1946, p. 1 & ff.
10. Minneapolis *Morning Tribune*, April 6, 1946, p. 4.
11. *Minnesota Labor*, February 1, 1946, p. 2.
12. Minneapolis *Sunday Tribune*, October 6, 1946, Section L, pp. 1 & 3.
13. Minneapolis *Sunday Tribune*, March 10, 1964, p. 10, and Minneapolis *Morning Tribune*, September 19, 1946, p. 15.
14. Washington *Post*, September 13, 1946, pp. 16-17.
15. *Minnesota Labor*, September 27, 1946, p. 2.
16. Minneapolis *Morning Tribune*, September 19, 1946, p. 15.
17. Minneapolis *Morning Tribune*, September 20, 1946, pp. 1 and 9.
18. *Time*, September 23, 1946, p. 21.
19. Minneapolis *Morning Tribune*, September 20, 1946, p. 1.
20. Minneapolis *Morning Tribune*, October 10, 1946, p. 9.
21. *Minnesota Labor*, May 3, 1946, p. 3.
22. Minneapolis *Morning Tribune*, October 23, 1946, p. 1.
23. Minneapolis *Morning Tribune*, September 1, 1946, p. 2.
24. *Minnesota Labor*, June 28, 1946, p. 1.
25. *Minnesota Labor*, November 1, 1946, p. 4.
26. Minneapolis *Morning Tribune*, October 31, 1946, p. 11.
27. *Minnesota Labor*, November 1, 1946, p. 4.
28. Minneapolis *Morning Tribune*, March 19, 1947, p. 1.

CHAPTER 9

1. Clifton Brock, *Americans for Democratic Action* (Public Affairs Press, Washington, D.C., 1962), p. 51.
2. Minneapolis *Morning Tribune*, March 19, 1947, p. 1.
3. Minneapolis *Morning Tribune*, July 1, 1947, p. 9.
4. Minneapolis *Sunday Tribune*, June 22, 1947, Section 1, p. 2.
5. Minneapolis *Morning Tribune*, March 22, 1947, p. 1.
6. Minneapolis *Morning Tribune*, June 30, 1947, p. 13.
7. G. Theodore Mitau, "The Democratic-Farmer-Labor Party Schism of 1948," *Minnesota History*, Vol. 24, No. 5, Spring 1955, p. 187 & ff.
8. *Ibid.*
9. *Will the D-F-L Party of Minnesota Be A Clean, Honest, Decent, Progressive Party?—Or—Will It Be A Communist-Front Organization?*, published by the Hennepin County D-F-L Volunteer Committee, 455 Loeb Arcade, Minneapolis, 1948.
10. *Ibid.*
11. From 1948 handbill.
12. Minneapolis *Morning Tribune*, April 29, 1948, p. 17.

13. Minneapolis *Sunday Tribune,* May 2, 1948, Upper Midwest Section, p. 1.
14. Minneapolis *Sunday Tribune,* June 13, 1948, Upper Midwest Section, p. 1.
15. G. Theodore Mitau, *op. cit.*
16. Minneapolis *Morning Tribune,* September 3, 1948, p. 1.
17. *Ibid.*

CHAPTER 10

1. Minneapolis *Morning Tribune,* July 12, 1947, p. 1.
2. Minneapolis *Sunday Tribune,* November 2, 1947, Upper Midwest Section, p. 1.
3. Minneapolis *Morning Tribune,* April 26, 1948, p. 25.
4. Minneapolis *Morning Tribune,* June 14, 1948, p. 1.
5. Clifton Brock, *Americans for Democratic Action* (Public Affairs Press, Washington, D.C., 1962), p. 93.
6. Minneapolis *Morning Tribune,* July 7, 1948, p. 3.
7. Minneapolis *Morning Tribune,* July 12, 1948, p. 2.
8. New York *Times,* July 15, 1948, p. 22.
9. Brock, *op. cit.,* p. 97.
10. Minneapolis *Sunday Tribune,* July 18, 1948, Upper Midwest Section, p. 1.
11. *Ibid.*
12. Minneapolis *Morning Tribune,* July 27, 1948, p. 6.

CHAPTER 11

1. Minneapolis *Morning Tribune,* January 30, 1948, p. 2.
2. Minneapolis *Morning Tribune,* August 11, 1948, p. 2.
3. Minneapolis *Morning Tribune,* October 15, 1948, p. 1.
4. Minneapolis *Morning Tribune,* March 12, 1948, p. 3.
5. Minneapolis *Morning Tribune,* October 28, 1948, p. 1.
6. *Ibid.*
7. Minneapolis *Morning Tribune,* August 19, 1948, p. 4.
8. Minneapolis *Morning Tribune,* October 19, 1948, p. 1.
9. Minneapolis *Star-Journal,* October 19, 1948, p. 13.
10. Minneapolis *Morning Tribune,* October 16, 1948, p. 6.
11. Minneapolis *Morning Tribune,* October 12, 1948, p. 1.
12. Minneapolis *Morning Tribune,* October 19, 1948, p. 1.
13. *Ibid.,* and Minneapolis *Star-Journal,* October 19, 1948, p. 1.
14. Minneapolis *Morning Tribune,* October 2, 1948, p. 1.
15. Minneapolis *Morning Tribune,* October 1, 1948, p. 2.
16. Minneapolis *Morning Tribune,* October 4, 1948, p. 11.
17. *Minnesota Labor,* August 8, 1947.

CHAPTER 12

1. *Congressional Record,* October 7, 1949, pp. 14121-14122.
2. *Congressional Record,* October 12, 1949, p. 14357.
3. *Reappointment of Leland Olds to Federal Power Commission,* Hearings before a Subcommittee of the Committee on Interstate and Foreign Commerce, U.S. Senate, 81st Congress, 1st Session, September 27-29 and October 3, 1949, Washington, D.C., p. 35.
4. *Ibid.*, p. 40.
5. *Ibid.*, p. 41.
6. *Ibid.*, p. 54.
7. *Ibid.*, p. 72.
8. *Ibid.*, p. 33.
9. *Ibid.*, p. 43.
10. *Ibid.*, p. 112.
11. *Ibid.*, p. 111.
12. *Ibid.*, p. 111.
13. *Ibid.*, p. 123.
14. *Ibid.*, p. 115.
15. *Ibid.*, p. 123.
16. *Ibid.*, pp. 291-292.
17. *Ibid.*, p. 135.
18. *Ibid.*, p. 303.
19. *Ibid.*, p. 150.
20. *Ibid.*, p. 305.
21. *Ibid.*, and *Congressional Record,* October 12, 1949, pp. 14384-14385.
22. *Congressional Record,* October 12, 1949, pp. 14365-14366.
23. *Ibid.*, p. 14375.
24. *Ibid.*

CHAPTER 13

1. *Congressional Record,* February 24, 1950, pp. 2328-2329.
2. *Congressional Record,* March 2, 1950, p. 2611.
3. *Ibid.*, March 2, 1950, p. 2610.
4. *Congressional Record,* March 1, 1950, p. 2536.
5. *Congressional Record,* March 2, 1950, p. 2612.
6. *Ibid.*
7. *Ibid.*, p. 2614.
8. *Ibid.*, March 2, 1950, p. 2622.
9. *Time* Magazine, September 4, 1964, p. 20.
10. *Congressional Record,* March 2, 1950, p. 2626.

HUBERT

CHAPTER 14

1. Washington *Post*, November 25, 1951.
2. *Town Meeting of the Air* radio broadcast, November 1, 1949.
3. Chicago *Tribune*, November 27, 1949.
4. *Congressional Record*, April 7, 1949, p. 4044.
5. ADA *World* (Volume 1, No. 12), November 21, 1947.
6. *Congressional Record*, April 7, 1949, pp. 4027-4031.
7. *Congressional Record*, February 7, 1950, pp. 1560-1561.
8. *Ibid.*, p. 1574.
9. *Ibid.*
10. Philip M. Crane, *The Democrat's Dilemma* (Henry Regnery Company, Chicago, 1964), p. 197.
11. *Ibid.*, p. 201.
12. *Congressional Record*, June 28, 1949, p. 8505.
13. *Congressional Record*, April 9, 1952, pp. 3842-3844.
14. *Time* Magazine, April 21, 1952.
15. *Congressional Record*, April 10, 1952, p. 3956.
16. *Ibid.*, p. 3825.
17. *Congressional Quarterly Almanac* (82nd Congress, 2nd Session), 1952, p. 323.

CHAPTER 15

1. *Congressional Record*, September 8, 1950, p. 14420.
2. *Ibid.*, p. 14421.
3. *Ibid.*
4. *Ibid.*, pp. 14420-14421.
5. *Congressional Record*, September 12, 1950, p. 14628.
6. *Ibid.*, pp. 14573-14574.
7. *Congressional Record*, September 20, 1950, p. 15260.
8. *Congressional Record*, September 22, 1950, p. 15520.
9. *Congressional Quarterly Almanac* (81st Congress, 2nd Session), 1950, p. 397.
10. *Congressional Record*, September 22, 1950, p. 15524.
11. *Ibid.*
12. *Ibid.*, p. 15525.
13. *Ibid.*, p. 15526.
14. *Congressional Record*, September 23, 1950, p. 15709.
15. *Ibid.*, p. 15710.
16. *Ibid.*, p. 15710.
17. *Ibid.*
18. *Ibid.*
19. *Ibid.*, p. 15712.

20. *Ibid.*, p. 15713.
21. *Ibid.*
22. *Ibid.*
23. *Ibid.*
24. *Ibid.*, p. 15717.
25. *Ibid.*
26. *Ibid.*
27. *Ibid.*, p. 15714.
28. *Congressional Record*, August 12, 1954, p. 14212.
29. Letter to Richard Landkammer, 869 Fourth Avenue, S.W., Faribault, Minn., June 19, 1964.

CHAPTER 16

1. James Burnham, *The Web of Subversion* (John Day Company, New York, 1959), p. 66.
2. *Ibid.*
3. *Congressional Record*, August 12, 1954, p. 14209.
4. *Ibid.*, p. 14210.
5. *Ibid.*, p. 14212.
6. *Congressional Record*, September 23, 1950, p. 15716.
7. *Ibid.*, p. 15710.
8. *Congressional Quarterly Almanac* (83rd Congress, 2nd Session), 1954, pp. 334-337.
9. New York *Times*, August 20, 1954, p. 1.
10. New York *Times*, August 21, 1954 (compilation of press comments).
11. *Ibid.*, p. 6.
12. *People's World*, November 16, 1954, p. 8.
13. *Time* Magazine, February 21, 1955, p. 28.
14. Minneapolis *Morning Tribune*, October 21, 1954, p. 6.
15. Baltimore *Sun*, August 20, 1954, p. 4.
16. Minneapolis *Morning Tribune*, October 7, 1954, p. 22.
17. Charles Bailey, *Candidates 1960* (Basic Books, Inc., New York), pp. 166-167.
18. *Congressional Record*, January 10, 1950, p. 266.
19. Michael Amrine, *This is Humphrey* (Popular Library, New York, 1960), p. 179.

CHAPTER 17

1. New York *Times*, August 13, 1956, p. 13.
2. New York *Times*, November 10, 1956, p. 1.
3. Los Angeles *Examiner*, August 18, 1956.

4. Minneapolis *Morning Tribune,* August 18, 1956, p. 2.
5. Victor Lasky, *JFK, The Man and The Myth* (Arlington House, New Rochelle, N. Y., 1966), p. 189.
6. Minneapolis *Morning Tribune,* August 18, 1956, p. 1.

CHAPTER 18

1. New York *Times,* January 10, 1957.
2. Earl H. Voss, *Nuclear Ambush* (Henry Regnery Company, Chicago, 1963), p. 125.
3. *Ibid.*
4. *Life* Magazine, January 12, 1959.
5. *Ibid.*
6. *Ibid.*
7. *Ibid.*
8. *Ibid.*
9. *Ibid.*
10. New York *Times,* December 3, 1958, p. 1.
11. New York *Times,* December 7, 1958, p. 26.
12. New York *Times,* December 12, 1958, p. 2A.
13. *Human Events,* December 15, 1958, p. 1.
14. Fulton Lewis, Jr., in the Los Angeles *Examiner,* October 11, 1960.

CHAPTER 19

1. New York *Times,* December 31, 1959, p. 10.
2. *Ibid.*
3. New York *Times,* January 1, 1960, p. 18.
4. New York *Times,* December 31, 1959, p. 1.
5. *Ibid.,* p. 10.
6. Victor Lasky, *JFK, The Man and The Myth* (Arlington House, New Rochelle, N. Y., 1966), p. 333.
7. New York *Times,* February 16, 1960, p. 23.
8. New York *Times,* March 13, 1960, p. 51.
9. New York *Times,* April 1, 1960, p. 16.
10. Washington *Evening Star,* April 27, 1960, p. 7.
11. *Time* Magazine, March 28, 1960, p. 23.
12. Washington *Post,* May 9, 1960, p. A13.

CHAPTER 20

1. Michael Amrine, *This is Humphrey* (Popular Library, New York, 1965), p. 84.
2. Winthrop Griffith, *Humphrey: A Candid Biography* (William Morrow and Company, New York, 1965), p. 133.

3. Minneapolis *Sunday Tribune*, April 16, 1944, Minnesota Section, p. 1.
4. Gene Newhall, bylined story in St. Paul *Pioneer Press*, May, 1960 (author has undated clip in files).
5. Scott Schoen, "Hubert Horatio Humphrey," *Human Events*, September 30, 1959.
6. Advertisement prepared and circulated by the Veterans' Good Government League, James Laughlin, Minneapolis Chairman, and published in the *Minnesota Legionnaire*, October 13, 1948.
7. *Northwest Industrial News*, September, 1964, p. 4.
8. *Ibid.*
9. *Ibid.*
10. Minneapolis *Times*, February 13, 1945.
11. Gene Newhall, *op. cit.*
12. Scott Schoen, *op. cit.*

CHAPTER 21

1. *Time* Magazine, September 11, 1964, p. 20.
2. Cleveland *Press*, September 28, 1964, p. 2.
3. Chicago *Tribune*, October 22, 1964, p. 3.
4. Speech made October 31, 1964, in Los Angeles.
5. New York *Times*, October 27, 1964, p. 21.
6. *Time* Magazine, September 25, 1964, p. 16.
7. Associated Press dispatch, Carbondale, Illinois, October 21, 1964.
8. Speech made October 31, 1964, in Los Angeles.
9. *Congressional Record*, January 9, 1957, p. 359.
10. *ADA World*, March 29, 1947, p. 2.
11. *Congressional Record*, February 27, 1950, p. 1574.
12. Clifton Brock, *Americans for Democratic Action* (Public Affairs Press, Washington, D.C., 1962), p. 65.
13. James Burnham, "Does the ADA Run the New Frontier?," *National Review*, May 7, 1963.
14. *The Worker*, June 23, 1963.
15. *Congressional Record*, June 20, 1957, p. 9807.
16. *Congressional Record*, September 22, 1964, pp. 21807-21813.

CHAPTER 22

1. Chicago *Tribune*, February 8, 1953, p. 20.
2. *Congressional Record*, July 7, 1959, p. 11752.
3. *Congressional Record*, April 15, 1953, p. 3133.
4. *Congressional Record*, August 13, 1957, pp. 14641-14643.
5. Los Angeles *Times*, April 6, 1957, Part III, p. 3.

6. *Congressional Record,* June 1, 1955, p. 7370.
7. *The Socialist Call,* May 7, 1948, p. 1.
8. Washington *Post,* May 25, 1949, p. 9B.
9. *Issues and Answers* television broadcast, April 29, 1962.
10. *The Wall Street Journal,* May 18, 1959, p. 14.
11. *Ibid.*
12. National Farmers Union Convention Banquet, Madison, Wisconsin, February 15, 1960.
13. *Congressional Record,* September 7, 1950, p. 14280.
14. *Ibid.,* p. 14323.
15. *Congressional Record,* March 9, 1956, p. 4409.
16. Chicago *Tribune* News Service, May 6, 1959.
17. "Food for Peace or Food for War," American Security Council *Washington Report,* March 6, 1967.
18. *U.S. News and World Report,* October 17, 1960, p. 17.
19. Chicago *Tribune,* May 30, 1964, p. 4.

CHAPTER 23

1. *Meet the Press* television broadcast, April 2, 1961.
2. Des Moines *Register,* November 23, 1950, p. 18.
3. *Congressional Record,* February 4, 1964, p. 1839.
4. *U.A.W. Solidarity,* November, 1959.
5. Chicago *Tribune,* November 21, 1964, p. 14.
6. Chicago *Tribune,* June 26, 1950, p. 18.
7. *Human Events,* December 23, 1959, and January 7, 1960.
8. Albert Lea (Minn.) *Tribune,* February, 1935, and St. Paul *Pioneer Press,* August 31, 1962, p. 2.
9. New York *Times,* November 14, 1959, p. 10.
10. Statement by Hubert Humphrey, November, 1959.
11. *Congressional Record,* June 17, 1954, p. 7346.
12. *Congressional Record,* September 17, 1963, pp. 17204-17208.
13. Ralph McGill, *The South and the Southerner* (Little, Brown and Company, New York, 1963), p. 16.
14. Associated Press dispatch, August 12, 1956.

CHAPTER 24

1. *Congressional Quarterly Almanac,* 1957, p. 577.
2. *Life* Magazine, January 16, 1956.
3. Chicago *Tribune,* January 13, 1956, p. 3.
4. Chicago *Tribune,* January 14, 1956, p. 6.
5. Peter Nehemkis, *Latin America, Myth and Reality* (Alfred A. Knopf, New York, 1964), pp. 119-143.

6. Holmes Alexander in the Los Angeles *Times*, January 11, 1960, Part III, p. 5.
7. News conference, Minneapolis, October 19, 1962.
8. Letter dated February 28, 1962.
9. *Congressional Record*, September 21, 1961, pp. 19368-19379.
10. *Time* Magazine, December 4, 1964, p. 30.
11. Washington *Evening Star*, April 6, 1961, p. 6.
12. *Congressional Quarterly Almanac*, 1955, p. 279.
13. Los Angeles *Times*, July 8, 1957, p. 26.
14. New York *Times*, February 25, 1955, p. 3.
15. *Face the Nation* television broadcast, September 16, 1964.
16. Letter to Hon. Walter H. Judd, dated June 17, 1964.
17. Washington *Post*, December 10, 1959, p. B-16.
18. New York *Times*, June 5, 1958, p. 14.
19. Chicago *Tribune*, October 17, 1961, p. 3.
20. Washington *Daily News*, February 18, 1960, p. 9.
21. *Congressional Record*, January 27, 1960, p. A727.
22. From address at the 64th Annual Convention of the Zionist Organization of America, Hotel Waldorf-Astoria, New York City, September 1, 1961.
23. Washington *Post*, October 17, 1961, p. 9.
24. New York *Times*, October 18, 1961, p. 19.
25. New York *Times*, October 19, 1961, p. 1.
26. New York *Times*, October 26, 1961, p. 3.

CHAPTER 25

1. Stewart Alsop, *Saturday Evening Post*, April 10, 1965, p. 18.
2. *Look*, April 6, 1965, p. 84.
3. *Newsweek*, March 15, 1965, p. 29.
4. Palo Alto *Times*, July 19, 1966.
5. *Fortune*, August, 1965, p. 143.
6. *Congressional Record*, August 7, 1967, p. H10027.
7. Eugene J. McCarthy, *The Limits of Power* (Holt, Rinehart and Winston, New York, 1967), p. 218.
8. William V. Shannon, *The Heir Apparent* (The Macmillan Company, New York, 1967), pp. 284-285.

INDEX

Index

INDEX

Index

INDEX

Index

INDEX

Index